BIOMETRIC USER AUTHENTICATION FOR IT SECURITY
From Fundamentals to Handwriting

T0205702

Advances in Information Security

Sushil Jajodia
Consulting Editor
Center for Secure Information Systems
George Mason University
Fairfax, VA 22030-4444
email: jajodia@gmu.edu

The goals of the Springer International Series on ADVANCES IN INFORMATION SECURITY are, one, to establish the state of the art of, and set the course for future research in information security and, two, to serve as a central reference source for advanced and timely topics in information security research and development. The scope of this series includes all aspects of computer and network security and related areas such as fault tolerance and software assurance.

ADVANCES IN INFORMATION SECURITY aims to publish thorough and cohesive overviews of specific topics in information security, as well as works that are larger in scope or that contain more detailed background information than can be accommodated in shorter survey articles. The series also serves as a forum for topics that may not have reached a level of maturity to warrant a comprehensive textbook treatment.

Researchers, as well as developers, are encouraged to contact Professor Sushil Jajodia with ideas for books under this series.

Additional titles in the series:

IMPACTS AND RISK ASSESSMENT OF TECHNOLOGY FOR INTERNET SECURITY:Enabled Information Small-Medium Enterprises (TEISMES) by Charles A. Shoniregun; ISBN-10: 0-387-24343-7

SECURITY IN E-LEARNING by Edgar R. Weippl; ISBN: 0-387-24341-0

IMAGE AND VIDEO ENCRYPTION: From Digital Rights Management to Secured Personal Communication by Andreas Uhl and Andreas Pommer; ISBN: 0-387-23402-0

INTRUSION DETECTION AND CORRELATION: Challenges and Solutions by Christopher Kruegel, Fredrik Valeur and Giovanni Vigna; ISBN: 0-387-23398-9

THE AUSTIN PROTOCOL COMPILER by Tommy M. McGuire and Mohamed G. Gouda; ISBN: 0-387-23227-3

ECONOMICS OF INFORMATION SECURITY by L. Jean Camp and Stephen Lewis; ISBN: 1-4020-8089-1

PRIMALITY TESTING AND INTEGER FACTORIZATION IN PUBLIC KEY CRYPTOGRAPHY by Song Y. Yan; ISBN: 1-4020-7649-5

SYNCHRONIZING E-SECURITY by Godfried B. Williams; ISBN: 1-4020-7646-0

INTRUSION DETECTION IN DISTRIBUTED SYSTEMS: An Abstraction-Based Approach by Peng Ning, Sushil Jajodia and X. Sean Wang; ISBN: 1-4020-7624-X

SECURE ELECTRONIC VOTING edited by Dimitris A. Gritzalis; ISBN: 1-4020-7301-1

DISSEMINATING SECURITY UPDATES AT INTERNET SCALE by Jun Li, Peter Reiher, Gerald J. Popek; ISBN: 1-4020-7305-4

SECURE ELECTRONIC VOTING by Dimitris A. Gritzalis; ISBN: 1-4020-7301-1

Additional information about this series can be obtained from http://www.springeronline.com

BIOMETRIC USER AUTHENTICATION FOR IT SECURITY
From Fundamentals to Handwriting

by

Claus Vielhauer
Universität Magdeburg, GERMANY

 Springer

Claus Vielhauer
Universität Magdeburg
Magdeburg, GERMANY

Library of Congress Cataloging-in-Publication Data

A C.I.P. Catalogue record for this book is available
from the Library of Congress.

Biometric User Authentication for IT Security
From Fundamentals to Handwriting
by Claus Vielhauer
Universität Magdeburg, GERMANY

Advances in Information Security   Volume 18

e-ISBN-10: 0-387-28094-4
ISBN-13: 978-1-4419-3873-2   e-ISBN-13: 978-0-387-28094-3

Printed on acid-free paper.

springeronline.com

Contents

Preface

Biometric user authentication techniques have evoked an enormous interest by science, industry and society in the recent past. Scientists and developers have constantly pursued the technology for automated determination or confirmation of the identity of subjects based on measurements of physiological or behavioral traits of humans. Many biometric techniques have been implemented into authentication systems of apparently mature functionality. Although all biometric systems are subject to an intrinsic error-proneness, vendors argue for the accuracy of their systems by presenting statistical estimates or error probabilities, which suggest to be reasonably low for particular applications. With intentions like an expected integration of biometric features in travel documents in the near future, large-scale application of biometrics is becoming reality and consequently, an increasing number of people working in the IT domain will be confronted with biometric technology in the future. Thus, with the increasing diverseness of the different techniques, it is becoming more and more important for academic teachers, students and researchers as well as for practitioners, application designers and decision-makers in the IT security domain to understand the basic concepts, problems and limitations of authentication by biometrics. The goal and the uniqueness of this book are to impart knowledge to these people by expanding in two dimensions.

The **horizontal dimension** will educate the reader about the common principles in system design and evaluation of biometric systems in general, over the spectrum of the most relevant biometric techniques. Here, we will introduce to the state-of-the-art in biometric recognition across the variety of different modalities, including physiological traits such as fingerprint and iris recognition, as well as behavior such as voice or handwriting, and put them in context of the general theory of user authentication in IT security. For the system design part, we look at the systematic development of a generic process model, and provide an overview of implementation examples, along with references to selected signal and image processing methods, as well as classification techniques. The part on evaluation discusses the fundamental causes of inaccuracy of biometric systems and introduces mechanisms for experimental determination of quantitative figures in terms of error rates. Specifically for the most relevant biometrics, state-of-the-art recognition rates and references to technical details are presented for physiological methods based on face, fingerprint, iris, retina, ear and hand modalities, as well as for behavior-based approaches for voice, handwriting, gait, lip movement and keystroke dynamics. This comparative discussion will enable the reader to differentiate technical principles, potential applications and expected recognition accuracy across the zoo of different biometric schemes

Away from the scientific disciplines of signal processing and pattern recognition, biometrics can also be viewed from the perspective of IT security. Here, biometrics represents just another possibility for user authentication, besides well-established possession and knowledge-based methods. For taking care of this aspect, the book will provide insights in a formal model for the user authentication problem, as well as security requirements within all types of authentication systems. As one of the view publications in this area, it will be demonstrated how biometrics fit into this IT security-based model and where security problems can be found here.

In the **vertical dimension**, the book expands into very detailed algorithm designs and evaluation methodology for active biometric modalities on the specific example of handwriting dynamics. These parts of the book present a new approach to systematic testing of biometric algorithms, based on modeling of different types of sensor hardware and a forgery classification of attacks. Furthermore, algorithm examples for user verification and cryptographic key generation from handwriting dynamics are presented mathematically and explained in detail. It will be discussed in a very detailed manner, how experimental evaluations in various parameterizations can be performed. While in these excursions, we expand on one single modality, online handwriting, the underlying concepts are by no means limited to handwriting and these reflections are thus relevant to other biometric methods as well.

Both dimensions of the book convey true novelties both in educational and in scientific aspects. The **perception of biometric user authentication from IT security** unveils very descriptively the necessity for not considering biometrics as a black box tool to achieve security in IT, but also the requirement of **securing biometric systems in themselves**. The presentation of a **new evaluation methodology** shows the reader how **experimental scenarios can be designed to simulate real-world scenarios** of skilled forgeries and varying sensor types. **Scientifically,** as well as relevant for application designers, the main novelties of the book consist of new findings on the **impact of forgery efforts and sensor characteristics** to the recognition accuracy of biometric systems and the presentation of a **new algorithm to secure biometric references**.

Acknowledgments

Writing a book is a project, which requires a lot of work, energy and resources over a long period of time. It requires passive and active support by numerous persons additional to the author, and I attempt to give credit to those, who have helped me most in my research activities and during the long months of writing.

My overall thanks go to my wife and family for their understanding, support and patience. A scientist working in author mode may become a very strange behaving creature at times, with very limited time for family business.

Further, Klara Nahrstedt and Ralf Steinmetz have given me incredible support in reviewing my Ph.D. thesis, and by pushing me to expand my work on the subject of biometrics. Substantial parts of this book are based on the work presented in this thesis ([Viel2004]), particularly the discussions on the user authentication system model in Chapter 3, as well as the details on handwriting biometrics in Chapters 4 onwards. I would like to thank Klara for her support in the area of formalization, test methodology and also for her never-ending patience in correcting my English. I am very thankful to Ralf for opening the gate to the scientific alley for me and for his trust, patience and guidance over the years.

Writing in a foreign language gives an additional challenge to a scientific book project and the only way to avoid the worst blunders is to ask a native speaker for a linguistic review. Thank you Ryan Spring for helping me in this for Chapters 3 onwards.

Of course, I would like to thank all of the students that have worked with me over the past years. Without their creativity, hard work and patience, particularly during endless hours of programming, debugging and test runs, I could not have completed this work. Especially Tobias Scheidat has helped me a great deal in implementing the test methodology and performing experiments over many days of test runs. These tests have been the basis for the experimental evaluations in the last three chapters of this book. My special thoughts are with Falko Ramann, who has devoted a lot of time to work with me and who contributed substantially to the user interface of the evaluation software. It is still very hard for his former colleagues and me to realize that Falko will not be able to share my joy about this book, as he was taken away from us far too early.

My thanks also go to all of my scientific colleagues at the Multimedia Communications Lab (KOM) in Darmstadt, Germany and at the Advanced Multimedia and Security Lab (AMSL) in Magdeburg, Germany, as well as to all my co-authors over the years. Our discussions were the basis of many inspirations and often influenced my scientific track.

Susan Lagerstrom-Fife and Sharon Palleschi from Springer Science and Business Media have provided terrific help in preparation and finalization of the book. I would like to thank both of them for their fulgurous responses, whenever I needed another hint to solve the many word processing problems.

Chapter 1

INTRODUCTION
Biometric User Authentication

1. INTRODUCTION

Biometric user authentication techniques have evoked an enormous interest by science, industry and society in the recent past. Scientists and developers have constantly pursued the technology for automated determination or confirmation of the identity of subjects based on measurements of physiological or behavioral traits of humans. Many biometric techniques have been implemented into authentication systems of apparently mature functionality. Although all biometric systems are subject to an intrinsic error-proneness, vendors argument for the accuracy of their systems by presenting statistical estimates or error probabilities, which suggest to be reasonably low for particular applications. With intentions like an expected integration of biometric features in travel documents in the near future, large-scale application of biometrics is becoming reality and consequently, an increasing number of people working in the IT domain will be confronted with biometric technology in the future. Thus, with the increasing diverseness of the different techniques, it is becoming more and more important for academic teachers, students and researches as well as for practitioners, application designers and decision-makers in the IT security domain to understand the basic concepts, problems and limitations of authentication by biometrics.

1.1   Requirement for User Authentication

The natural recognition of individuals by biometric features is a very common and trivial task in human-human interaction. Identification of individuals from a circle of acquaintances by looking at facial images, for examples on photographs, is a well-established capability of most human beings and usually works quite robustly, even over a larger period of time. Other examples for human-to-human recognition are identification of persons by their voices, for example over the telephone, as well as from sound transmitted from discussions in a neighboring room, or recognizing the style of handwriting. The later is the case particularly amongst people who are quite familiar to each other, allowing them to identify the originator of a handwritten note, such as a shopping list, simply by the appearance of handwriting.

All these natural recognition capabilities appear trivial to us, but in fact constitute excellent cognitive skills, which are highly desirable also for automated recognition of persons in many applications.

Considering for example a general physical access control application, such as border control, the main two authentication tasks here are to check the validity of travel documents (document authentication) and to confirm the binding of such documents to the identity of the actual person aspiring access (person authentication). Before the availability of techniques such as photography, permits were issued in form of certificates by trusted third parties, usually confirming the identity of the travelling person by signature and seal of a governmental executive. While these mechanisms provided reasonable means for authenticating the documents, the confirmation of identify of the traveling person was difficult and relying on descriptive information in the documents and methods like interrogation or third party testimonials.

The development of new technologies has provided new means of authentication. With respect to document authentication, for example protection methods based on watermarks and holograms have emerged. Also; with the availability of techniques such as photography, the first biometric features have been included in travel documents around the end of the 19th century and today, we find a variety of additional biometric data on passports, including fingerprints and signatures in some countries. All this data, which so far has been included as analog data such as images, have increased the amount of information available for the authentication task of an immigration officer and should thus allow for more accurate decisions.

The ultimate goal of any biometric user authentication is to adopt the concepts for natural recognition or authentication of subjects, find techniques to automate this process and to implement these techniques in such way that a minimum of authentication errors occur. Applications goals for these techniques include many additional areas besides the border control scenario already discussed. These areas stretch from additional access control applications to buildings or computer systems over multimedia authentication, for example of authors, copyright holders and consumers of digital media in DRM systems. They lead to automatic identification of persons moving in pervasive environments, or operating systems with embedded computer technology like cars, with goals such as convenience, safety or forensic surveillance.

1.2 Authentication by Possession, Knowledge and Biometrics

As discussed in the previous section, the automation of user authentication is a desirable goal with a variety of potential applications. Also, we have shown that practically all automated user authentication approaches are motivated from natural processes. These natural schemes are based on very different concepts and can be classified into three non-exclusive categories: knowledge, possession and biometric authentication schemes, as illustrated in Figure 1.1. The non-exclusivity can be seen here already, meaning that the combination any two or more schemes for a user authentication process is quite possible

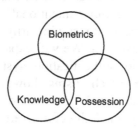

Figure 1-1. Three basic schemes for user authentication and their overlap

In this section, we want to briefly introduce to examples of authentication mechanisms in each of the three categories, both for conventional, non-automated authentication, as well as paradigms in the digital world. Furthermore, we want to briefly motivate some combination possibilities by looking at possible application scenarios.

A historical paradigm for **knowledge based user authentication** schemes is the concept of military watchwords, where specific phrases are assigned to single persons or groups of subjects. This concept is based on the idea that such watchwords remain secret within the group, i.e. they are neither get compromised nor , nor can be guessed of engineered from other knowledge by persons outside the group. This concept was adopted to computerized systems into password-based access control very early with the emerge of multi-user systems. Today, password-based mechanisms are by far the most common user authentication methods and familiar to almost every user of computers.

The second approach of **authenticating individuals by possession** also has a long tradition in the non-digital world. First developments of locks can be found back in ancient Egyptian and Roman eras. In ancient Egypt, pin tumbler type locks were in use, and the first full metal locks were introduced in the first centuries of the last millennium. Obviously, the concept of lock and key is the assumption that only authorized persons will have physical access to a device, by which access to a particular space, e.g. a building or a room within a building, can be gained. Considering the age of this technique, key-based access control still is enormously common. Probably every single person living in our civilization is possessing a varying number of keys for accessing housing, work spaces or cars. Again in the computerized world, this basic scheme was adopted and devloped into concepts like smart-card based access control or more recently Radio Frequency Identification (RFID) transponders.

Both of the two authentication schemes have one **severe disadvantage**, the **transferability of the credentials**. Knowledge and possession are not intrinsically linked to persons and can thus be transferred between different subjects. Such transfer can be either intentional, for example by lending a house key to a temporary visitor, or involuntarily, for example by theft of a keycard or spoofing of a password. We will expand more systematically on these threats, or attacks to authentication systems later in Chapter 4. **Biometric authentication mechanisms** however, as physiological or behavioral properties of individuals, do **provide intrinsic links between credentials subjects**. They may therefor overcome the disadvantage of transferability, however at a trade-off, which is a certain inaccuracy in the recognition. In this book, we will discuss this inaccuracy, leading to the two principal error classes of falsely rejected authentic users and falsely accepted intruders, early in our discussions on fundamentals in biometrics. This principal of inaccuracy holds true for all biometric modalities, regardless whether for example fingerprints or signatures are the source of biometric information. The major **disadvantage of biometrics** as a single scheme for user authentication is given by the fact that they are supposed to be **unique and not replaceable**, that is, once a specific biometric feature is compromised for an user, it cannot be replaced easily by another.

An interesting aspect is the combination of more than one authentication scheme for user authentication. For example, it can be considered to store biometric references only on devices that are supposed to remain in possession of authentic users, for example smart cards. A successful user authentication in these cases will then require firstly the possession of the device and secondly the ability of the subject to present the biometrics. Consequently, a transfer of the object holding the credential to another person will not result in a positive authentication result. This scheme may be easily extended by a knowledge-based component, whereby the biometric reference on the smart card needs to be activated for example by a Personal Identification Number (PIN) prior to a biometric authentication, in which case all three authentication schemes are used.

Particularly for behavior-based biometrics like voice or handwriting, the combination of knowledge and biometric trait appears very interesting. For example a spoken or handwritten secret could be used as authentication credential rather than just the specific characteristics of the voice or handwriting style. This approach is particularly interesting, as it may compensate for disadvantages in both schemes: the transferability of knowledge and the non-replaceability of biometrics. From Chapter 5 onwards, we will consider such combination of knowledge and biometrics by introducing to alternative semantic classes for handwriting based biometrics.

1.3 Security Issues in Biometric Systems

So far in this introduction, we have shown that biometrics can serve, as a single authentication scheme or in combination with knowledge or possession, as a means to provide one specific security aspect to computerized systems: verification of authenticity of subjects. From the perspective of IT security, biometric user authentication thus can be one building block of a more complex system.

On the other hand, biometric systems in themselves require security provisions. Particularly the biometric reference data, which are required from each user enrolled to an authentication system and which are used for comparison during subsequent authentication processes, need to be protected from malicious use. For example looking at biometric systems based on fingerprint images, it is required to avoid unauthorized access to reference images, which could potentially be used by attackers for the production of digital or even physical fingerprint forgeries (e.g. rubber stamps). In password and possession based authentication schemes, this problem arising from attackers having read access to the reference information can be solved elegantly by cryptographic methods such as hash functions or digital signatures, as we will show in Chapter 4. However, the protection of sensitive data in biometrics today still is a challenging problem, which we will address particularly in Chapter 6, where we will point to state-of-the-art work in this domain and expand upon a new approach for handwriting based biometrics.

1.4   Organization of this Book

The first chapter introduces to the requirement of user authentication and provides a summary of biometric and non-biometric techniques for this purpose, as well as an anticipation of the problem of securing biometric systems. After the introduction, the book is divided into two parts. The first part addresses biometrics in general and across the variety of different modalities, whereas the second part expands upon one specific modality, handwriting, in detail.

In Part I, Chapter 2 first elaborates fundamentals in biometrics, by defining the scope of user authentication, expanding on the general layout, parameters and signal processing and pattern recognition basics. From the general view, the book then leads over to an examination of authentication schemes based on different biometric modalities in Chapter 3. Here, the reader learns to distinguish between active and passive schemes and becomes acquainted with references to specific signal and image processing algorithms for the most important biometric modalities. An auxiliary aspect, the fusion of different biometric sub systems into multibiometric systems, has attracted a lot of scientific work recently. We accommodate this development by a short section, introducing to multibiometrics. Further, the motivation for the particular modality of handwriting dynamics, which is pursued in greater detail in the remaining chapters of the book, is given in this chapter by two selected case studies. Chapter 4 changes over to the perspective of the user authentication from the discipline of IT security and introduces a generic model for user authentication, abstracting from possession, knowledge and biometrics. This model is used for a security analysis with respect to possible attacks and consequently, security challenges are derived from this analysis.

In Part II of the book, the following three chapters then focus on the exemplary modality of handwriting dynamics. In a new evaluation methodology for the exemplary modality of handwriting, which is presented in Chapter 5, the concept of a systematic design for an evaluation framework and a well-designed structure of test data is introduced. Further, a basic handwriting verification algorithm (Minimum Quadratic Envelope Distance, MQED) is presented in detail, along with results of the application of the new test method to this algorithm. Chapter then 6 addresses the problem of securing biometric reference data and suggests a new algorithm for generation of cryptographic keys from handwriting input, the Biometric

Hash function. Again, this algorithm undergoes experimental evaluation by the new methodology, to demonstrate how testing can performed and how results can be interpreted. Based on the concept of biometric hashes and again evaluated by the same evaluation scheme, Chapter 7 develops and describes a fully functional user verification system by introducing distance measures and a threshold-based verification decision model. The functionality of this model will conceptional shown by discussing test results in terms of error rates and information entropy.

1.5   How to read this Book

The book addresses readerships in academic, scientific and industrial areas. Besides this introduction to the topic, which should be read by all readers to understand the scope of the book, Chapters 2 to 4 are particularly intended to provide the fundamental understanding of biometrics. All readers with a fundamental background in signal processing, pattern recognition and the underlying mathematical principles, but with no or little knowledge in biometrics should therefore carefully read them. This category of readers may include college and university students, participating in introductory courses to biometrics, as well as technicians who want to get more familiar with the subject.

Even readers already having a substantial technical background in the basics of biometrics, but limited experience in IT security should consider having a look at Chapter 4. By introducing to general concepts of user authentication from this perspective, this section sensitizes and supports understanding of security issues in context of, and intrinsic to, biometric systems.

For comprehensive insights and deeper knowledge about algorithm design, systematic evaluation approaches and security mechanisms for active biometrics, readers should refer to Chapters 5 to 7. From the methods presented here for the particular modality of handwriting, conclusions can be derived for other biometric modalities as well, which is important know-how for all technicians, scientists and technically oriented decision-makers, who are or will be in the situation to design or evaluate biometric applications. A comprehensive summary of the literature and Web resources, referred to throughout the book, is provided in the last Chapter 8, allowing for extensive further studies.

PART I: FUNDAMENTALS - OVERVIEW

Chapter 2

FUNDAMENTALS IN BIOMETRICS
Automated Processing of Bodily Measurements

2.   FUNDAMENTALS IN BIOMETRICS

In the recent past, multimedia systems have undergone enormous developments and with the technological advances in the area, a great number of multimedia applications have emerged. The developments in computer hardware as well as software in terms of performance, capacity and cost have been the enabler for the movement of many concepts of this originally scientific discipline, allocated in the domain stretching from signal processing in electrical engineering to computer science, from theory to practice. One important factor for the success of this technology was the movement from the concept of personalized computers in the early 1980's towards the paradigm of globally networked, ubiquitous infrastructures, which we find today. In the context of challenges arising from this evolution, the new research domain of Multimedia Communications has emerged. Among the various areas of interest in this domain, recently two categories have attracted increasing activity: **quality and security for multimedia services** such as IP telephony, Video-on-Demand and Digital Watermarking, as shown for example in [StNa2004a] and [StNa2004b]. With respect to security in multimedia services, we find numerous aspects, which need to be addressed in many application scenarios. These aspects include **confidentiality/privacy, integrity and authenticity** of multimedia content, see Section 2.3. Also, quite often, the **logical binding of multimedia content** to **human identities** is desirable, for example for protecting copyrights in digital media or for the authorization to use a specific multimedia service.

For this task of **user authentication**, as the process of confirming or determining the identity of users, we find three concepts based on **possession, knowledge and biometrics**. Possession- and knowledge-based authentication schemes have been used for access control mechanisms for centuries, for example, by the military concept of watchwords or the invention of mechanical key locks in the middle ages. Compared to these authentication schemes, biometrics is a very recent scientific discipline.

The **term biometrics** is composed of the two **Greek terms "bios"** for life and **"metros"** for metric. Consequently, in a wide interpretation, the term biometric describes the science of measurement of creatures. Historically, there are two main goals, which are pursued with this measurement: elaboration of biological or medical knowledge and identification of persons. First approaches for a systematic registration of such measures by Chinese merchants was reported by the Portuguese explorer João de Barros in 1563, where he describes the stamping of palm and foot prints of infants [Garf2001]. While at that time, these biometric records were considered as deeds of sale, the requirement for more precise measurements came up with the establishment of systematic criminalistic methods. For this purpose, Alphonse Bertillion introduced the technique of *anthropometric signalment* or *"man measurement"* in 1877, which was based on eleven different body and head measurements: body height, span width of the arms, seat height, head length, head width, length and width of the right ear, length of left foot, and lengths of left middle finger, left little finger and left forearm. These features were used for an indexing technique based on file cards. Figure 2-1 illustrates some of the features of the Bertillion measurements, as it was been used in the United States until the early 1900's.

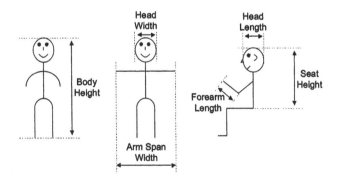

Figure 2-1. Example for six features of Bertillion's system of bodily measurements, as used in the United States in the early 1900s

Bertillion's concept can be considered as the first successful biometric identification system; a first suspect could be arrested in 1881 and until 1903, more than 120.000 comparisons have been performed in several police stations in France and the United States. However, a false identification of a suspect person by anthropometric techniques, the Will West case, marked the end of application of this identification method in 1903 for the benefit of fingerprint recognition techniques in criminology [CMSU2004].

Since then, a wide number of authentication techniques have been suggested, many of which have been adopted for automated biometric authentication methods recently.

In this chapter, we want to give a brief introduction to the domain of automated biometric user authentication, which will be denoted as biometric user authentication, or biometric authentication for simplification in the following discussions. We do so by pointing out the four most relevant application domains for biometrics in Section 2.1, followed by a more narrow definition of biometrics in the context of authentication systems in Section 2.2. Section 2.3 identifies IT security objectives and elaborates on these objectives, which can be pursued by biometric authentication. General terminology and accuracy parameters are summarized in Section 2.4 and this chapter concludes with a short summary of signal processing and pattern recognition concepts for biometric authentication in Section 2.5 and a summary of the terms and abbreviations introduced in this chapter in Section 2.6

2.1   Biometric Domains

Biometric methods are utilized in many domains and for many purposes. In this section, we want to give a very brief overview on the different perspectives and position our particular intention of user authentication among the other disciplines.

2.1.1   Medical Biometrics: Biological Symptoms

In **Bioinformatics**, denoting the application of computer science in the area of biology and medicine, the term *Biometrics* is often used synonymously for a more descriptive term of *"Biomedical Data Sciences"*. In analogy to other biometric disciplines, measurements of biological and/or medical phenomena are collected; however the goals in this research community are quite different from those in user authentication and include, for example, **statistical evaluations of larger populations such as automated classification of gene, proteins and diseases** or categorization of proteins into relevant families [Bioi2004].

2.1.2   Forensic Biometrics: Physical Evidence

Wechsler defines the term forensics as follows [Wech2004]:

"FORENSICS - the science and technology of using and interpreting physical evidence for legal purposes.(..) are related to processing and interpreting image data for applications related to biometrics, image enhancement, detection of characteristic landmarks, monitoring and surveillance, and motion analysis and interpretation (...)."

From this definition and in accordance to our introduction to this chapter, it becomes obvious that many of the modalities, which are used for biometric authentication today, originate from forensics. The most prominent example is the fingerprint comparison technique, which has been introduced as a manual mechanism to identify persons in the 19th century, has been developed over the years. Today, Automated Fingerprint Identification Systems (AFIS) automatically perform the matching of fingerprint traces against registered samples on very large scales, serving law enforcement in many countries of the world [Inte2004]. Another example for a forensic biometric method is Forensic Speaker Identification; see for example [Rose2002].

In comparison to biometric user authentication, while goals and methods in both disciplines are quite similar, an important difference lies in the perspective of forensics. In contrast to **forensics**, where **a person other** than the **person observed** intents to prove or disapprove the authenticity for criminalistic purposes, **biometric authentication serves an individual to prove her or his authenticity** by a biometric authentication system. An example of biometrics with an entirely forensic motivation is automated video surveillance combined with automated face recognition [Eff2004], as the recognition here is performed without the user's explicit consent.

2.1.3   Convenience Biometrics: HCI

A more recent usage of biometrics can be found in the domain of **Human-to-Computer Interaction (HCI)**. The goal here is to **enhance performance and accuracy** of such interfaces, by **recognizing users and adapting to user specific characteristics for recognition tasks**. Today, we observe many research activities towards multi-modal interfaces for HCI, with the perspective of seamless and ubiquitous human-machine interfaces for future applications [Simi2004].

One paradigm from the wide variety of concepts is user specific speech recognition. If a user can be identified by the characteristics of her or his voice, a speech recognition system may automatically adopt to a particular speaker model, thus improving the recognition accuracy. While in single speaker environments, the benefit of automated speaker recognition appears limited, a clear advantage of user-aware recognition can be expected, for example, in multiple speaker environments, such as conference scenarios.

2.1.4 Security Biometrics: User Authentication

Biometric authentication serves to **determine or confirm the identity of a user**. Goals of authentication include gaining of logical or physical access to an infrastructure (access control), or binding digital information to identities (information authentication). Access control mechanism encompasses many applications, from logical access to small personal electronic devices like memory storage devices secured by biometrics (e.g. Flash Memory drives protected by fingerprint verification), via user authentication for personal computers and computer networks to physical access control to buildings and areas. Authentication of information includes applications like electronic signatures for documents or protection of copyrights in multimedia content. A significant difference to the other biometric sub-disciplines in this section is the intentional perspective: in biometric authentication, we imply the **explicit content and awareness of users** about the authentication process and the physical phenomena measured for this purpose.

In this book, we will address exactly this particular objective of biometrics and introduce to the variety of methods based on different human traits, which can be automatically processed for this purpose. We will further extent upon this aspect for one specific biometric modality, handwriting. In the remaining chapters, we will very often make use of the term biometrics. At this point we want to clarify that, unless stated otherwise, in this book, we will always use it in the sense of biometric user authentication.

2.2 Definition of a Biometric Authentication System

The **term Biometrics**, in a wide definition, describes the science of

"Statistical analysis of biological observations and phenomena" [NIST2003].

Originally organized under the discipline of Biology, the term Biometrics has been adopted by other scientific domains over the past years, as this definition does not claim specific objectives with the discipline. Besides biological biometrics, which is a highly relevant field to medical sciences and therefore commonly referred to as medical biometrics, another branch originating from computer science has adopted the term Biometrics, as seen from the previous section. This science explores the possibility to use numeric measurements based on biological observations and phenomena to determine the authenticity of individuals or to derive specific individual physical or behavioral properties from this authentication. Wayman gives a definition of this discipline as follows [Waym2000]:

"The automatic identification or identity verification of an individual based on physiological and behavioral characteristics"

Although the precise terminology should be "Biometric Authentication", the common notation synonym "Biometrics" is commonly used in computer science.

The automated authentication of individuals by physiological or behavioral traits is of high interest mainly due to two reasons: Firstly, underlying methods are well known from human-to-human interaction. Manual identity authentication by properties like facial image, voice recognition or handwriting analysis are well accepted methods and find application areas ranging from high security access control down to trivial recognition of known persons in private life. The second main motivation lies in the steady increase of security and convenience requirements, which are arising from applications based on new technologies. Examples here are electronic signatures, which require user authentication, electronic access control to computer systems, physical buildings or immigration points. Although today in computer science, biometric technology is mostly found for security applications, additional research potential lies, for example, in the area of convenience. Biometrics may be used to improve human-machine interfaces, for example, by involving biometric measures in speech or cursive handwriting recognition to optimize recognition rates or automatic person-specific configuration of devices like cars.

From the variety of biometric methods, the analysis of the process of writing by hand and the resulting writing script seems to be of special interest. Especially in application areas, where traditional processes involving hand-written signatures of persons are migrated into electronic workflows, information about the writing process can be recorded digitally and used for an automated writer authentication. Besides the possibility to identify a writer, the human signature traditionally serves a number of additional social and legal functions like warning and finalization aspects [Kais2001]. In the context of document handling in new electronic media it is very desirable to make use of an automated authentication technology, which preserves these properties. The derivation of behavioral characteristics from handwriting is not limited to the writing process of a signature and may be analyzed from arbitrary textual content. This observation along with the increasing availability of computers with built-in pen-based digitizer devices provide the technological basis for new access control mechanisms, which make use of means based on knowledge, possession and biometrics. From these intrinsic qualities of the human handwriting, a substantial significance among other biometric techniques can be foreseen for the future, especially in the domain of electronic document processing.

All biometric methods known today are non-deterministic and need to be based on heuristic approaches. Although significant improvements can be observed in the area with respect to recognition accuracy for literally all of the published biometric methods, a number of unresolved problems today still exist in the area. The aim of this work is to point out significant open areas and to present and evaluate new approaches towards the increase of overall accuracy of biometric technology based on dynamic handwriting.

2.3   IT Security Objectives

Biometric authentication methods are mainly referred to in context of IT security. In this section, we briefly discuss the placement of biometric user authentication in view of the other general goals in this domain. The main goals in IT security are based on the three components of computer security defined by Bishop [Bish2003] as follows:

- **Confidentiality**: concealment of information or resources. This aspect includes the requirement for keeping **information secret (Privacy)** as well as obscuring the identity of communication partners exchanging information, preserving **Anonymity**.
- **Integrity**: refers to the trustworthiness of data or resources and includes aspects of integrity of data, which can be verified by **Data Authentication**, as well as sources of information, which in cases where this source is a subject, can be confirmed by **User Authentication**. Both authentication mechanisms can be combined to ensure **Non-Repudiation**.
- **Availability:** refers to the ability to use the information or resource desired. Besides **Reliability**, protections against Denial-of-Service Attacks are important aspects to ensure this goal.

Many of the mentioned security goals can be achieved by the use of mathematical methods provided by cryptography. For example, symmetric and asymmetric encryption schemes are powerful means to provide confidentiality, cryptographic hash functions can be utilized for verification of data integrity.

Additional objectives arise, whenever data and user authentication needs to be combined. This is the case, for example, when the content of some information (which may or may not be confidential) needs to be linked to the identity of subjects in a non-deniable way. A commonly known example for such situations are signed documents, where both the textual content of the agreement needs to be authentic as well as the identities of signers and their declarations of intent. In the analog world, well-defined legal procedures exist for such processes and for the last few years, electronic signatures have been promoted as means to transform legally accepted signature processes in the digital world. Electronic signatures are based on cryptographic mechanisms for data authenticity, non-repudiation and confidentiality, but an existing problem is a precise user authentication [ViSt2003].

Not only for ensuring integrity, reliable proofs of the identity of subjects are required. Bishop identifies access control mechanisms as one possibility to support confidentiality [Bish2003]. The great majority of access control mechanisms authenticate users by possession or knowledge. In the following chapter, we will show that there are disadvantages to these two concepts, which may be overcome by utilizing biometric methods for user authentication.

In summary, the purpose of biometric user authentication in the broad context of IT security can be described as a means to provide **identity-based access control** and to authenticate **integrity of information with respect to subjects involved**.

2.4   General Aspects of Biometric Authentication

In this section, we firstly introduce the two basic operation modes of biometric authentication systems, Enrollment and Authentication, in Section 2.4.1, as well as the two methods of authenticating individuals by verification and identification, in Section 2.4.2, and clarify our terminology in these contexts. We then formulate the most relevant requirements in the selection of biometric features, which are required in the context of this book (Section 2.4.3). Further, we introduce measurements for system accuracy of biometric authentication systems (Section 2.4.4) and discuss the impact of thresholds in biometric authentication (Section 2.4.5). At this point, we limit our overview to those aspects, which are relevant for our specific work. Our views presented here are based publications on fundamentals in biometrics, [Waym2000] and [Zhan2000], where much more comprehensive discussions can be found.

2.4.1 Operational Modes: Enrollment vs. Authentication

All biometric authentication systems basically operate in two modes: firstly all users need to be registered with the system, this process is called **Enrollment**. In this enrollment process, **reference features** for each individual user are stored in the system environment and associated with the identity of the subject. Figure 2-2 illustrates this process, which starts on the left with the acquisition, i.e. measurement and analog-digital conversion, of behavioral or physiological traits. The **digital information representation** after this process step is denoted as *Enrollment Samples*, or simply *Enrollments*. As shown in Figure 2-2, copies of Enrollment Samples may be stored in some evaluation environment (gray rectangle) in order to allow later reproductions of the original writing processes. From these original Enrollments, features are then extracted after pre-processing. These extracted features are stored as references to a storage location of the authentication system (Reference Storage).

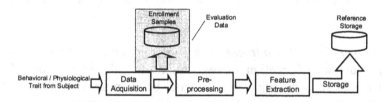

Figure 2-2. Enrollment mode of a biometric authentication system

The complementary mode to Enrollment, **Authentication**, denotes the process of identity verification or determination by the authentication system (see Section 2.1.4). In order to come to an authentication result, the system performs a comparison of the data from the actually presented traits to stored references. Figure 2-3 illustrates the authentication process, where from left to right the process steps are identical to those of the Enrollment mode, until reaching the completion of the feature extraction process. Here, in the Authentication mode, the features derived from the actual sample presented for authentication are compared to stored references from the reference storage. Based on the result of the comparison, the system will then perform a classification[1]. In analogy to the enrollment process, copies of verification samples can be stored after A/D-conversion for further usage by an evaluation system.

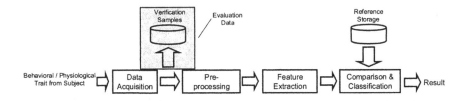

Figure 2-3. Authentication mode of a biometric authentication system

As indicated by the rectangles labeled "Evaluation Data" in Figures 2-2 and 2-3, the collection of evaluation data is performed by creating copies of the digitized traits directly after the A/D-conversion both for Enrollment and Verification Samples. Evaluation plays an important role in the context of this book and with respect to evaluation data, we use the following terminology:

- *Enrollments* or **Enrollment Samples** (abbreviated **ES**) denote the reproducible information representations, which are recorded directly after the data acquisition and have not been preprocessed at all. As no further processing of the A/D-conversion is performed, the data can be considered as raw information.
- *Verifications* or **Verification Samples** (abbreviated **VS**) are also information represented in raw format, but this information is recorded during Authentication processes.
- **References** or *Templates* denote the data representations resulting from an earlier Enrollment process, which are written to the Reference Storage

Enrollment and Verification samples are recorded for evaluation purposes only, because in a real-world user authentication system, availability of such data would enable replay attacks and consequently imply security risks. In an evaluation context, References can be reproduced by

---

[1] Note that generally for biometric user authentication problems, two classification concepts exist: **Identification** automatically classifies the given biometric features to one of the stored identities, thus identifies the user, whereas **Verification** will classify, if the biometric features match a declared identity or not, yielding a binary result. These two classification schemes are related to each other, which is explained in Section 2.4.2. All further discussions of this book are based on Verification.

repeating the Enrollment process from samples stored in the evaluation database. However, the reverse transformation, a reproduction of Enrollment Samples from References, is not necessarily possible (and more importantly not desirable, which is shown later).

For one specific exemplary biometric modality, fingerprint recognition, we want to provide the following examples for the type of information resulting from these two operational modes: data representations of Enrollment/Verification samples can be digitized image data (e.g. bitmaps) of pictures taken during Enrollment and Verification processes respectively, whereas references can be structural information extracted from the Enrollment images, such as type, location and orientation of minutiae [MMJP2003].

2.4.2 Authentication Functions: Verification vs. Identification

Biometric user authentication can be achieved in two alternative classification modes. In user **Verification**, the authentication system classifies, if a set of biometric features is similar enough to a set of reference templates of a person of claimed identity, to confirm the claim or not. The result of biometric user verification is always a binary yes/no decision, confirming an identity or not, possibly along with a confidence or matching score, reflecting the degree of similarity.

Identification describes the process of determining the identity of a subject based on biometric features. Here, the classification will assign the biometric features to one out of all the classes of persons, registered with a particular system.

One possibility to implement identification is exhaustive verification, where the actual biometric features are compared to all registered references and the identity is determined by the origin of references of greatest similarity.

Verification can be considered as a one-to-one comparison, where one actual biometric sample is compared to reference data of one single registered user. In this view, identification can be accomplished by a systematic verification between an actual biometric sample to references of all registered users in a biometric system. The result of this process then yields the identity linked to those references showing greatest similarity. Consequently, the process of identification can be modeled as sequences of one-to-all verifications. As the fundamental underlying mechanism is always verification, we abstract from the problem of finding adequate identification in this book and focus our views on verification problems.

2.4.3   Selection Criteria for Biometric Features

A number of criteria for selection of adequate features for biometric authentication have been suggested in the literature, for example in [Waym2000] and [Zhan2000]. From these selections, we introduce those four important criteria, which appear most important in the context of this book: **Variability**, **Discriminatory Power**, **Ascertainability** and **Performance**.

<u>Variability</u>
All biometric features are subject to natural variability, i.e. they vary in values from event to event, even for the same, authentic person. This effect is called Intra-Personal or **Intra-Class variability**, in consideration of the formulation of biometric authentication problems as classification problems. Reasons are the non-deterministic nature of biometric measurements due to varying operating conditions as well as systematic errors during analog-digital conversion of the trait, as well as aging effects in the human trait.

<u>Discriminatory Power</u>
The discriminatory power of biometric authentication systems is determined by the degree of uniqueness of the biometric features utilized for the comparison. Obviously, features reflecting a high degree in distinctiveness are required for biometric user authentication algorithms with a high discriminatory power, implying a high **Inter-Class variability** of feature values.

Figure 2-4 illustrates these requirements. The left graph represents an exemplary probability distribution of features of an authentic subject (in this case an assumed Gaussian distribution, as drafted), the so-called Intra-Class distribution, whereas the right graph symbolically shows the hypothetical distribution of the same feature for all other, non-authentic users of a biometric system (Inter-Class distribution). Apparently, good biometric features should possess low Intra-Personal and high Inter-Personal variability.

The degree of intra-personal variability is reflected by the width of the Gaussian distribution for authentic subjects, whereas the discriminatory power can be estimated from the intersection region of both graphs, as illustrated by the rectangular area of False Classifications in Figure 2-4. While features having complete discriminatory power would show no overlap at all, practical features exhibit this property to varying degrees, which may lead to false classifications.

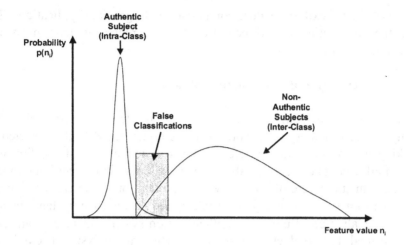

Figure 2-4. Example of variability and discriminatory power of a single biometric feature n_i

Note that the diagram shown in Figure 2-4 only shows the selection criteria for one single biometric feature n_i and thus demonstrates a one-dimensional simplification of a problem of higher dimensionality.

In the context of this book the term **Stability** denotes a qualitative characterization of biometric feature sets, possessing a high Inter-Class and low Intra-Class variability, allowing for precise generation of individual feature values[2].

Ascertainability

In order to design a functional biometric authentication system, features need to be ascertainable. Today, this criterion is mainly predetermined by sensor technology and the question is, if the desired feature can be acquired in acceptable time and sufficient quality. Examples for features, which are hard to ascertain are DNA patterns, which today can be only retrieved by chemical and radioactive processing of cellular material and thus are hardly acceptable for automated user authentication purposes.

Performance

As indicated in our views of ascertainability, a biometric feature must be processable in acceptable time. These timing aspects include not only the time required for acquisition from the sensor and any pre-processing, but

---

[2] Note that the definition of a stability measure is not required at this point. We will define a metric for the quantitative description of the degree of stability at a later point in this book, where it is required for experimental evaluations in Chapter 6.

also refer to complexity in feature comparison in large-scale applications. To fulfill the later criterion, aspects of efficient representations must be considered in feature selection.

2.4.4   Accuracy and Performance Measures

Biometric authentication systems attempt to determine or verify the identity of each member of a group of users registered with these systems, by taking into account appropriate measures as features for distinctiveness between all users and the repeatability over each individual user. Due to the non-deterministic nature of this process, as pointed out in an earlier section, a formal proof of an accuracy level is impossible for such systems today. Technical evaluation of biometric authentication systems therefore can only be performed by conducting tests and statistical analysis of empirical measurements.

For the specific modality of handwriting, the border between laboratory experiments and empirical analysis is fuzzy, if the test sets reach a specific size, the test samples have not been collected with the purpose of one specific experiment alone and are stored in a way that allows reproduction of the experiment under different parameterizations or with different algorithms. Later, in Chapter 5, we describe our test methodology in the context of this work and as all these aspects are all fulfilled, the term empirical is often used as a synonym for experimental.

Throughout the scientific work of more than two decades, a general consensus on five most significant test measures has been reached [Waym1999], which are briefly summarized in the following Table 2-1.

Table 2-1. Measures for technical evaluation of biometric systems

Measure	Description
False Match Rate (FMR)	Ratio between numbers truly non-matching samples, which are matched by the system and total numbers of tests.
False Non-Match Rate (FNMR)	Ratio between numbers truly matching samples, which are not matched by the system and total numbers of tests.
Equal-Error-Rate (EER)	The point on the error rate diagrams where the false match and false non-match rates are equivalent.
Binning Error Rate (BER)	Ratio of falsely not matched samples due to partitioning errors (applies to systems involving partitioning of large template databases).
Penetration Coefficient (PC)	Average percentage of the size of the database to be scanned for each authentication process (applies to systems involving partitioning of large template databases and supporting assignments of samples to multiple partition classes).

Table 2-1 (cont.).

Measure	Description
Transaction Time (TT)	Time required for a single authentication transaction, composed of sum of data collection time and computational time.

The first two measures (**FMR** and **FNMR**) are the most common evaluation criteria for all biometric systems and describe the actual accuracy of a biometric algorithm. They are typically recorded over different operating points, or parameterizations, of the algorithm. Two common visual representations are the error rates as function of some operating point (typically determined by a **decision threshold value** T) and FNMR as a function of FMR at discrete operation points. Figures 2-5 and 2-6, illustrate two examples for these representations, where the first diagram in Figure 2-5 visualizes an example of the interpolated graphs of FMR and FNMR measurements from discrete operating points during a test. Here, the FNMR curve represents the function of falsely non-matched transaction ratios, whereas the FMR curve depicts the percentage of falsely matched events. As can be seen from the diagram, the overall accuracy of a biometric verification system is a trade-off function of the system parameter, where a decrease of error rates of one class cause an increase in the other class and vice versa. A theoretically significant operation point is the point where FMR equals FNMR, thus minimizing the tuple (FMR, FNMR), which is called **Equal Error Rate (EER)**. Although there is no practical justification to operate a biometric authentication system at exactly this point, it is often referred to as first order measure of system accuracy. Figure 2-5 illustrates a typical error rate diagram, showing the dependency of FNMR (dashed graph) and FMR (dotted graph) as function of a decision threshold parameter T.

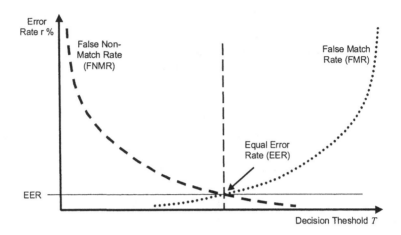

Figure 2-5. FNMR, FMR and EER as exemplified functions of decision threshold

Another example for a concise visualization of the error characteristics is presented in Figure 2-6, in the form of a **Receiver Operating Characteristic (ROC)**. Graphs in the figure outline possible error rate characteristics of four different biometric systems, labeled Verification System A to D. This exemplary ROC is motivated by one of the publications on biometric evaluation by Wayman [Waym1997] and are presented here for demonstration of the concept of a ROC visualization.

In this diagram, a single point at the point of origin, having both error measures equal to 0, would represent a theoretical system with optimal accuracy. Systems parameterized to accept higher FNMR at lower FMR can be found in the upper left part of the main FNMR=FMR diagonal, whereas the complementary case can be allocated in the lower right half. Note that for the exemplary Verification System A in this figure apparently only one single FMR/FNMR was determined, thus is it represented as a point rather than a graph in the ROC diagram.

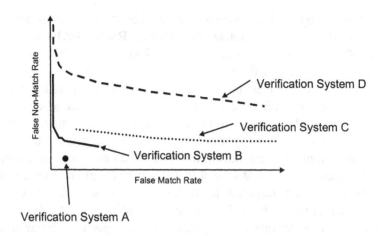

Figure 2-6. Exemplified ROC of four different fingerprint verification systems

The third and fourth measures from the previous Table 2-1 are relevant for testing biometric authentication systems on large reference data sets, employing partitioning of templates. Here, prior to the comparison of the biometric features, each test sample is classified into one or more partitions of the entire template set with the objective of reducing search time in databases of large scale. As the partition classification in such systems can only be based on biometric features exposed to natural inter-personal variance, false classifications can occur during this stage. In these cases, the **Binning Error Rate (BER)** reflects the percentage of samples not placed in a partition related to the original templates, thus causing false-non-matches. The **Penetration Coefficient (PC)** denotes the average number of comparisons for each sample in relation to the overall reference database size and represents a measure for the search complexity.

Practically, both BER and PC measures are relevant to biometric identification systems with a great number of users or long computation times. On the one hand, search problems in biometric authentication systems working in verification mode with given identities are trivial and on the other hand, exhaustive search or in small data sets can be acceptable, if a single comparison can be performed computationally fast. Thus for verification systems, BER becomes zero and PC becomes the ratio between number of single comparisons for an authentication decision and the total number of reference templates; typically, this number is $1/N_{References}$, with $N_{References}$ denoting the total number of all stored references in a biometric authentication system. For evaluations in the context of this book, we focus our views on user authentication by verification, thus determination of BER and PC becomes obsolete.

It is necessary to mention that in a wide number of publications, accuracy measures are referred to as **False Acceptance Rates (FAR)** and **False Rejection Rates (FRR)**. In contrast to the FMR and FNMR measures, which are determined based on discrete decisions of the comparison of features of each actual test sample with exactly one biometric template, FAR and FRR rates are determined at a more abstract level of the authentication process. For example, many biometric authentication systems base an overall accept/reject decision on the comparison of the actual sample with more than one template. Here, during the cause of an authentication process, several false-matches and/or false-non-matches may occur and in such cases, decision strategies are required to come to an overall decision. Other distinctions between FAR/FMR and FRR/FNMR respectively can be justified due to a wide variety of system-intrinsic specifics. Examples for such characteristics are a-priori quality filters which may or may not be invoked after the data acquisition process in the authentication process, erroneous rejections due to system outages or temporal and regional authentication policies, for example, implanted by biometric systems used for access control. However, many scientific publications suggest simplified systems, not involving any of these factors, where the overall system response is based solely on a single biometric comparison. In these simplified cases, both conditions (FAR==FMR) and (FRR==FNMR) hold true and in this book, we follow this simplification. For the sake of completeness however, it needs to be stated that these systems represent special cases with respect to a general model for evaluation of biometric authentication systems.

Also, for cases of system evaluations in identification mode, quite often the measure of **False Identification Rates (FIR)** is referred to, denoting the ratio of truly non-matching identifications and the total number of identification tests. Sometimes, this value is also given as the complementary value of **Correct-Identification Rate** (i.e. 100%-FIR). As stated earlier, in our discussions on evaluation of biometric systems in coming chapters of this book, we will limit our views to tests in verification mode, thus FIR will not be used as an accuracy measurement.

Performance measurement is a rather straightforward term to describe in comparison to accuracy. Here, the fifth measure presented in Table 2-1, **Transaction Time (TT)**, denotes the period required for a single authentication transaction. This temporal measure consists of the sum of the times required for data collection time (both actual sample and reference template), $T_{Collect}$ and computational time required from the input of sample and template to output of the comparison result, $T_{Compute}$. Wayman has shown, that in large scale identification systems, $T_{Collect}$ can be much greater than $T_{Compute}$, where collection times are in the range of seconds to a couple of minutes. $T_{Compute}$ is a function of hardware processing rate and the number of transactions required for each comparison and is typically measured in the range of milliseconds to a few seconds. The TT measurement is mainly of practical relevance, when high operational capacities in view of authentication processes have to be handled under real-time constraints. For our scientific evaluation tasks, the TT does not play an important role, thus we refrain from analyzing this performance measurement.

The above discussion on four accuracy measures FMR, FNMR, BER and PC indicates the key terms of the very complex problem of testing biometrics systems. An exhaustive discussion does not lie within the scope of this book, but a comprehensive collection of scientific work in the area can be found for example in a publication by the National Biometric Test Center [Waym2000].

2.4.5 Security Levels: Thresholding Trade-Off

As shown on the abscissa of the diagram in Figure 2-5, the decision accuracy of a biometric authentication system is a function of a system parameter of a biometric authentication algorithm, the decision is threshold usually denoted by the Greek letter T (pronounce *"taw"*). A lower value of T will cause a lower matching probability for non-authentic persons, at the cost of increase non-acceptances of authentic users, whereas a higher threshold value will cause the opposite effect. From the perspective of IT security, this effect can be utilized to configure a desired security level, if this level can be defined in terms of false match probabilities. In order to do so, the system simply needs to be parameterized by the threshold value of T corresponding to desired false match probability on the ordinate of the error rate diagram.

Higher FNMR are bothersome for authentic users, as they increase the probability of false rejections. Consequently, from an application point of view, this thresholding represents a trade-off between convenience and user acceptance on one side and security level on the other.

2.5 Biometric Signal Processing and Pattern Recognition

The task of biometric user authentication requires methods from the scientific disciplines of signal processing and pattern recognition, as shown in the following Figure 2-7.

Signal processing is required for the analog-digital conversion of the biometric traits (Data Acquisition) and preprocessing steps as shown in the left part of Figure 2-8, whereas pattern recognition techniques are required to extract adequate features, to perform comparisons to references and to finally classify the incoming trait.

In Section 2.4.2 of this chapter, we have shown that user authentication can be achieved by verification and identification. Consequently, the pattern Recognition problem can be formulated either as a two-class or a multiple-class problem.

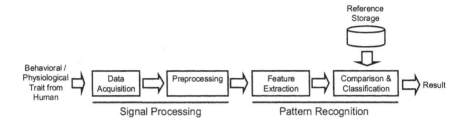

Figure 2-7. General model for biometric user authentication

The variety of techniques in each of the process steps is enormous and depends on the actual modality used. Thus we will limit ourselves to a very few examples of methods for non-handwriting modalities by the discussion of different biometric traits in Chapter 3.

2.6   Notations and Abbreviations

Table 2-2 summarizes notations and abbreviations introduced in this chapter in alphabetical order.

Table 2-2. Summary of notations and abbreviations introduced in Chapter 2

Designator	Name	Description	Introduced in
BER	Binning Error Rate	Ratio of falsely not matched samples due to partitioning errors (applies to systems involving partitioning of large template databases)	Section 2.4.4
EER	Equal Error Rate	The point on the error rate diagrams where the false match and false non-match rates are equivalent	Section 2.4.4
ES	Enrollment Samples	Set of information representing the biometric measurement after data acquisition in the operational mode of Enrollment.	Section 2.4.1
FIR	False Identification Rate	Ratio of truly non-matching identifications and the total number of identification tests.	Section 2.4.4

Table 2-2 (cont.)

Designator	Name	Description	Introduced in
FMR	False Match Rate	Ratio between numbers truly non-matching samples, which are matched by the system and total numbers of tests	Section 2.4.4
FNMR	False Non-Match Rate	Ratio between numbers truly matching samples, which are not matched by the system and total numbers of tests	Section 2.4.4
HCI	Human-to-Computer Interaction	Human-to-Computer Interaction	Section 2.1.3
$N_{References}$	Total Number of References	Denoting the total number of all stored references in a biometric authentication system	Section 2.4.4
PC	Penetration Coefficient	Average percentage of the size of the database to be scanned for each authentication process (applies to systems involving partitioning of large template databases and supporting assignments of samples to multiple partition classes)	Section 2.4.4
ROC	Receiver Operator Characteristic	Graphical representation of FNMR as function of FMR for the error rate characteristic of a biometric system	Section 2.4.4
TT	Transaction Time	Time required for a single authentication transaction, composed of sum of data collection time and computational time	Section 2.4.4
VS	Verification Samples	Set of information representing the biometric measurement after data acquisition in the operational mode of Verification.	Section 2.4.1

Chapter 3

BIOMETRIC MODALITIES
Different Traits for Authenticating Subjects

3.   BIOMETRIC MODALITIES

This chapter will expand our views on the different modalities that are involved with automated biometric authentication systems today. We will do so, by discussing the principles of acquiring biometric information from humans. The goal of this chapter is to introduce to the variety of different biometric traits, classify them into two main categories. Modality by modality, we explore the most significant technical concepts and characteristics, enabling the reader to identify these concepts for each of the traits introduced. Furthermore, the reader will be introduced to important related work and will be enabled to follow up more detailed by the literature references provided.

As introduced in the previous chapter, the term *Biometrics* is a term, which is an artificial composition of two the Greek words *"bios"*, meaning life and *"metros"* for metric. We have shown that identifying subjects by various biological measurements have been under investigation for centuries. Further, we have pointed out that one of the basic challenges in research on biometrics is finding adequate modalities, fulfilling the three main aspects of Ascertainability, low Intra-class variability and high Inter-class discriminatory power as introduced earlier in this book in Chapter 2.

There exist three principles for obtaining information about personal traits for measurement of biometrics:

1. **Physical removal of organic material** from human bodies for biological analysis. This method has become very common in criminal forensics,

where parts of the human body (e.g. samples of hair or dander) undergo **Deoxyribonucleic Acid (DNA) analysis**. DNA carries the genetic instructions for the biological development of cell forms, as well as for many viruses. Today's DNA analysis is based on a model introduced by Watson and Crick [WaCr1953], where the genetic instruction are coded as sequences of building blocks called bases. By comparing order and length of two or more of such sequences, based on different samples, it is possible to authenticate persons. However in biometrics for automated user authentication, DNA analysis is not yet used mainly due to two reasons. First, extraction of the DNA sequences still requires biochemical processing, which cannot be fully automated today and is quite time-consuming. The second reason is the fact that organic material carrying DNA may be lost easily. Consequently, it may be collected and re-used by other subjects easily, for example by collecting a sample of a lost hair from a brush or leavings of saliva from a glass.

2. **Behavior of subjects** is mainly characterized by three categories of individual traits: the **biological construction** of the organs producing behavior, the **learned characteristics** of how to produce behavior and the purpose or **intention**, which action exactly to be produced. For example in speech based biometrics, various aspects of the biological construction of mouth, vocal cords and glottis influence the individual sound characteristics of speech generation. On the other side learned characteristics include linguistic aspects like vocal tones, pronunciation and speech tempo, which are heavily influenced by the way the speaking capability has been acquired, typically during infancy and school days.

3. **Physiological traits of persons** represent biological structures, which are individual and which may be acquired without taking physical samples, e.g. by optical means. These can be seen as visible or at least measurable physical results, naturally grown as programmed by the genetic construction code. For example, the structure of the ridges on fingertips has proven to be individual and persistent for most human beings.

Measurements of these different categories, which are called **biometric modalities,** form the basis for techniques in various biometric domains, like medical biometrics, forensics, convenience and security, see Section 2.1 of Chapter 2 in this book. In this chapter, we will focus on IT security and within this domain more precisely the task of user authentication. We will do so by discussing in more detail the later two categories of biometric principles, **behavior** and **physiology**. Based on these two classes, we will develop a taxonomy of active and passive features for biometrics in Section 3.1. This taxonomy will allow to classify today's most common biometric techniques into active traits, based on measurement of behavior and passive quantities based on physiology. Some relevant representative techniques in each category are presented in Sections 3.2 and 3.3, where for each of the methods, the underlying modality is introduced and some selected state-of-the-art technical approaches, along with typical recognition characteristics and selected literature references are presented. This modality-by-modality review is supplemented by some additional observations for each trait, for example with respect to potential application scenarios. Besides using one single biometric trait for user authentication, it is possible to use multiple modalities for this purpose. Section 3.4 will introduce to this special discipline in biometrics, called **Multibiometrics**. Finally, we take an application-oriented approach by looking into two **case studies** in Section 3.5. Here, we outline an assessment of biometric modalities with respect to their qualification in two scenarios: Declaration of Intention and Scene Observation. This chapter closes with a summary of notations and abbreviations in Section 2.6.

3.1   Principles of Biometrics: Behavior and Physiology

In the previous Chapter 2, Section 2.4, we have shown that all biometric user authentication systems require data from sensors, which perform analog-digital conversation of the traits to be collected from the users. Obviously, the task in this process, which is called *Data Acquisition*, is to transform traits into information, for further digital processing by a computer system. We also refer to this process as *biometric measurement*. From the introduction to this chapter, we see that there are two fundamental schemes for obtaining such information for user authentication in context of IT security: behavior and physiology. The third option, sampling of organic material for DNA analysis, will not be discussed further in this context, mainly because today, it does not appear mature enough for the purpose of automated recognition of subjects.

To start our discussions on the principles, we will refer to two definitions from of the terms from a medical dictionary ([Sted1995]), which we take representatively from the immense number of definitions that can be found in the literature:

"be-hav-ior:
1. . The actions or reactions of persons or things in response to external or internal stimuli.
2. The manner in which one behaves."

and

"phys-i-ol-o-gy:
1. The biological study of the functions of living organisms and their parts.
2. All the functions of a living organism or any of its parts. "

The first definition of behavior contains two substantial properties for behavior, which are well qualified for a distinction between the two terms: *"(...) action or reaction (...) in response to external or internal stimuli."* Obviously, while physiological traits can be studied from external without requiring any specific stimuli, just by observing the organism of the user, this is not the case for behavior.

From the point of view of the user of biometric systems this classification can be described as differently. Here, the acquisition of the biometric data either requires some action (or re-action) or the subject may remain passive. Consequently, by adoption of this terminology, we use the terms **active biometrics synonymously** for those based on **behavioral traits** and **passive biometrics** for those designed from **physiological measurements**.

In the following Figure 3-1, we introduce our taxonomy for the most commonly known biometric modalities. In this figure, active traits are shown as biometric features in the left branch, whereas passive features are shown on right. Leaves denote some examples for modalities in each category.

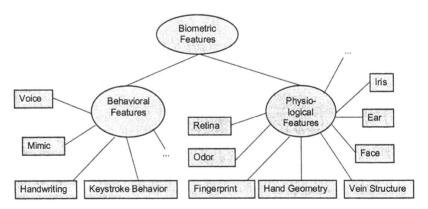

Figure 3-1. Taxonomy of active vs. passive biometric features

Before going into detailed discussions for representative traits in each category, the following subsections will address the differences between the two categories with respect to the data acquisition and the problem of liveness detection.

3.1.1 Data Acquisition

For behavioral biometrics, there are two possibilities for measurement of traits. Either the **entire process** of the activity is observed, recorded and measured or the authentication system refers only to the **result of an actual behavior**. In the first case, as today's digital computer technology does not allow processing of continuous signals directly, the sequences of observation during such processes need to be reconstructed from temporal sequences of discrete observations. For example the acoustic oscillations produced by a speaker can be digitally reproduced by sequences of numbers representing the volume of the analog signal at each discrete sampling time, recorded by a microphone and digitized by an analog-digital converter. Figure 3-2 illustrates an example for a short voice recording, where each of the gages in vertical direction represent discrete values of the sampled voice over a number of sampling times, shown on the time axis on the abscissa.

This method, called **signal sampling**, will be discussed in further detail in Chapter 4, Section 4.2, where we introduce signal categories for modeling a general authentication system.

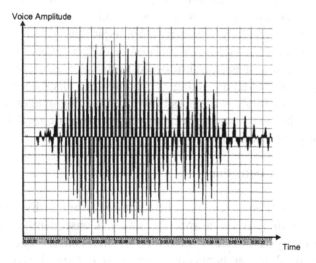

Figure 3-2. Example of an audio sample, represented as temporal sequence of discrete value measurements of the voice amplitude over time

In context of this chapter, discussing our taxonomy, the important conclusion is that for measuring the entire process, a finite-length sequence of single **measurement values in temporal order** is required. The process for generating such a digital representation from an analog observation is called signal sampling and the **subcategory** of methods implementing **behavioral biometrics** this way is called **online methods**.

In contrast to online methods for acquiring behavioral biometrics, **offline biometrics** address the result of a particular process, not the dynamic properties of it. One example for this category is offline handwriting analysis, whereby scans of handwriting, for example a signature on a document, are scanned. From the digital image resulting from the scan process, the authentication system may then extract characteristic features for the recognition task. As can be seen from this example, the biometric modality is digitized after completion of the underlying behavior and it is **digitized without any temporal context**. In context of this book, we call this kind of digitalization **capturing** (see also Chapter 4, Section 4.2 of this book).

For the case of handwriting as a biometric trait, we need to mention that there also exist techniques for online sampling of the writing process. This category of online handwriting biometrics will be discussed in further detail later in this chapter.

Note that offline features may be derived from online information, but not vice versa. Online handwriting data, for example, includes information about the pen movement over time, besides other physical measurements. This movement is typically represented by sequences of horizontal/vertical coordinates, each of which is associated with a time stamp. From this temporal description, it is straightforward to derive a 2D representation by simply graphically interconnecting the points and displaying them on a canvas. Another example is the possibility of extracting images from a video stream, which then can be used for image-based biometric modalities such as face or fingerprint recognition.

3.1.2   Liveness Detection

Physiological biometrics may be captured from individuals without requiring them to perform a specific action. Consequently, this kind of information may be obtained without their explicit consent, because many of the features used for authentication are present regardless of the user's consent, awareness or even health conditions. Furthermore, **attacks** to biometric systems may include the possibility of **spoofing**, i.e. the production of a fake modality. One example for such attacks to fingerprint based systems are 'Gummy" finger attacks, which lead to successful false acceptances, at least in some systems [MMYH2002].

All these observations led to the forming of liveness detection, being a sub-discipline in biometrics [Vale2002]. One important property of behavioral modalities is the intrinsic proof of liveness. As explicated in the introduction to this section, behavior requires an action from a subject, and consequently, we can assume that behavioral traits can only be sampled, if the person was aware and willing to provide them.

For physiological biometrics, the problem of liveness detection cannot be solved by means intrinsic to the modalities, and researchers have been addressing this weakness over the past years. Amongst the approaches suggested to solve this problem, we find design suggestions like ([IBGr2005]):

- **Randomization of verification data**, where users are asked to multiple samples of one modality (e.g. multiple fingerprints) to the system,
- **Retention of identifiable data**, to establish an audit trail, whereby original biometric data shall be kept for later examination in case of doubtful authentication,
- Multiple biometrics, as will be discussed in Section 3.4 - **Multibiometrics** - of this chapter,
- **Multi-factor authentication**, i.e. the combination of biometrics, possession and knowledge. This approach may also help to detect liveness of subjects (see Section 4.2 of the following chapter). Particularly by linking knowledge to the authentication process, one can assume liveness if the user is able to present correct knowledge along with the physiological measurement.

Liveness detection is not necessarily a requirement for all applications. Considering for example user authentication in supervised scenarios, such as border control areas, liveness may be ensured by other means than the biometric modalities themselves. However, particularly in unsupervised environments, liveness detection is a desirable goal and an integration scheme for this should therefor be considered already in the design of an authentication system.

3.2 Active Biometric Traits

In this section, we will introduce to the most active relevant biometric modalities: voice (subsection 3.2.1), handwriting (subsection 3.2.2) and gait recognition (subsection 3.2.3). For each of these three modalities, we will provide a look at the sampling process for biometric information, outline some fundamental approaches to feature extraction and classification and present some state-of-the art recognition rates, which are achieved today. Additionally to these three selected active schemes, we will briefly look at two additional behavioral traits, keystroke and lip movement, in subsection 3.2.4.

3.2.1   Voice Biometrics

Speech processing has been an area of high interest for researchers and scientists in the signal process domain over many decades. In the 1990's, the development towards multimedia enabled PCs has started and today, literally every new PC sold is equipped with a digital audio-processing unit called sound card. At the same time, the computational resources even of standard PCs are well sufficient for digital signal processing and therefore, use of digitized voice as biometric appears very attractive. Besides the task of **Automated Speaker Recognition (ASR)**, there exist other, different goals for voice processing, including textual speech recognition or estimating emotions from voice characteristics. In context of this book however, we will limit our views to the particular task of authentication subjects by their voice.

Over the years, a vast number of technical approaches have been published and a great number of commercial and academic biometric ASR systems have been implemented. An exhaustive discussion of the different techniques would be out of the scope of this book; thus we limit our review to some fundamental techniques in this discipline. Readers, who are interested to learn more details about this modality, are encouraged to refer to the comprehensive literature available. A selection of books, tutorials and articles can be found, including [RaJu1993] [Furu1994], [LeSP1996], [Camp1997], [Naik1990] and [Reyn2002].

One fundamental classification in voice modality is based on the textual content of utterances used for recognition. In text-dependent speaker recognition, each user of an authentication system speaks one specific text for authentication. A text may be a word or more complex structures like sentences or passphrases. This text-dependency implies that one single user may register more than one characteristic with an authentication system, allowing use of different utterances in different contexts. Text-independent speaker recognition, constituting the other category of ASR, attempt to recognize subjects solely by the characteristics of their voice, without dependency to the textual content or other features like temporal length of the spoken sequence. Obviously, the later category is of particular interest for forensics, where it may be desirable to recognize people without the requirement to have them speaking a specific utterance. Although for user authentication, typically text-dependent ASR is used, the technical principles are almost identical and both methods are qualified for authentication in principle. Therefor, we will not further differentiate between text-dependent and text-independent approaches for the remainder of this section.

Data Acquision

Typically in voice based biometrics, the analog waveforms generated from utterances are directly digitally recorded at the authentication device, using built-in sound cards of computers. These sound cards perform the analog-digital conversion using built-in D/A processors, with typical modulation resolutions of 12-16 bits and sampling rates up to 44 kHz. Since the analog transmission line in this scenario is very short, the main quality aspects of recordings depend on the physical characteristics of the microphone, (e.g. frequency response, sensitivity), which usually can be rated high quality [Camp1997]. However in verification scenarios over telephony networks, significant degradations in signal quality have to be expected, mainly due to the limited bandwidth. Given a typical sampling rate of 8kHz in digital telephony, the Nyquist theorem limits the available frequency bandwidth in the digital domain to half of the sampling rate; thus the actual bandwidth is less than 4kHz [Nyqu1928]. With a typical frequency range of 250 Hz to 6000 Hz for human speech, obviously some frequencies may not be represented in such telephony applications.

Feature Extraction

The basis of most feature extraction approaches is the observation, that the speech spectrum shape encodes significant information about the speaker's vocal tract. This appears to be mainly the case due to two reasons. First, the human vocal tract forms a resonator and second, the glottis is a source of pitch harmonics [Reyn2002]. Consequently, most feature extraction approaches aim at extracting spectrum-based features and typical methods for extracting first-order features are Linear Predictive Coding (LPC) or Fourier Transformation (FT). Based on these first-order spectra, many approaches compute higher order cepstral features, such as Mel-Frequency Cepstral Coefficients (MFCC). Cepstral analysis is based on the idea of inverse transforming the logarithmic spectrum from frequency to temporal domain, thus the cepstrum of a signal can be defined as the inverse FT (IFT) of the logarithm of the FT of the original signal.

Spectral or cepstrum features are extracted for temporal subsections of the entire audio signal, called windows. These windows are usually shifted sequentially over the entire signal and are characterized by a window size (in milliseconds, ms) and a window-to-window offset in milliseconds. Figure 3-3 illustrates this typical feature extraction process for voice biometrics, starting from the signal acquisition on the left and leading to the cepstrum feature signal representation on the right. Note that in this illustration, no preprocessing is included. However, in many practical systems, such preprocessing includes techniques like filters for reducing background noises or other methods for emphasizing those signals that are relevant for biometric features. These filters are typically implemented as transfer functions in frequency domain.

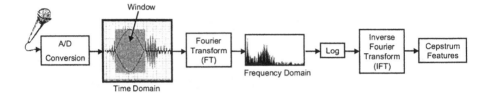

Figure 3-3. Example for a cepstral feature extraction in voice biometrics

Comparison and Classification

For the comparison of feature values after feature extraction of an actual test sample, mainly two different models are used in speech biometrics: template models and stochastic models. In the first category, cumulated distances are calculated between the features of the actual test sample and the stored reference features. Amongst the variety of different methods for measuring distances in feature space (see Chapter 7, Section 7.1), mainly Euclidean and Mahalanobis distances are used in voice biometrics. Based on such distance values, the verification process can be implemented, for example, simply as a threshold-based decision function whereby the distance between reference and sample may not exceed a given threshold value.

Stochastic models formulate the classification problem differently, i.e. by measuring observation likelihood given a particular speaker model. In this case, observation denotes a feature vector from the collection of features of the actual speaker and the speaker model refers to the enrollment. Each feature vector possesses a Probability Density Function (PDF), which is individual to the speaker and their parameter may be estimated from training vectors obtained during enrollment. Very popular models for stochastic methods are Hidden-Markov Models (HMM), which consist of finite-state machines, where a statistic model is associated with each given state. This statistical model defines the transition probabilities $a_{ji} = p(s_j|s_i)$, i.e. the probability a_{ji} of a state transition to state s_j given state s_i. Figure 3-4 illustrates a simplified example for a three-state HMM consisting of states s_1, s_2 and s_3 and the six resulting transition probabilities. Initially, HMM have been used in speech recognition, but they have been successfully applied for speaker verification as well, for example in [ReCa1995]. The result of such stochastic methods is quite different from those bases on distance measures, as they are of true probabilistic nature, i.e. the comparison result is represented in terms of a probability value, whereas distances denote values in different spaces, depending on the type of features. Thus, intuitively, the use of stochastic methods appears to be reasonable.

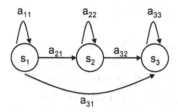

Figure 3-4. Example for a HMM consisting of three states: s_1, s_2 and s_3

Recognition Accuracy

Literally for all published ASR systems, including academic approaches as well as commercial products, figures regarding the recognition accuracy have been published as a measurement for their recognition capability. In order to get a general overview about the state-of-the-art in ASR, one would be required to look at the wide spectrum of different systems, and perform a comparative study of their published recognition rate. However, such comparison between figures appears to be difficult, because most of the published results are based on tests of proprietary data sets, which may vary widely with respect to the quality, quantity and characteristics of voice samples.

Due to this lack of comparability, some organizations have started to collect corpora of voice data for comparative evaluations of ASR systems, for an overview see for example [CaRe1999]. These data are categorized by properties such as number and gender of subjects, sampling device (e.g. telephone network, direct sampling), number and duration of samples per user, as well as type of speech (conversational or prompted text). Based on collections in such corpora, some institutions have performed comparative evaluations. One of the experienced groups in evaluation of various biometric systems the National Institute of Standards and Technology (NIST). Besides other biometric modalities, the ASR group has been evaluating text-independent speaker identification systems since 1996 extensively. NIST Evaluations include aspects of different application scenarios like telephony voice over landline or cellular networks. Recent evaluations based on more than 59.000 trials from 291 speakers in identification mode, have reported an accuracy in the range of 1% false recognition rate at a 5% miss rate (i.e. a 1% FIR plus a 4% non-identification rate), for the most accurate amongst the 16 participating systems. Further observation include a continuos increase in recognition accuracy over the years and a degradation of accuracy, for voice data collected over cellular telephone networks as compared to landlines, see [PrMa1998] and [MaPr2002].

3.2.2   Handwriting Biometrics

The active modality of handwriting is widely associated with signature verification in context of biometric user authentication systems. Later in this book in Chapter 5, we will elaborate on additional types of handwriting samples such as passphrases or Personal Identification Numbers (PIN), which may be used for this purpose as well. We call these kind of alternative handwriting samples *semantics*.

From an application point of view, handwriting appears quite intuitive, since the signature has been in use for authentication purposes in the analog world for centuries. Even in our digitized world today, the process of signing a document is very common to many people and performed frequently, for example when signing credit card receipts or documents like car rental contracts. Furthermore, many ID documents today already contain the image of the holder's signature amongst other biometric information.

Two different approaches exist for the analysis of handwriting biometrics: **online authentication methods**, which have access to signals *sampled during the process of writing*, whereas *offline methods* refer to the result of a *completed writing process*. The majority of handwriting-based authentication systems make use of online methods, whereas offline methods are more common in forensics, for example for verification of signatures on documents like bank checks. From Chapter 4 onward, we will discuss online handwriting in great detail, therefore, at this point, we will briefly summarize the most important differences between online and offline methods.

Data Acquision
In **online handwriting biometrics**, physical measurements are taken during the writing process, which is typically achieved by digitizer tablets. These tablets measure dynamic features like pen position, pressure and angle, convert them from analog to the digital domain and make them available as a sequence of discrete measurement values. More details on such digitizer devices can be found in Sections 4.2 to 4.5 of Chapter 4 in this book.

Offline handwriting methods do not use temporal information for the authentication process and since the handwriting samples are usually taken from printed material, the most common data acquisition technique is image scanning. Scanning is typically performed at resolutions around 300 dots per inch (dpi) and 256 gray levels per pixel, which can be easily achieved by industrial, low cost image scanners.

Feature Extraction

Due to the two different types of biometric data, for the types of features, which can be extracted after preprocessing, a categorization into features including temporal information (online features) and features considering only spatial information (offline features) exists. Furthermore, within each of the two categories, a differentiation between the scopes of the feature analysis can be made: either features are extracted on entire samples (global features) or for parts of the writing sample.

Figure 3-5 illustrates this taxonomy and further refines online features by their representation, which can be either statistical scalar terms (parameter) or functional descriptions of signals (functions).

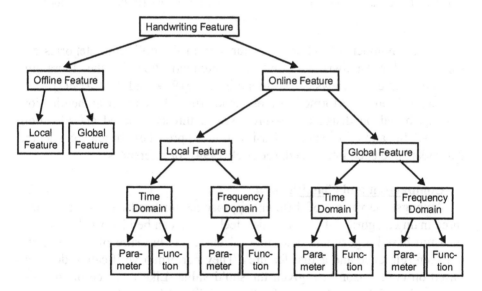

Figure 3-5. Feature taxonomy for handwriting biometrics

Examples for basic offline features are pixel density and curvature, which can be determined either on a global scope, i.e. from the entire image of the handwriting trace, or locally, for example by dividing the entire image into a fixed number of rectangular areas. Figure 3-6 illustrates such features, where hypothetical **pixel count parameters** (PCP_1, ..., PCP_{12}) are calculated for a segmentation into 4 columns by 3 rows. Functional features for online handwriting parameters include normalized signal representations of the **horizontal and vertical pen movement** ($x(t)$ and $y(t)$ respectively), which are used for signal comparison, for example by correlation and distance measurement methods. An example for such feature representations for a global analysis of the signals will be given in our introduction to the Minimum Quadratic Envelope Distance Algorithm (MQED) in Section 5.6. The statistical parameters of the Biometric Hash function, which will be discussed in Chapter 6 of this book, represent global parameters from the time domain.

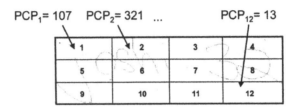

Figure 3-6. Example for offline features: Pixel Count Parameter (PCP$_1$ ... PCP$_{12}$) for 12 rectangular areas

A great number of additional features from the different categories are suggested for handwriting-based user authentication in the literature, comprehensive overviews can be found in [PlLo1989] and [GuCa1997].

Comparison is performed in most handwriting-based user authentication systems based on distance measures with a threshold-based classification process. In addition, some classification approaches based on neural networks have been introduced, see [LePl1994] for references.

Comparison and Classification

Amongst the variety of different approaches for handwriting biometrics, three main categories of classification techniques can be identified. Distance measure based algorithms determine distances as measure of dissimilarity between reference and actual features. They perform a verification decision based on comparison to a given threshold value. Like in voice biometrics, statistical models are also used for the modality of handwriting, particularly HMM have been suggested widely. Again, such statistical models result directly in matching probabilities rather than differences in measurement.

The third category of classification schemes uses neural networks for this purpose by training them with different types of features, along with identities of users during enrollment. In this case, the neural network usually outputs directly the determined identity, if designed for identification, rather than distance or matching probability scores in the two other categories. Further details of handwriting based biometric algorithms will be reflected in detail in Section 5.2 of Chapter 5.

Recognition Accuracy

Signature or handwriting biometrics is widely believed to be a less accurate discipline compared to other biometric modalities. However, significant improvements in recognition rates have been reported over the years, however most of them have been justified based on evaluations on proprietary test sets. Only recently, a first open contest has been performed based on 33 different algorithms; all of them tested by using one identical reference database [YCXG+2004]. Here, the best system has shown an EER of slightly above 2%, which appears to be rather low for an active biometrics. However, in this initial test, only the verification mode has been analyzed and the ROC along with EER have been published. Identification scenarios have not been considered, making it difficult to compare, particularly to the results of NIST voice evaluations, for example.

3.2.3   Gait Biometrics

A fairly recent active biometric modality is gait recognition. Here, the goal is to find specific characteristics in movement of subjects from video streams. This discipline has been motivated by experimental observations, where individuals were able to identify other people known to them only by looking at the projection of silhouettes of their body movements. Besides movement characteristics, the proportions of human limbs appear to be of significance to human in this natural recognition experiment.

Gait biometrics aims at adopting this recognition capability by automated systems. This approach is of particular interest in observation scenarios, for example for automatically identifying subjects wanted by law enforcement authorities. Other areas of application are Human-Computer-Interaction scenarios, where ubiquitous systems sensor for moving subjects and attempt to identify them, for example to provide individualized service to them.

Data Acquision

Since gait biometrics addresses features of the moving body, video recordings are the media to provide biometric information. For the video sampling, standard digital video techniques are typically used, with varying resolutions (around 720x576 pixels) and frame rates starting from 25fps. The video recording usually can be performed in three setups regarding a static camera perspective: frontal walk, canonical walk and free perspective. In the frontal walk scenario, the subjects approach the camera in a frontal manner, following the straight line of the optical axis of the camera. Canonical walk denotes a scenario whereby subject follow a line orthogonal to the optical axis, i.e. they move in a left-to-right or right-to-left manner in the video, with a sidewise view to their bodies. The main advantage for these first two settings is the limited isometric deformation in the resulting images, allowing for simple compensation of the isometric effects. In the third scenario, where the camera may have an arbitrary position relative to the person, the isometric distortions are more complex to model and when considering a moving camera, the problem gets even harder due to the dynamic of both observer and observed subject. Figure 3-7 illustrates the two scenarios of frontal and canonical walks.

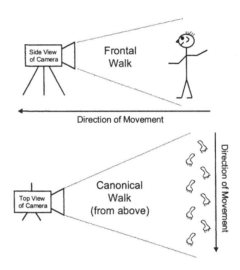

Figure 3-7. Two setups for recording of gait: frontal walk (top) and canonical walk (bottom)

Feature Extraction

The extraction of movement features from the video firstly requires detection of the bulk movement of the target body. To do so, typically pre-processing for removing background information is performed, followed by an edge detection to identify the bodily shape in each of the video's frame. Once the target body is tracked, a wide spectrum of features can be extracted using image-processing methods. Besides the possibility to calculate static measurement of body and stride such as vertical distance between head and foot, head and pelvis or left and right foot [BoJo2001], a wide spectrum of dynamic features have been suggested. These include early approaches like a five-stick model to the detected silhouette, as shown in Figure 3-8. Here, a simplified model consisting of five sticks is fitted into the silhouette, where for example stick 1 represents the body corpus including head, sticks 2 and 3 represent the left and right thighs and sticks 4 and 5 the shanks. After normalization of the resulting vectors for each image frame, translation patterns over time (XYT patterns) are extracted from the outer points of limbs, see for example [NiAd1994]. Over the years, many more feature extraction methods have been published, including, but not limited to eigenvalue decompositions, and spectral features. A comprehensive overview, including recent feature extraction approaches is given in [NiCa2004].

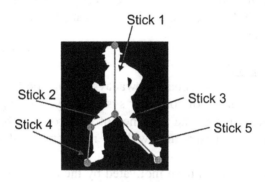

Figure 3-8. Example for a five-stick model extraction from the bodily silhouette as suggested in [NiAd1994]

Comparison and Classification

Early approaches like [NiAd1994] used Euclidean distance measures and threshold-based decisions for the classification of test samples. In recent activities, probabilistic approaches have shown promising results, for example maximum likelihood estimation or Gaussian models within Bayesian decision networks [AbCD2002]. These Bayesian classifiers have recently also shown good performance in model-based estimations with feature vectors of higher order [BaNi2005].

Recognition Accuracy

As for most other biometric modalities, an exhaustive comparative overview of state-of-the art in gait recognition is difficult, due to the varying test sets used in evaluations, but also due to the different setups for the video acquisition. Nixon and Carter [NiCa2004] show that recognition accuracy furthermore depends on camera viewpoint and the kind of shoes worn by the test subjects. Here correct identification rates between 76% (wearing different shoes) and 99% have been reported for 5 different databases, some of which containing videos of more than 100 subjects.

In verification mode, recent work reported an improvement in EER from 8.6% to 7.3% by using Bayesian probability rather than Euclidean distance [BaNi2005]. These results were obtained based on relatively large databases, consisting of 1079 video sequences from 115 persons [SGNC2002].

3.2.4   Other Active Traits

Besides voice, handwriting and gait, there a few other modalities, which have been researched for use in biometric user authentication. Here, at the end of subsection 3.2, we want to briefly summarize some of these additional approaches for the two selected areas of keystroke dynamics and lip movement and reference some of the relevant related work for further studies by the reader.

<u>Keystroke Dynamics</u>
With every computer keyboard nowadays, a specific kind of biometric sensor is provided to users of computer systems. By referring to an internal clock and time stamping of the sequence of keystrokes, a biometric signal may be sampled very easily and without requirement of special sensor hardware.

Keystroke dynamics has been motivated by the observation that users of computer keyboards tend to develop specific timing patterns during typing of text. Such timing patterns can been observed in the timing of the letter sequences of frequent words as well as on the level of combinations of letters occurring frequently within words of a given language. Examples for such combination in English language are the sequences *"th"* and *"ing"*. With this observation, it is possible to generate user-specific timing models and to use those for feature extraction and authentication. Depending on the nature of textual input, like in voice and handwriting biometrics, text-dependent and text-independent recognition can be performed.

Features of keystroke sequences are typically extracted based on **digraph**, **trigraph** or, more generally, **n-graph segments** of the entire text. Here, one n-graph denotes a sequence of n characters in the key stream. If this technique is applied step-by-step from left to right with an offset of one character, any text sequence of length l characters will result in $l-n+1$ n-graphs. Consequently, for $n=2$ such sequences are called digraphs and for $n=3$ trigraphs. For each keystroke, two measurements can be taken: one time stamp at the switching point of the key down event, $t_{KeyDown}$, and one at the key release event t_{KeyUp}. These measurements are illustrated Figure 3-9 for an exemplary phrase *"hello world"*, resulting in a total of 22 time stamps: $t_{1,KeyDown}, \ldots, t_{11,KeyDown}$ and $t_{1,KeyUp}, \ldots, t_{11,KeyUp}$. Grouped to n-graphs, these timings can be used for example to generate latency and key press duration patterns [JoGu1990]. While in case of digraphs, four possibilities exist for generating latency diagrams by combining the two types of time stamps for the two keys, typically the offset between the two key-down events is looked at. Figure 3-10 shows such a diagram containing latency patterns for an enrollment and an actual test sample for the *"hello world"* example. The ordinate shows the 10 resulting digraphs and on the abscissa, the latency duration is shown in milliseconds.

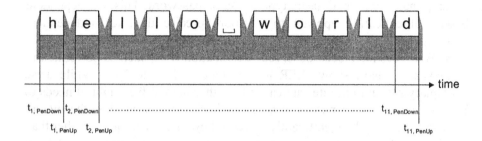

Figure 3-9. Keystroke time measurement for an exemplary key sequence "*hello world*" of length *l=11*

Diagrams like shown in Figure 3-10 can be generated by mathematical toolboxes [MoRu2000] or by freeware tools like *jKeyStroke* [BBEC+2004].

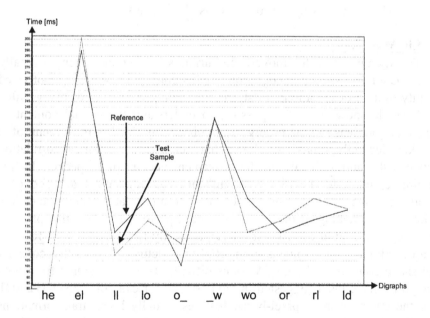

Figure 3-10. Digraph latency diagrams for reference and test sample based on an exemplary key sequence

For the classification task, similar techniques like for other biometric modalities have been evaluated, including various distance measures and probabilistic classifiers such as Bayesian-like classifiers. Furthermore, the usage of neural networks has been investigated at an early stage already, for example in [BrRo1993].

One of the possibilities to measure recognition accuracy in keystrokes is a test scenario, where all users type the same password. This text-dependent based authentication appears to be more precise than text-independent schemes, see for example [MoRu2000], where recognition rates in the range of 83% to 92% have been observed. Verification tests, such as performed in [MoRW2002] have shown EER in the range of 15% to 20%. While these exemplary recognition rates appear to be rather high at first sight, it needs to be considered that in password-based authentication scenarios, the overall security level may be significantly increased by such techniques. Rather than verifying only the correctness of the password, the authentication system may additionally verify the biometric in the specific typing style, i.e. on a second authentication level. A successful imposter in this case would need to both find the password of an authentic user and reproduce the original's typing characteristics, in order to get authenticated. This argument and the ease of system integration in knowledge-based authentication schemes appear to be major advantages of keystroke biometrics.

Lip Movement

The dynamics of lip movement during speaking has been originally investigated for speech recognition applications [ChDM2002], motivated mainly by two observations. First, the lip-reading capability of many, often deaf people shows that it is possible to understand the textual content of utterances at least in part only from observing the lip movement of a speaker. Secondly, it has been shown that there exists a statistical correlation between the audio signal and the movement vectors of a speaker. In this discipline, input to the biometric authentication system is a video of a speaking subject. From this video, first of all a face region detection, followed by tracking of the lip movement is performed. After this process, resulting in a **region of interest (ROI)**, basically two categories of features can be extracted: video pixels in the ROI or structural features that consider the shape contour of the lips. Various different types of features from both categories have been suggested in the past, see for example [PNGG+2003]. For the comparison of pixel-based features, usually linear transformations for dimensionality reduction are used, such as eigenvalue decompositions, called "Eigenlips" for this kind of modality. In the other category of contour-based features, frequency-based comparison approaches for example based on the Discrete Cosine Transform (DCT) coefficients of movement vectors have been investigated additionally to statistical comparisons recently, particularly for application in user authentication, see [CYET2004].

Lip movement is usually not intended for use as a single modality for user authentication, but rather as one component of a special category of multimodal systems, called **audio-visual speaker recognition**. For further discussion s of multimodal, or multibiometric systems, see Section 3.4 of this chapter.

This multimodal approach is rather suggestive, since video recordings are usually not limited to the lip region, but cover the entire face and an audio stream typically is available also for speech recordings.

Some recently published test results with respect to recognition accuracy of lip movement alone indicate the EER between 5.2% and 6.8% can be achieved for test subject populations of 50 users and 5 repetitions for each of them during enrollment and verification ([CYET2004]).

3.3   Passive Biometric Traits

This subsection will introduce to the three most common passive biometric traits: fingerprint (subsection 3.3.1), face (subsection 3.3.2) and iris (subsection 3.3.3). Like we did for the active modalities in the previous section, we will first look into data acquisition aspects, outline feature extraction and classification approaches and finally discuss some recent observations with respect to recognition accuracy for each modality. This subsection closes with a short summary of additional passive modalities based on hand and retina in subsection 3.3.4.

3.3.1   Fingerprint Biometrics

The analysis of fingerprints has a long tradition in forensic identification of persons, and has widely replaced the method of anthropometric measurement since the early 20th century (see introduction in Chapter 2). The basis for this biometric modality is the skin structure of fingertips of humans, which is of unique structure. It is a phenotypic biological feature, i.e. a specific manifestation of a trait, making it unique, even for identical twins. Ridges and valleys make up an individual structure and it has been observed that the characteristic structure of these ridges and valleys usually does not change over time. Today, three levels of structures can be derived from fingerprint images:

- *Global- (or Course-) Level Features*: classify a global pattern built from the entire collection of ridges of one fingertip image into two **Wirbel classes** (whorl and twin loop) and the four **Lasso classes** (arch, tented arch, right loop, or left loop), see [BaSE1997].

- *Minutiae-based Features*: these features are based on characteristics of and interrelation between local ridges in the spatial domain. The classification originates from features used in forensics since more than a century and specific occurrences here include bifurcations (i.e. branching), islands, termination (i.e. end-points), crossovers, spurs, lakes and independent ridges.
- *Sweat-pore-based Features*: pores, i.e. openings of a sweat gland are visible on the surface of the finger ridges and make up a distinct pattern formed by spots on top of ridges, see [RoSt1997]. Acquisition of these features, sometimes also called third-level features, require sensors providing high spatial resolution.

Figure 3-11 illustrates the taxonomy of Global Level Features (upper part), the specific Minutiae Features as well as a pane of a fingerprint image showing the tagged positions of sweat-pores.

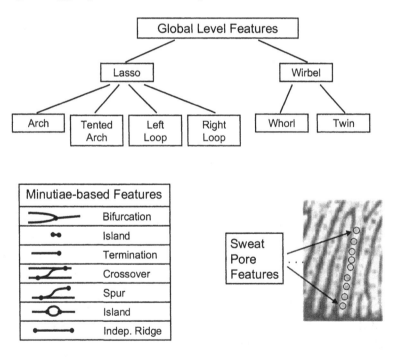

Figure 3-11. Global Level Features (top), Minutiae-based features (lower left) and sweat pore feature examples (lower right) for fingerprint images

In this section of the book, we may only outline the very fundamental approaches for analyzing fingerprints towards automated user authentication. Amongst all biometric modalities, fingerprint analysis has probably attracted the greatest number of researchers and consequently, an enormous number of publications can be found in this area, allowing for more detailed further studies. Some book reading suggestions for details in fingerprint technology include [MMJS2003] and [RaBo2003].

Data Acquisition

For automated processing in user authentication, an image of the fingertip (then called fingerprint) is taken by sensor devices. The scanning technology can be divided into two categories: optical and on-optical sensors. Sensors of the first category expose the fingertip, which mostly has to be affixed on top of a glass surface, to light and take images of the optical response. Non-optical sensors capture information about the elevation profile on the skin surface of the fingertip by other means than light. Here, we find capacitive approaches, where an electrical voltage field is established between the sensor surface and the skin and a height profile of the ridges and valleys on the skin is derived from capacity measurements of an array of tiny sensor electrodes. Other non-optical sensors measure a thermal profile of the skin from a specific distance and extract elevation information from this 2-D thermogram. Also, piezo-electric sensors are used, which generate voltage when exposed to pressure. In all cases, the data acquisition results in a 2-D array of scalar measurements, which are usually interpreted as gray-scale images in varying resolutions and sizes. Typically in automated fingerprint recognition, image sizes are in the range of 0.4 Inches to 1 Inch in height and 0.4 Inches to 0.6 Inches in width. Scanning resolutions of these sensors are in the area of 200 to 1000 dpi, see [MMJS2003].

Feature Extraction

As shown earlier in this subsection, we can differentiate into three levels of features: Global, Minutiae and Sweat-pore based features. Although features of the first and third category have shown good accuracy in biometric recognition (see [BaSE1997] and [RoSt1997] respectively), the majority of approaches base on minutiae detection. At this point in the book, we shall only briefly outline the most common image processing techniques for finding and classifying such feature points, based on the seven types of minutiae shown earlier. The result of the feature extraction process is typically a map of spatial location, type and orientation of features, relative to the original image.

Minutiae detection requires numerous preprocessing steps, which usually start with some image enhancement filters, for example histogram equalization to emphasize those frequencies in the image, that are relevant for the fingerprint patterns. Another image enhancement that has shown high efficiency in fingerprints is direction-based frequency filtering, e.g. by

Gabor filters, which emphasize ridges in a local orientation. Further, some standard image processing routines are usually applied for smoothing and sharpening, followed by a binarization process to obtain true black and white images. Based on the binary image, thinning and erosion algorithms lead to an image representation, whereby the ridges have a line width of 1 pixel, called skeleton. Figure 3-12 shows some exemplary images for each of these processing steps.

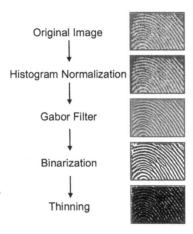

Figure 3-12. Preprocessing of fingerprint images

Based on the resulting skeletonized images, minutiae detection is a rather simple task, which can be achieved for example by defining 8-neighbor rules. Here, each pixel of the image is analyzed in context of its 8 neighboring pixels and, for example, if a particular pixel has only 1 neighbor, it can be classified as a termination minutia.

Note that besides minutiae techniques, other types of features, such as ridge and correlation-based features exist, which require different kinds of preprocessing. Particularly correlation-based methods, which are sensitive to transformations, require size and orientation normalization.

Comparison and Classification

One major advantage in minutiae-based fingerprint recognition is the scale and rotation invariance of the detected feature points. Rather than measuring positions and directions of features in an absolute coordination system, relative positions of minutiae points can be compared during the matching process. A simplified illustration of two bifurcations is shown in Figure 3-13. Here, (x_1, y_1) and (x_2, y_2) denote the absolute positions of feature points 1 and 2 respectively, Θ_1 and Θ_2 denote their orientations. One possible approach for comparison of minutiae is to compute a map of positions of each individual point to all other minutiae in the image. Such a model can be achieved for example terms of polar coordinates, where distances and angles to all other feature points are enumerated for each minutia. For the example in figure 3-13, we yield:

$$\delta_{1,2} = \sqrt{(y_2 - y_1)^2 + (x_2 - x_1)^2} \tag{3-1}$$

and for the angular orientation as shown in the plot:

$$\alpha_{1,2} = \Pi - \arctan(\frac{|y_1 - y_2|}{|x_2 - x_1|}) \tag{3-2}$$

Furthermore, the difference between the two orientations yields $(\Theta_1 - \Theta_2)$. Thus we have three scalar distance measures between the feature points, independent of the orientation of the coordinate system.

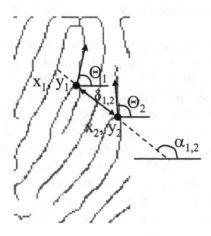

Figure 3-13. Two exemplary minutiae feature points of type bifurcation. Their respective coordinates and orientations are given by (x_1, y_1, Θ_1) and (x_2, y_2, Θ_2)

There are a wide number of additional methods for extraction of local distances, which we refrain to referring to for the sake of briefness. Regardless of their type, collections of local distance measures can be cumulated (e.g. by addition) during the matching process and consequently result in one overall similarity measure. This distance, as a term of dissimilarity, then again may be used for a threshold-based comparison during the verification or identification process.

Note that the method briefly introduced here is just an example to illustrate one possible approach for minutiae feature matching. Distance measures and classification strategies are strongly depended on the underlying feature category, and a great number of very different approaches have been published. In order to get more detailed insights in fingerprint recognition, it is necessary to study additional literature. Some suggested references have been given earlier in this subsection.

Recognition Accuracy

One important source to assess the recognition accuracy of fingerprint biometrics is the Fingerprint Verification Contest (FVC), which has been conducted for the third time in the year 2004, see [MMCW+2004]. Here test data has been collected on three different sensors and the data set has been expanded by computer generated (artificial) fingerprint images. A total number of 67 algorithms have undergone a unique test protocol and the detailed evaluation results have been presented in [FVC2004]. The best algorithm here achieved an average EER of 2.07% and more of 30% of the algorithms yield EER less than 5%. Besides EER, FVC 2004 has considered other performance measurements, such as rejection rates during enrollment or FRR at zero FMR.

When looking at these recognition results, it is of importance to mention that the underlying evaluation concept does not consider skilled forgeries. It has been shown that dummy fingerprints can circumvent some fingerprint recognition systems, see [MMYH2002] and [Sass2004]. This attack is based on the production of rubber masks, which can be produced from digital images of fingerprints. Such images can be taken from for example from polished surfaces such as glass, but can also be reverse-engineered from minutiae representations, as shown in [CEMM2000]. Although recently mechanisms for life detection address this vulnerability, it needs to be considered in general that even abstract feature descriptions such as minutiae diagrams may not robustly prevent this kind of attacks.

3.3.2   Iris Biometrics

Basis for iris biometrics are images of the iris, being the most visible part of eyes of humans. The iris is a flattened ring consisting of pigmented tissue, which controls the contraction of the pupil. It is ring-shaped, almost circular and delimitates the pupil area. The iris itself is embedded in a white outer coating of the eye, called sclera. Figure 3-14 shows a simplified layout of this anatomy.

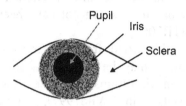

Figure 3-14. Outline of the anatomy of an eye

The iris is usually strongly pigmented and it has been observed that these pigments form very specific, individual textures. These textures are the basis for analysis methods, which lead to a very accurate biometrics for user authentication.

Data Acquision

Capturing of images of irises requires close-up photographs of the opened eye. It has been shown that a resolved iris radius of 80-130 pixels is a typical value, sufficient for iris recognition today. In order to get appropriate images of the iris texture, the eye needs to be illuminated during capturing. In order to avoid annoyances, Near-Infrared Radiation (NIR) in the 700-900 nanometer band is used for this purpose, which can be efficiently captures by monochrome Charge-Coupled Devices (CCD). Most iris cameras today are based this technology and provide resolutions of at least 480x640 pixels. Consequently, the captured iris should cover at least 30% of the horizontal area of the image, which requires a very close positioning of the camera during the acquisition process and a precise positioning of the subject's eye in relation to the camera. Mainly due to this reason, data acquisition is a crucial process in iris recognition, because the handling of sensors has been found rather difficult, see for example [Sass2004]. Current research addresses the question of improving user interfaces for capturing iris images in authentication systems, and more convenient devices are to be expected.

Feature Extraction

In iris biometrics, the first problem to be solved prior to feature extraction is the location of the actual shape and position of the iris in an image. This can be done for example with edge detectors as known from image processing, because due to the white color of the sclera and the dark image of the pupil on eye photographs, the edges between the three structures are usually well defined. One technique suggested by Daugman uses Integro-differential operators, which further exploit the circular geometry of structures and behave like a circular edge detector, see [Daug1993]. Some additions to this concept have been suggested, such as Hough transform in [TMTR2002].

Once the iris area is identified from the image, the texture can be localized and feature values may be extracted from it. For this purpose, different feature extraction algorithms have been suggested, for example correlation-based approaches in [Wild1997], multidimensional Hilbert transform in [TMTR2002], Gabor wavelet decomposition in [Daug1993] and others. Daugman's approach, which has been patented in the year 1994 ([Daug1994]), shall be reflected here very briefly, due to its high practical significance in a number of products and practical applications. Further details of this technique are given for example in [Daug2004]. The feature extraction leads to a very compact feature representation consisting of 2048 bits, the so-called *IrisCode*.

Very simplified, the generation of IrisCode features is performed in the following steps:

- Transformation of the extracted iris region from Cartesian to polar coordinate systems.
- Projection of local regions of the iris onto quadrature 2D Gabor wavelets.
- Coding of the real and imaginary parts of each phase portion (the amplitude portion does not contain sufficient discriminatory information) of the complex-valued coefficients onto 2 bits of IrisCode. This coding is called Phase-Quadrant Demodulation code.

These processing steps are repeated across the iris with various wavelet sizes, frequencies and orientations 1024 times and thus yield a 2048 bit feature vector by concatenation of each of the 2 bit demodulation codes.

Comparison and Classification

For the example of IrisCodes, a very simple and computationally efficient comparison can be implemented by using the Hamming distance. Since feature representations are binary vectors of fixed length, the

Hamming distance between two IrisCodes in a vector representation is defined by the number of non-identical bits at each vector position. In can be easily determined by a bit-wise *xor*-operation between the two vectors and a cross-sum of nonzero bits in the resulting vector. For a more formal discussion of the Hamming Distance and other distance functions, see Section 7.1 in Chapter 7 of this book.

In case of the 2048-bit IrisCode, resulting distance values have the property of being in the range [0,...,2048], thus allowing a very straightforward threshold-based classification.

Recognition Accuracy

Compared to other biometric modalities, iris recognition methods have been tested very comprehensively and experimental results, as well as discussions on the statistical significance with respect to very large populations have been discussed very thoroughly, for example in [Daug2004]. Here, experiments based on 7070 different pairs of same-eye images, but captured by different types of cameras, have been conducted by exhaustive determination of all Inter-class and Intra-class Hamming Distances. The result of these experiments was that it was possible to operate the system at threshold values, which actually led to zero-EER, i.e. no False Matches and no False Rejections. Further, it has been shown in [Daug2004], that the statistical distribution of intra-class distances can be approximated by a binomial distribution, allowing predicting odds of False Match Rates for much larger populations. It may be concluded from these results, that even False Match probabilities in the range of 1 in 10^{13} (i.e. 10^{-11} %) can be achieved by the system at very low one-digit FNMR.

However in these tests, the biometric system has not been exposed to skilled forgeries. Like for fingerprint methods, it has been conceptionally shown that iris recognition systems may be circumvented by forgeries, even the attacked systems were instances of early generation systems, see [MaHS2004]. Ongoing research addresses strategies for anti-spoofing, e.g. by liveness detection.

3.3.3 Face Biometrics

The face modality has an advantageous property of not requiring any sort of contact or complex user processes during the acquisition of images. Standard digital cameras can usually be used for acquiring images of faces, which are the source of biometric authentication. Besides verification of subjects, for example in access control applications like border control, automated identification of persons by their facial images is of high interest for example in surveillance scenarios in search for suspects.

With the emerging technology of 3D scanning, recently another sub-discipline based on 3D meshes measured from faces of persons has developed in face recognition. Methods used in 3D-face recognition are often quite similar to those used in 2D recognition and an enormous number of different approaches can be found in the literature. In this overview part of the book, we may only introduce to some very fundamental aspects in this area of high research activity and we have to limit our views to 2D technologies. For detailed study of this topic, a number of comprehensive publications may be referred to, including [WePB+2002], [ZCPR2003] and [GoMP2000].

Data Acquision

Sensors used in face recognition are digital cameras, which usually are operated at specific frame rates, i.e. the biometric system is provided with a series of images. Today, almost all cameras are equipped with CCD arrays of various spatial resolutions (up to several millions of pixels) and different frame rates. Although high spatial resolution is usually referred to as quality criterion for digital cameras, it is not necessarily desirable in biometric face recognition. Due to the computational complexity of the underlying image processing algorithms, this discipline faces a trade-off problem between recognition performance and the image resolution, see [WaZS2004].

The capturing processes of images can be classified in various modes, depending on the circumstances of the capturing process. A practical approach is to differentiate with respect to three aspects ([Phil2004]):

- *Indoor* scenarios, with control over lighting conditions versus *outdoor, uncontrolled* imaging.
- *Single* still setups, where only one frontal image of the subject is us used for authentication versus *Multiple Stills*, where the face is photographed from multiple positions (e.g. frontal plus two side profiles).
- *Cooperative* applications, where it can be assumed that the users will follow guidelines for a successful capturing versus *non-cooperative* scenarios, where users are not assumed to act in a cooperative manner, for example because they are not even aware of the capturing (e.g. in observation scenarios).

Feature Extraction

According to [WaZS2004], mainly two categories of feature extraction can be found in face recognition today: *global* and *component* based approaches. In the first category, typically all or part of the original image is used as one single feature vector, which requires alignment between the images in all cases. Such an alignment can be performed for example by detection of corresponding key points in the facial part of the photograph and a subsequent warping of one of the images towards the other(s).

The other category of features addresses geometrical properties of the face, such as relation and size of eyes, nose and mouth in the image. Another approach is to identify additional key points on the face and expand an elastic graph model between them. Since the number of feature types used in face recognition is very large, we refrain from further enumeration. References to a number of additional features suggested can be found for example in [WaZS2004] and [ZCRP2003].

Comparison and Classification

At this point, we want to briefly refer to two exemplary classification methods from the variety: *Eigenfaces* and *Elastic Graph Matching* (EGM).

The *Eigenfaces* method, as introduced by Turk and Pentland in [TuPe1991], uses sets of normalized and equally sized images (256x256 pixels of 8 bit gray level intensity information). These images are interpreted as face vectors and a Principal Component Analysis (PCA) of the difference vectors between an average face vector and each individual reference sample is performed. The PCA results in an ordered set of those eigenvectors, possessing the highest eigenvalues. Due to their visual similarity to faces in image representations, these eigenvectors are called eigenfaces and from the relatively large number of 65535 eigenfaces, only the most useful first $M \ll 65535$ are considered. During the verification process, these eigenfcaes allow the transformation of an actual image into the face space and result in weight measure vector for each of the $1, ..., M$ eigenface components. Comparison of such weight vectors to those of stored reference images is then performed by Euclidean distance and the verification decision is based on an empirical threshold.

Elastic Graph Matching methods as discussed for example in [LVBL+1993] and [WSKM1997] apply Gabor filters as key point detectors, utilizing their properties of differentiating local regions of the face showing low variation in intensity (such as cheeks) from those of high variance (e.g. pupils). Based on a chosen set of filters (for example, [WSKM1997] suggest 8 Frequencies at 5 orientations, i.e. a total of 40 responses), feature vectors are calculated based on the Gabor coefficients of the filter responses. These feature vectors are used as attributes to the nodes of a graph model, whereby the nodes are located at distinctive points (noise, mouth, eyes etc.) in the facial image. The comparison in EGM can be performed in an iterative manner. First, a global positioning between an actual model and a test model is performed by globally moving over the test sample. For each position, the localized feature vectors are calculated and compared to the ones from the reference, using some distance measurement (e.g. based on amplitude and/or phase of the Gabor coefficients, like suggested in [WSKM1997]). The goal is to find a global alignment as a starting point for the second iteration. In this second iteration then, each of the node positions in the graph model is modified in its position separately, and the distance measurement is re-calculated. Such movements of the graph nodes result in changes in the lengths of edges to neighboring nodes, and since this is applied successfully to all nodes in the model, it undergoes elastic deformations, thus the term EGM. Using this scheme, after determination of a local minimum, user authentication can be achieved by comparison to threshold values.

Recognition Accuracy

In the initial evaluation of eigenfaces, the system has shown a correct identification rate of up to 96% for a population of 16 subjects and a total of more than 2500 images. However it has been observed that the recognition rate significantly reduces down to 40% correct recognition, when different orientation, sizing and lighting conditions apply.

In [WSKM1997], some comparative evaluation results have been presented for an EGM approach, based on images from 250 subjects. Here high recognition accuracy was observed for the case of frontal images of the face used for building the reference model as well as for the actual test sample. The authors report degradation down to 27% recognition rate, when considering models generated from half profiles and compared to probe images from full profiles.

The National Institute of Standards and Technology (NIST) has performed an extensive evaluation of commercially available face recognition systems in 2002 and amongst other observations, the best system achieved a 95% recognition rate in indoor condition and FNMR of 10% at a configured FMR level of 1%, see [PGMB+2003].

3.3.4   Other Passive Traits

Fingerprint, Iris and Face are the most common passive biometrics modalities today. However, a number of other physical traits have been elaborated for biometric authentication purposes and this section will close with a brief look at some of these schemes.

Hand Biometrics

We have already discussed the use of fingertips and fingerprints resulting from their skin structure for biometrics as one particular portion of the hand. The hand however offers additional sources for biometric information, for example:

- *Palm Print*: quite similarly to fingerprint techniques and also originated from forensics are individual structures in the palm skin. The characteristics here are three **principal lines**, colloquially denoted as "heart line", "head line" and "life line", as well as **wrinkles** and **ridges**. Like for fingerprint, we find an enormous number of different approaches, most of which have been taken for other modalities as well, including eigenpalm features (see [LuZW2003]), geometrical analysis or Gabor wavelets. The recognition accuracy of palm print as a single modality appears to vary widely, with the best systems having EER below 1% ([PaRR2004]). More details on palm print recognition may be found for example in [Zhan2004] and [PaRR2004].

- *Hand Geometry*: In hand geometry, the goal is to extract geometrical features from images of the entire hand. Usually, images of the hand are taken in a specific apparatus, with pegs for guiding the positioning of hand and fingers. From images taken in such way, image-processing algorithms can be used for contour detection and from the contour, geometrical features can be extracted. Some exemplary features include absolute and relative length of fingers or diameter of the palm. Furthermore, contour-based features such as gradients between reference point on the contour can be considered. In the system presented in [GoMM1997] for example, a total of 17 geometrical features are extracted from the top-down view of the hand and the hand profile image. The accuracy of hand geometry appears to be relatively high: [GoMM1997] have reported an EER of approximately 0.0012 %, based on 800 images taken from 100 subjects, however other approaches appear to be less accurate (e.g. 5.29% FMR at 8.34% FNMR, see [PaRR2004]).

- *Vein Structure*: by using infrared cameras, it is possible to retrieve images of the vein structure of the hand. The fundamental concept here is the observation that the vein pattern of the back of the hand has unique, individual structures and may thus be used for biometric authentication ([CrSm1995], [IKHK+2001]). Again, we find geometrical approaches for feature extraction, as well as global image based methods. Although vein structure analysis apparently does not attract too many research activities, some advances in research have been reported recently. For example, an approach based on Feature Point Vein-Patterns has been suggested in [FaLL2003], with reported EER between 2.3% and 3.75%.

Ear Biometrics

Ears, like other bodily measurements have a tradition for identification of subject in forensics. It had been observed already in the late 19th century that the structure of ears is quite unique to individual persons. Apparently, it took until the end of the 21st century, until the idea of using ear images as modality for automated biometric authentication was taken up, in an initial design of a graph-matching based recognition technique introduced by Burge and Burger in [BuBu1999]. Other research approaches use several classifiers based on shape, wrinkles and macro features from a compression network ([MoSV1999]). Recently, force field transformations have been looked at and have shown high accuracy of up to 99.2% in identification tests, as compared to a maximum of 68.8% for a PCA method, based on eigenvectors approach, similar to eigenfaces (see Section 3.3.3 of this chapter). The test database in these experiments consisted of 4 ear images for each of the subjects in a population of 63.

Retina Scan

The retina, a structure of blood vessels located on the back of the eye, is believed to be the most accurate biometrics, according to a detailed article on this technology, [Hill1999]. Basic concepts for automated recognition of persons by their retina were developed already in the 1970's, techniques have been patented for this purpose (e.g. [Hill1978]) and products are available on the market today. Although the recognition accuracy has been reported as rather high (e.g. zero FMR at 1% FNMR), the practical distribution of retina based authentication system is limited. Main reasons for this is the complex data acquisition process, which requires costly special sensors, has high demands regarding the user cooperation and is also subject to perceived health threats.

3.4   Multibiometrics

Recently, a new sub-discipline has emerged within the domain of biometrics: **multimodal biometrics** or **multibiometrics**. The concept of this research area is inclusion of multiple biometric modalities in one authentication process. Ross and Jain identify five main motivations for multibiometric systems in [RoJa2004]:

1. *Noise* in the biometric data, which may occur due to temporary inferences in the biometric trait such as scars in the skin of a fingertip or changes in voice due to a cold. Also noise may occur due to defective sensors or environmental conditions such as acoustic background noise in voice recordings or unfavorable lighting of faces.

2. ***Intra-Class variations*** due to incorrect interaction of users with the sensor. Other causes for high Intra-Class variations can be intrinsically to particular groups of users, for example some persons tend to show high variability in the way they perform signatures.
3. ***Inter-Class similarities***, which may particularly occur in systems used by a large number of users, where there might be a collision of features by multiple users of different identity.
4. ***Non-Universality***, where not all users in the population are able to produce the particular biometric characteristic of one single modality, for example persons not showing a sufficient number of minutiae in their fingerprint due to skin defects.
5. ***Spoof or replay attacks***, which are particularly relevant to behavioral biometrics, such signature or voice biometrics. As discussed earlier in this chapter, these schemes are potentially vulnerable to trained or recorded forgeries. However also biometric systems based on passive traits can be exposed to forgeries, see Section 3.3.1 for attacks to fingerprint systems and Section 3.3.2 for attacks to the iris modality.

In general, the architecture of a multibiometric system consists of several biometric subsystems for different modalities (e.g. fingerprint and iris). After feature extraction, each of the subsystems may, but does not necessarily have to, consist of the components ***data acquisition, preprocessing, feature extraction*** and ***classification***, as introduced in Section 2.4 of Chapter 2 in this book. The existence of the components depends on the actual fusion strategy of the multibiometric system, which will be discussed in the following subsection 3.4.1. Subsection 3.4.2 will then, from the variety of suggestions to be found in literature, refer to selected multibiometric approaches of three categories.

3.4.1   Fusion Strategies

In general, a multibiometric system can be based on three alternative fusion levels: ***feature extraction level, matching score level*** or ***decision level***, see [RoJa2004] and [RoJa2004].

In the ***feature extraction level*** the information extracted from sensors of each different modality is stored in feature vectors separately by modality. These feature vectors are then combined to a joint feature vector (e.g. by vector concatenation), which is the basis for the subsequent matching and classification processes. Obviously in feature level fusion, the biometric subsystems are not required to implement separate matching and classification modules. Furthermore, this concept does not require separate reference representations for each modality, as these reference data, being input to the matching process, are already of multimodal nature. One of the potential problems in this strategy is that in some cases a very high dimensional feature vector results from the fusion process.

Matching score level fusion is based on the combination of matching scores after separate feature extraction and comparison between reference data and test data for each subsystem. Based on the matching scores or distance measures of each subsystem, a joint matching score is calculated based on strategies such as linear or nonlinear weighting. This result of the fusion is a new matching score, which is the basis for the classification decision of the entire system.

With the fusion on the *decision level*, each biometric subsystem completely completes the processes of feature extraction, matching and classification autonomously. Each participating modality performs it's own decision and at the end of these multiple processes, the individual decisions are combined to a final decision. Decision strategies here are usually of Boolean nature, such as binary conjunction of results, where all modalities have to yield a positive authentication result, or majority votes, where the authentication yields the majority decision amongst all subsystems involved.

Figure 3-15 illustrates an example for a multibiometric system composed of two modalities. Subsystem 1 is allocated in the upper gray rectangular area, Subsystem 2 in the lower. For simplification, the model shows all three fusion levels in the same architecture. The three different fusion strategies (Feature Level, Matching Score and Decision level) are located from left to right in the white horizontal layer between the subsystems.

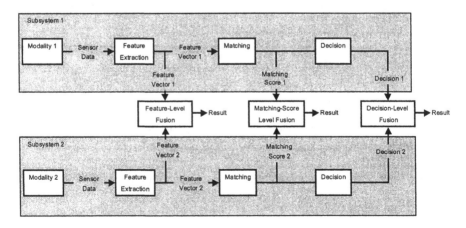

Figure 3-15. Example for a multibiometric architecture composed of two monomodal subsystems: Subsystem 1 (top gray box) and Subsystem 2 (bottom)

In this general model for multibiometric systems, various possibilities regarding the combinations exist. The most obvious is the fusion of two different modalities, for example hand and fingerprint. However, there are additional possibilities of using the concept of a multibiometric system, for example to use one single modality, but with an authentication decision based on multiple sensors or recognition algorithms. The later case, where sensor data of one single sensor forms the input to multiple independent experts is also called *multialgorithmic biometric system* ([SCVD2005]).

3.4.2   Selected Multibiometric Systems

In this subsection, we will introduce to three design approaches for multibiometric systems. Multibiometrics is currently a field of very active research and numerous additional concepts have been presented or are emerging at this point in time. Therefore the examples given here are not exhaustive and the purpose of our discussion is to introduce to three main trends in this domain.

The first trend is characterized by a *single sensor, multiple modality scenario*, which does not require the user to pass through several sensors during the authentication process. Here, we find various approaches based on hand modalities. Kumar et al. for example combine line matching features of the palmprint and hand geometry and report zero FMR at a FNMR of 1.41% for a fusion on decision level, based on almost 500 hand images of 100 subjects [KWSJ2003]. They have also observed that feature level fusion in the same system lead to less accurate decisions (FMR of 5.08% at a FNMR of 2.25%). Pavesic et al. use three modalities of the hand: finger length, palm geometry and palmprint texture features. In their experiments, they report EER of 0.41% for a test database of 110 persons with 7 hand images each ([PaRR2004]).

Simultaneous recording of speech and face video does require two different sensors: video camera and microphone. But with respect to convenience, this concept is advantageous, because both sensors are contactless and can be operated by a user simultaneously. Frischholz and Dieckmann use this data acquisition concept for a **three-modal authentication system** called BioID, which essentially is a commercial development of an earlier research project called SESAM ([FrDi2000] and [DiPW1997]). The system uses two active and one passive modality: speech, lip movements and facial image and the fusion strategy can be configured either to one of three decision level criteria, or application specific weighting on matching score level. The published experimental results shown in

[FrDi2000] base on tests by 150 persons. They report a FMR of less than 1%, but do not disclose the FNMR observed at this system setting.

In the last category of multibiometric system examples, we want to look at multialgorithmic systems for a single modality, but having different independent classifiers. Jain et al. for example investigate the combination of multiple fingerprint matchers based on Hough Transform, String Distance and 2D Programming-based matching. They were able to show and significant improvement by a matching-score level fusion, based on a logistic transform fusion strategy. They observe an improvement relative to the best single matcher in the range of 5% by combining either all three, or the two most relevant matchers. For the modality of online handwriting biometrics, Scheidat et al. have investigated the fusion of alternative matchers, based on different distance measures (City-Block, Euclidean, Hamming and Canberra distance, see Section 7.1 of Chapter 7 in this book). They compare one decision level fusion strategy (best-of) to four matching-score level methods (equally weighted, two empirically determined linear weights and one non-linear weighting strategy). They have evaluated the system on a database of more than 1700 signatures from 22 users and were able to show an EER improvement from 9.1% to 8% for the non-linear fusion strategy, as compared to the best single matcher.

Apparently, multibiometrics has a lot of potential for future authentication applications. Besides the examples mentioned, many other scenarios for multibiometric systems can be found in the literature with quite different combinations of biometric traits, for example face and fingerprint. Further references work in this area may be found for example in [RoJa2004].

3.5   Case Studies

The discussion of different biometric modalities is often based on solely technical terms such as recognition accuracy, computational time or population sizes. While these terms are certainly of great importance when assessing authentication systems, it is also necessary to consider application-specific factors. Some of these factors have been mentioned earlier, for example discussing the accuracy of face recognition in outdoor scenarios, where not control over the lighting conditions can be assumed during the authentication process. Besides technical aspects, a number of additional factors have to be considered, when discussing biometric authentication in context of specific application scenarios. These aspects include, but are not limited to environmental conditions such as lighting and temperature, human factors like system acceptability and possible constraints due to the integration of biometrics in a particular workflow. At the end of this chapter reviewing the wide variety of different modalities, we want to two discuss hypothetical case studies, to illustrate what kind of non-technical aspects may be relevant, in dependency of an aspired application scenario.

3.5.1   ID Documents

Biometric information has been present on ID documents for a long time. Facial photograph, signature and in some countries even fingerprints are visibly included parts in passports, for example. Today, we find an increasing number of countries, which have already, or are planning to, include digital biometric features in travel documents as well. In these cases, besides problems of securing the biometric data on the documents and privacy issues, which will not be addressed here, the question arises, which biometric modalities are adequate for this application.

Regardless if based on analog or digital data, the purpose of ID document is mainly proof of identity of persons, in some cases associated with credentials, for example the authorization to operate specific types of vehicles in case of driver's licenses. While usually for the authentication, which takes place for example when passing immigration at international borders, users can be assumed to act cooperatively, this is not always the case. In some scenarios, it is desirable to be able to authenticate persons without their cooperation, e.g. for identification of unconscious subjects. Following the discussion earlier in this chapter, passive biometric traits are required to fulfill these requirements. If furthermore, the modalities of the digital and analog data are identical, for example by storing a digital representation of the face as well as a printed version, integrity checks between the visible and the digital features are possible. For example in a border control scenario, an officer could manually compare both the visibly printed image on the document to the visualization of the retrieved image data from the stored digital data. Alternatively, an automated face verification system could perform this task and provide decision support the officer.

According to the current suggestion of the International Civil Aviation Organization (ICAO), which will be the basis for the implementation of the first generation of biometrics in passports, only such passive features are considered. The recommendation requires digital facial images as mandatory features, with additional but optional fingerprint and iris features. For details of the specification, see [ICAO2004]. In future, it could be desirable to complement this set of modalities by active biometrics, which may be useful in situations, where an explicit declaration of intention is desired during the passport-based authentication. A possible application scenario for this could be the use of passport authentication in context of electronic signatures, see for example [ViKD2002], or other scenarios requiring explicit consent of the user, as discussed in the following subsection.

Some further discussions on biometrics in context of ID documents can be found for example in [PiTV2004], [SKVK2005] and [CFVS2002].

3.5.2   Declaration of Intention

The validation of document authenticity and integrity has been of importance since many centuries. Before the digital age, there have been manual methods for ensuring these security goals. For example the envelope of important letters were sealed using wax and stamp prior to dispatch, to allow the recipient to verify integrity of the content of the letter. With respect to authenticity, handwritten signatures and stamps have been the classical techniques to verify the origin of a document.

The techniques mentioned have become legally and socially accepted over the centuries and for this reason, they are still widely used today. With emerge of electronic workflow and, along with this, the digital document management, the requirement for electronic equivalents to the classic means of document security has become increasingly important in the past years. **Cryptography** has provided technologies based on **Public-Key-Infrastructure (PKI)**, which provide mechanisms to fulfill the requirements of integrity and authenticity on digital data. These methods, known as **digital signatures**, have been legally put on par with the classic means in many countries (e.g. in the EU, see [WuCo2000]) and a huge number of products are available for application in industrial or private use are available today [Garf2002].

The cryptographic solutions for digital signatures require public key pairs, i.e. at least one pair for signing digital documents, the other for encryption. The general function of an asymmetric cryptographic signature is outlined in Chapter 5 of this book and as we will discuss there, the authentication of the digital signature relies on the assumption that the private portions of keys are and remain secret. This secrecy requirement is a problem in practice, because keys are too long and too complex to be memorized by individuals and the number of keys to be memorized will grow with the number of different scenarios and applications. In practice, it is intended to solve this problem by usage of chip cards, where each participant of a digital signature community possesses a card storing all the required keys. For keeping these keys confidential, each chip card needs to be activated by a PIN.

As a logical consequence, in this chip-card based scenario, the authentication and declaration of intention, which is often implied with it, now relies on three assumptions: the card remains in possession of the authentic user, the knowledge of the PIN remains secret and the user purposely and voluntarily makes use of the card and PIN at time of signature. Of course, this assumption can not be ensured in all cases, because the transfer of possession and knowledge cannot be avoided generally. Biometric user authentication may help to overcome this weakness, as it may complement the binding of cryptographic keys to a specific user. The combination of biometrics and digital signatures has been an area of discussions earlier and in [ViKD2002] for example, the usage of handwriting or signature based biometrics has been suggested mainly because of three reasons:

- it appears to be *socially and historically well accepted*,
- besides the authentication function, signatures fulfill additional functions like *Finalization*, *Evidence*, *Identity* and *Warning*, because it is an active biometrics,
- by using *active digitizer display technology*, like those in Tablet PCs, the biometric modality *signature can be linked to a visible document*. The user can for example sign in a particular field of a form, which is displayed on the screen. An explicit declaration of intention can thus be assumed, and the entire signature process becomes intuitive.

Although the usage of passive biometrics in this scenario is generally possible as well and might be more accurate in terms of recognition accuracy, the use of signature verification as an active trait appears to be advantageous. In any case in this scenario, there remains a trade-off between less accurate, but intuitive biometrics on one side and higher accuracy and less intuitive biometrics, leading to less seamless integration on the other side. In a practical design, the required security level might be a decision criterion for such a scenario.

3.6 Notations and Abbreviations

Table 3-1 summarizes notations and abbreviations introduced in this chapter in alphabetical order.

Table 3-3. Summary of notations and abbreviations introduced in Chapter 3

Designator	Name	Description	Introduced in
a_{ji}	Transition Probability	Probability a state transition to state s_j given state s_i in a Hidden Markov Model.	Section 3.2.1
ASR	Automated Speaker Recognition	Scientific discipline of biometric user authentication by the modality of voice.	Section 3.2.1

Table 3-1 (cont.)

Designator	Name	Description	Introduced in
CCD	Charge-Coupled Devices	Image sensors used for capturing of images and video frames in digital cameras. Used in all image and video based biometrics.	Section 3.3.2
DCT	Discrete Cosine Transform (DCT)	Transformation function from temporal to frequency domain, based on cosine decomposition.	Section 3.2.4
DNA	Deoxyribonu-cleic Acid	DNA carries the genetic instructions for the biological development of cell forms. DNA analysis is used for forensic authentication by comparing order and length of sequences of bases.	Chapter 3
EGM	Elastic Graph Matching	Face Recognition techniques based on a graph model between feature points detected on the facial image.	Section 3.3.3
HMM	Hidden Markov Models	Classification method used for example in voice or online handwriting biometrics.	Section 3.2.1
IFT	Inverse Fourier Transform	Transformation function from frequency to temporal domain.	Section 3.2.1
FT	Fourier Transform	Transformation function from temporal to frequency domain.	Section 3.2.1
LPC	Linear Predictive Coding	Feature extraction technique used in voice biometrics.	Section 3.2.1
MFCC	Mel-Frequency Cepstral Coefficients	Higher order cepstral features, used for example in voice biometrics.	Section 3.2.1
n-graph	n-graph	Localized timing feature in keystroke biometrics between 2 or more keystroke events.	Section 3.2.4
NIR	Near-Infrared Radiation	Region in the infrared radiation band having wavelengths between 0.7 and 1.4 μm. Used for illumination in iris biometrics.	Section 3.3.2
NIST	National Institute of Standards and Technology	Non-regulatory federal agency within the U.S. Commerce Department's Technology Administration. Part of NIST's mission is to develop and promote standards.	Section 3.2.1
PCA	Principal Component Analysis	Statistical feature selection method used for example in face recognition (Eigenfaces) and lip-based biometrics (Eigenlips).	Section 3.3.3

Table 3-1 (cont.)

Designator	Name	Description	Introduced in
PCP	Pixel Count Parameter	Feature in offline handwriting biometrics, based on spatial segmentation.	Section 3.2.2
PDF	Probability Density Function	Individual property of a feature vector, may be estimated from training feature vectors obtained during enrollment.	Section 3.2.1
PIN	Personal Identification Number	Textual knowledge as a sequence of numbers for knowledge-based user authentication.	Section 3.2.2
ROI	Region of Interest	Spatial localization of feature areas in image- and video-based biometrics.	Section 3.2.4
$s_i, s_j.$	Logical States	Logical States in a Hidden Markov Model.	Section 3.2.1
$t_{KeyDown}$	Key down event time	Timestamp of a recorded key down event in keystroke biometrics.	Section 3.2.4
$t_{KeyUp}.$	Key up event time	Timestamp of a recorded key up event in keystroke biometrics.	Section 3.2.4
x(t)	Horizontal pen position signal	Sampled signal of the horizontal writing position as provided by digitizer tablets.	Section 3.2.2
y(t)	Vertical pen position signal	Sampled signal of the vertical writing position as provided by digitizer tablets.	Section 3.2.2

Chapter 4

FUNDAMENTALS IN USER AUTHENTICATION
Techniques for Binding Identities to Information

4. FUNDAMENTALS IN USER AUTHENTICATION

As shown earlier in this book in Chapter 2, the assurance of integrity and authenticity is one of the main goals in IT security. In communication via digital systems, users quite often require some level of confidence in the identity of their communication partners. Such confidence can be provided by integration of user authentication functionality in IT infrastructures.

A general definition of the term **authentication** is given by Bishop [Bish2003]:

"Authentication is the binding of an identity to a subject".

This definition represents a narrow interpretation of the term for the domain of computer security. Wider definitions, e.g. from the domain of telecommunications, do not necessarily bind authentication to subjects [ANST2000]:

"[Any] Security measure designed to establish the validity of a transmission, message, or originator, or a means of verifying an individual's authorization to receive specific categories of information. (...)"

As the work in the context of this book addresses exclusively IT security aspects, we base our interpretation of the term authentication on the view of Bishop, binding users to identities. Thus we use the terminology user authentication and authentication synonymously.

It can be derived from this definition that any authentication process operates on information of two categories. Firstly, an identification string logically and uniquely assigned to a subject and secondly, some kind of information related to the subject allowing a decision on authenticity, i.e. is the person the one she or he claims to be. This information may come from one or more if the following properties related to the person directly [Bish2003]:

- from *"what the entity knows (such as passwords or secret information)"*, i.e. **knowledge** of the subject,
- from *"what the entity has (such as a badge or card)"*, i.e. **possession** of the subject, or
- from *"what the entity is (such as fingerprints or retina characteristics)"*, i.e. **biometric traits** of the subject (e.g. structure of fingerprints, handwriting style).

Furthermore, additional environmental conditions such us temporal information (e.g. authentication for access control only at specific dates/times) or spatial position of the subject (e.g. authentication only for specific terminals) may be taken into account for authentication, but are not intrinsically linked to the subject's nature. Bishop presents a formal description for an authentication system consisting of five component sets. These components are summarized in Table 4-1.

Table 4-1. Five components of Bishop's authentication system [Bish2003]

Component	Designator	Description
Authentication Information	A	Set of specific information with which entities prove their identities
Complementary Information	C	Set of information that the system stores and uses to validate the authentication information
Complementary Functions	F	Set of functions that generate the complementary information from the authentication information, i.e. $f \in F, f{:}A \to C$, also used in functional notation: $c=f(a)$, for all $a \in A$ and $c \in C$
Authentication Functions	L	Set of functions that verify identity, i.e. $l \in L, l{:}A \times C \to \{true, false\}$, also used in functional notation: $l(a,c) == \{true, false\}$, for all $a \in A$ and $c \in C$
Selection Functions	S	Set of functions that enable an entity to create or alter A and C

With the definition of these components, Bishop introduces two categories for information and functions: two sets of information (A and C) and three sets of functions (F, L and S). **Authentication Information** $a \in A$

can be used as argument of the **Complementary Functions** $f \in F$ to obtain **Complementary Information** $c \in C$. Information of each of the two information categories A and C are the arguments of the **Authentication Functions** $l \in L$, having a binary result. **Select Functions** $s \in S$ are introduced by Bishop for the creation or alteration of A or C, without explicitly specifying arguments for these functions. A number of arguments can be taken into consideration for the parameterizations of S, for example, entity name to select from, device for capturing the information or a value determining if the select function is used for the generation or alteration of A or C. For our further discussions, we make the following assumptions, written in algebra notation for the sake of consistency with Bishop's definitions:

- the set of Select Functions S contains subsets for select functions to generate C for an enrollment of an entity or subject, denoted as $S_{Enroll} \in S$ and subsets for the generation of A for verification of users, $S_{Verify} \in S$,
- select functions have **no arguments**: $s \in S_{Verify}$, $s \to A$, and $s \in S_{Enroll}$, $s \to C$.

Consequently, the two modes of biometric authentication systems, enrollment and verification, can be described by the model as follows:

- Enrollment: $s \in S_{Enroll}$, $s \to C$,
- Verification is equal to the generation of A by some $s \in S_{Verify}$, with a subsequent application of an authentication function $l \in L$: $s \in S_{Verify}$, $s \to A$, and $l: A \times C \to \{true, false\}$

While this model represents the authentication task in principal well, it abstracts from component details such as media origin of information, structure of representation and methods how to extract information from media. Based on this observation, our motivation is to enhance Bishop's model for user authentication by introducing an extended, signal-based model for user authentication systems, which includes considerations of physical phenomena as well as formal structures.

We start by **analyzing information flow** and media transitions in user authentication processes in Section 4.1, applying signal-based modeling for the information transmission. The goal is to identify location, type and direction of information required in a generic authentication process, determine and enumerate channels between system components for exchange of this data and to find an assignment between the logical information flow and the channel enumeration.

This flow model, which abstracts from a particular authentication modality, is then discussed in the context of three different information categories for authentication. In order to do so, we present a detailed discussion on the integration of three user **authentication modalities**: knowledge, possession and biometrics in a general signal-based model in Section 4.2. This discussion is conducted separately for each modality under consideration of appropriate digital data representations and information loss conditions. As a result of the first two sections, we introduce a new generic model for the authentication process, based on signals representing different modalities. This model is the means to systematically identify potential **attacks**, which is done in Section 4.3. By comparison of properties of different authentication modalities in the general authentication system we reveal open **research challenges** in Section 4.4 and we formulate these challenges, which are further pursued for the modality of handwriting biometrics in later chapters of this book. Finally, Section 4.5 concludes with a summary of notations and abbreviations for this chapter.

4.1   Information Flow Analysis for Authentication Systems

Any user authentication process in the context of IT security takes place between two entities: a **human subject *H*** and an **automated authentication system *U***. For the authentication task, *U* needs to obtain information about *H*. This information needs to be presented by *H*, transferred from *H* to *U* and to be processed by *U*. Also, it may become necessary for both sides to exchange synchronization information in both directions. Thus, an authentication system *U* needs to perform bi-directional communication with a subject *H*.

Furthermore, the authentication system requires a device to capture Authentication Information *A* and a storage location for the complementary information *C* of each of the registered users. This complementary information acts as a reference for the authentication functions $l \in L$. Although *C* may be physically integrated in the system *U*, we explicitly model the **external reference storage *R***, because the integration assumption does not hold true for all practical implementations. Information exchange is necessary between *U* and *R* in both directions, as *U* needs to request complementary information from *R* and *C* need to be transmitted back to *U*.

As for all digital communication systems, this communication between the two entities requires communication channels and interfaces to and from the two entities' systems. The communication is established by sending media signals via an outbound interface of the sender of information, over the channel to the inbound interface of the receiver. The signals, which are transmitted over the channel, represent media information.

For our authentication scenario, we define and specify the following channels [ViKa2004]:

- Authentication Submission Channel (***ASC***),
- Synchronization Forward Channel (***SFC***),
- Synchronization Reverse Channel (***SRC***),
- Reference Information Control Channel (***RCC***),
- Reference Information Submission Channel (***RSC***),
- Authentication Result Channel (***ARC***).

The Authentication Submission Channel *ASC* is responsible for transmission of **user authentication information *A*** from the **subject *H*** to the **authentication system *U*** while the Synchronization Forward and Reverse Channels *SFC* and *SRC* take care of the exchange of synchronization data, which is an optional feature and is not required in systems where the user presents the authentication information without challenge by the system.

Table 4-2 describes the information flow between the introduced components during an authentication process formally in a protocol description, where only transactions relevant for the authentication process itself are included, abstracting from any possible synchronization messages which might exist, for example, on lower network layers. The notation of the protocol description in Table 4-2 is as follows:

- the temporal sequence of the protocol step is given by the sequence number in the left column. Optional steps are denoted as (*Optional*).
- In the column Information Flow, arrows denote the direction from the sending entity to the receiving entity, for example, $H \xrightarrow{ID} U \mid_{SFC}$ denotes a message *ID* send from entity *H* to entity *U* using channel *SFC*.

For an authentication process, which is initiated by the subject, *H* first initiates the process by sending an authentication request message $M_{Authentication}$ from *H* to *U* via the Synchronization Forward Channel *SFC*, which may or may not be followed by a **declared identity *ID*** via the same channel. In the next step, *U* will send a solicitation message $M_{RequestAuthenticationInfo}$ to *H* via *SRC*, requesting the presentation of authentication information (or a conditional error message). Subsequently, *H* will provide the authentication information *A* to *U*. In an analogous manner, the complimentary information is requested by transmission of a message

$M_{RequestComplimentaryInfo}$ from U to the Reference Storage R via the Reference Information Control Channel RCC and the requested information C is returned via the Reference Information Submission Channel RSC in the opposite direction. Finally, after execution of the authentication functions L within U, the authentication result $l{:}A \times C$ is provided to an external system via the authentication result channel ARC.

Table 4-2. Formal information flow protocol in the authentication process

Step	Information Flow	Description
1.(Optional)	$H \xrightarrow{M_{Authentication}} U \big|_{SFC}$	Authentication request sent from H to U using channel SFC
2.(Optional)	$H \xrightarrow{ID} U \big|_{SFC}$	H sends declared identity ID to U using channel SFC
3.(Optional)	$H \xleftarrow{M_{RequestAuthenticationInfo}} U \big|_{SRC}$	U requests presentation of authentication info A by sending $M_{RequestAuthenticationInfo}$ to H via channel SRC
4.	$H \xrightarrow{A} U \big|_{ASC}$	Submission of authentication info A from H to U via channel ASC
5	$U \xrightarrow{M_{RequestComplementaryInfo}} R \big|_{RCC}$	U requests Complementary Reference Information from R by sending $M_{RequestComplementaryInfo}$ via RCC channel
6.	$U \xleftarrow{C} R \big|_{RSC}$	R supplies U with Complementary Reference Information C via the RSC channel
7.	$U \xrightarrow{l:A\times C \rightarrow \{True, False\}} External\ World \big|_{ARC}$	U presents the result of an authentication function $l{:}A \times C \rightarrow \{true, false\}$ to the external world via channel ARC

User authentication systems are typically designed as components of more complex computer systems with the function integrated into the entire system. Therefore, from the point of view of the authentication system, the result is processed by an external system, which then utilizes the result of an authentication function $l{:}A \times C$ to proceed with further authorization steps, e.g. processing of access control lists in operating systems [Bish2003].

Typically such a communication is initiated by the human being, indicating an authentication request along with a declared identity to the IT system. In this case, authentication is performed based on identity verification, and steps one to three of the above information flow description become mandatory. Alternatively, the authentication request may be initiated by the authentication system U itself, or initiated by the subject H, but without declaring a claimed identity. In such cases the authentication is performed based on identification of the user (see Chapter 2, Section 2.4.2), and at least step two from the above description becomes obsolete. Furthermore, if the authentication process is initiated by the system, even step one can be omitted. Practically, the later requires an authentication system, which is in the position to automatically detect that a subject attempts to enter a logical or physical area requiring authentication. Consequently, the identification process can be modeled by a subset of functions and information of a verification system, thus identification can be considered as a specialization of verification processes. Within the context of this book, we will therefore focus on verification-based authentication. However, the observations and results are by no means limited to this method and may be adopted for identification as well.

The following Figure 4-1 illustrates our model, based on Bishop's components and our extensions for the information exchange protocol during an authentication process. Note that the temporal sequence in this protocol is represented by top-down order of the processes.

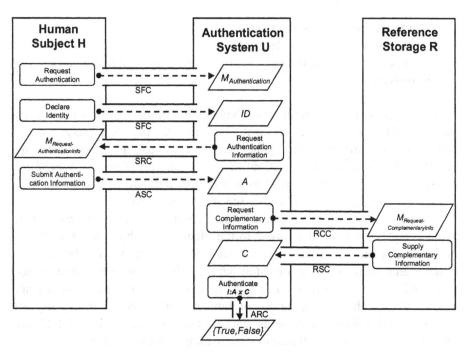

Figure 4-1. Information flow model for a general authentication system

Our new information flow model for authentication systems abstracts from the physical origin of the information, authentication modalities and the functional methods for the authentication process. Its purpose at this point is to expose entities and communication channels of generic authentication systems, which will be referred to in later sections of this chapter, where we analyze potential attacks to such systems.

4.2 General Model for User Authentication Modalities

In the previous Section 4.1, it has been shown that the authentication process requires information exchange between human subjects, authentication systems and reference storages. The information for this purpose is required to be adequate in the sense that it allows:

- reliably confirm the identity of each of the users of the system,
- allow distinction between non-identical users of the system.

In the context of user authentication there are three elementary categories of origin of information, which can be presented by a subject:

- information based on **possession,**
- information based on **knowledge,**
- information based on **being,** i.e. physiological or behavioral properties (**biometrics**).

For the necessary information exchange via communication channels, as shown earlier, it becomes evident, that media transitions have to be considered. Regardless of the authentication modality, the problem can be described by the following question: *"How can subject H present something to system U, in a way to allow U to access sufficient information about it to evaluate the authenticity of H with a reasonable precision?"*

This problem description makes two assumptions: Firstly, it implies that "something" is intrinsically linked to the identity of subject S. Secondly, it presumes that an error-free decision cannot be achieved by an authentication system and therefore any decision will be bound to some confidence threshold, leading to a reasonable precision. These two limiting factors are mainly due to the analog nature of human beings. While practically all computerized systems operate as digital state machines based on binary primitives, information originating from human subjects is represented in various analog media, which are subject to natural Intra-Class variability [Waym1999]. In the modeling of general authentication systems, we proceed as follows in the coming subsections: firstly, we will determine appropriate digital representations for signals in Section 4.2.1, followed by an examination of the communication channels in Section 4.2.2, which are pointed out in the information flow model presented earlier in this chapter.

We then will focus on channel models for the Authentication Submission (*ASC*), based on the three different modalities of possession (Section 4.2.3), knowledge (Section 4.2.4) and biometrics (Section 4.2.5) plus a short reference to hybrid systems in Section 4.2.6, which combine different authentication modalities.

4.2.1   Digital Signal Representations

For the signal-based modeling of authentication systems, it is necessary to determine the type of signals, which are relevant in this scenario, and to define appropriate digital representations. In our model, we find three categories of signals that need to be considered, depending on the nature of information they represent: sampled signals (representing temporal information), captured signals (representing spatial information) and switched signals (representing conditional information). In this section, we define our terminology used for the signal models in this book. It is based on commonly used terminology in telecommunications and signal processing. Note that for our digital signal model, we assume a given quantization, i.e. the transformation of real values from an analog sampling process to a countable numeric data representation, for example, by Integer variables. We justify our assumption by the observation, that many device drivers of common analog-digital converters for user interfaces today provide quantized data of physical traits, taking into account information loss due to quantization noise [StNa2004b].

Our goal is to find suitable signal models for the representation of Authentication Information A for different authentication modalities and we therefore denote the three signal categories by the letter a. However, depending on the specificity of Complementary Functions F, Complementary Information C may be modeled using the same signal definition as well.

Sampled Signals
We base our terminology for Sampled Signals on the definition of signal sampling in signal processing [ANST2000]:

"Signal sampling: The process of obtaining a sequence of instantaneous values of a particular signal characteristic, usually at regular time intervals."

A sampled signal $a(t)$ is the digital discrete representation of quantized physical measurements of a continuous phenomenon. The process of sampling amplitude measurements of the physical waveform at discrete times *t*, quantizes the measurements and represents them as values of finite precision and temporal resolution (sampling rate), in our case as *Integer* values. Although in many cases, signals are sampled in equidistant time intervals for *t*, for the analysis of biometric signals the assumption of equidistance is too narrow and cannot always be justified, we define a Sampled Signal *a(t)* according to the following definition:

$$a(t) \in Integer \ for \ all \ t \in \overline{T},$$

$$with \ \overline{T} \ being \ the \ ordered \ set \ of \ discrete \ sampling \ instances$$

(4-1)

where *a(t)* represents each of the sampled and quantized values of the physical waveform at each of the $t \in \overline{T}$ finite discrete measurement times *t*.

An example for a sampled signal is the digital representation of audio, where the sampled values *a(t)* represent the quantized amplitude of the audio waveform measured at the analog-digital (A/D) converter at specific (and in this case usually equally distanced) times $t \in \overline{T}$.

Captured Signals

Captured signals denoted as *a(x,y,z)* are serialized digital representations of discrete information. Like for sampled signals, the information is represented by sequences of quantized, discrete values represented by an integer range. The main difference compared to sampled signals *a(t)* is that the information in this case is related to spatial coordinates rather than on temporal semantic. The conversion of data from a discrete representation into sequential data is performed in order to supply the authentication system *U* with the information, thus building the information channel. For this book, we will abstract from technical implementation details of such serial communication and will make use if the following definition for captured signals:

$$a(x, y, z) \in Integer \ for \ all \ x \in \overline{X}, y \in \overline{Y} \ and \ z \in \overline{Z}$$

$$with \ \overline{X}, \overline{Y} \ and \ \overline{Z} \ being \ the \ sets \ of \ spatial \ coordinates$$

(4-2)

The dimensionality in coding of captured signals is media dependent, i.e. it can be based on one, two or three dimensions. In case of images for example, *a(x,y,z)* can represent the luminance values of pixels at horizontal (*x*) and vertical (*y*) positions, sequenced, for example, by a line-by-line scan process. In this two-dimensional case, the *z* argument is not required and can be set to a constant value, for example, *z=1*. An example for a captured signal representing a one-dimensional information is a textual string. Here, *x* could represent the position index of each character within the string, whereas y and z are not required and can be set to a constant value, for example, $y=1$ and $z=1$.

Note that in the context of discussion of authentication systems the significant differentiation between sampled and captured signals is that in the first case, the information represents both sampled values and temporal information, whereas in the later case, the sequential arrangement of the transmitted values carries no temporal information content.

Switched Signals

The third category of signals *Switch(a)* is defined by a conditional state rather than the interpretation of sequential information. Here, the information is modeled by two states: the presence or the non-presence of a signal, as formalized in the following equation:

$$Switch(a) = \begin{cases} a, if\ SwitchingCondition = TRUE \\ 0, otherwise \end{cases} \quad (4\text{-}3)$$

where a can be any category of signals (sampled or captured) and *SwitchingCondition* denotes the switching condition physically controlled by an interface.

An example for a switched signal is a key-operated switch, where the *SwitchingCondition* is the presence and activation of a key matching the lock.

4.2.2 Loss Considerations for Channel Modeling

From our previous observations, it is evident that bi-directional communication is required in the authentication process and for the bi-directional channels between the human subject H and the authentication system U presented in the previous section, analog-to-digital (A/D) and digital-to-analog (D/A) conversion has to be taken into account. Due to the known physical problems in the digitizing process, such as finite sampling rates, quantization noise and coding limitations [StNa2004b], the conversions are lossy by nature, leading to lossy channels. For the communication between the authentication system U and the reference storage R and for the Authentication Result Channel *ARC* however, it can be assumed that channels themselves do not cause any losses, because they are of a purely digital nature[3]. The following Figure 4-2 illustrates the channel categories based on the information flow model introduced by us in [ViKa2004], including the three principal authentication modalities of possession, knowledge and being. We observe three categories: lossy A/D conversion channels, lossy D/A conversion channels and lossless digital channels, marked by different patterns in Figure 4-2.

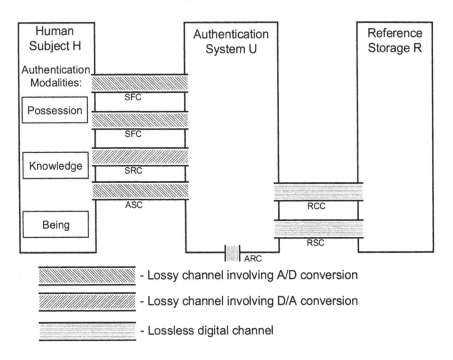

Figure 4-2. Basic modalities and channel categories for a user authentication system [ViKa2004]

It becomes obvious that the different modalities, which can be used to provide authentication information, will lead to quite different types of signal representations. In order to structure our analysis on signal representations of modalities, we will develop a focused view at a signal level for the communication between *H* and *I*, separately for each of the three categories. This differentiation however does not mean that any authentication process would be limited to singular modalities. The

---

[3] Note that at this point, we are making two assumptions in our model: firstly, we do not take into account intentional attacks to the channels and secondly, we consider information transmission over digital channels error free, abstracting from the technology requirements to achieve error-free digital data transmission.

combination of multiple modalities at a logical level is quite possible, but will require different instances of the channel types defined earlier.

4.2.3 Possession-based Authentication

Possession-based Authentication schemes rely on the assumption, that possession of some object is intrinsically linked to the identity of its owner. Here, the authentication process requires presentation of the object via the *SRC* channel with a preceding declaration of identity. The authentication system U then verifies if the possession represented by A is logically assigned to the subject H, referring to the complementary information C. This authentication concept is derived from the classic metaphor of possession-based access control by key (representing A), allowing physical access (authentication) to whoever is the actual holder of it by matching a lock (representing C). In view of our model however, this paradigm of key and lock however is a simplified example for a generalized possession-based authentication scenario, because it does not include an explicit declaration of an identity by the user H (see Table 4-2).

In the digital world, electronic key devices have adopted classic key functionality in a wide variety of applications. Typical representatives from this category include embossed cards, magnet-stripe cards, optical cards and chip-cards. Recently, especially cards from the later category have become increasingly popular. They are intended for contact-based or contact-free interfacing with stationary terminals. A wide variety of different types of memory cards and microprocessor cards exist today, a comprehensive overview of recent technological advances is provided in [RaEf2003].

Signal Modeling

For our signal-based model, three basic physical media can be observed: mechanical contact, electrical contact and electromagnetic oscillations (including radio frequency and optical oscillations such as infrared). The following Figure 4.3 illustrates the signals that may be derived from the physical presentation of objects of each category and the type of interface required for their generation. For keys based on mechanical contact, such as car keys or plastic cards with physical embossing (e.g. early generations), the resulting signal is a binary switch signal. In case the key matches the lock, the interface will close the electrical contact; otherwise the switch remains open, implementing the functionality of a switched signal *Switch(a)*, as defined earlier in this section. One lock may match more than one key, even if the shapes of the keys are not identical. Therefore, in these cases, identification of the key actually activating the switch is impossible.

In the second category, electrical contact, the objects carry some information and/or logic, which is made available to the authentication system via captured signals, denoted as *a(x,y,z)* in Figure 4.3, to be interpreted as series of binary information. The information provided by this signal represents either a predefined identification number (in case of pure memory cards) to be represented, for example, as a textual string, or some cryptographic response. Functions for such cryptographic responses can be implemented, for example, on smart cards equipped with programmable microprocessors and memory [RaEf2003]. Here, the response signal is solicited by the interface as a function of some input signal, denoted as cryptographic response in Figure 4.3. An example for such a function is the cryptographic signature of a message by the device. For this category of possession-based systems, the authentication objects implement functions for the cryptographic signature of an input message and the presentation of the signed information as output data. Both input data and result of the cryptographic response function are discrete values, thus can be represented by captured signals *a(x,y,z)* and interpreted as a sequence of binary data.

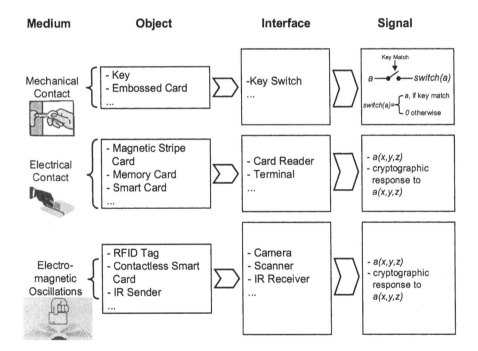

Figure 4-3. ASC signals based on possession-based authentication information

The third media category, electromagnetic oscillations, includes chip cards with contact-free interfaces to the external world. Interfaces can be implemented based on radio frequency technology (e.g. transponder technology like Radio Frequency Identification RFID or capacitive coupler), optical technologies operating in invisible (e.g. infrared) or visible frequency bands (e.g. bar code reader). In comparison to the electrical contacted objects, the main difference is the type of interface to the terminal, therefore we find the same categories of signal representations, $a(x,y,z)$ or cryptographic response, for the second and third category, see Figure 4.3.

Reference Storage

Explicit reference storage is required only for possession objects from the non-mechanical contacts. For mechanical contact, the reference (complementary information C) and the authentication system U comprise one single unit; only a key matching the lock will activate the electrical switch.

For the two remaining categories, two basic concepts for reference storage can be determined: either identification codes of each authentic subject among all possible users are stored along with object identifiers in the Reference storage R or (in case of microprocessor cards) cryptographic mechanisms such as signatures are used for the authentication process. In the later case, asymmetric cryptographic key pairs are shared between the authentication system U and the device in a way that the card has access to a private key and the reference storage R holds the associated public key for each of the authorized devices. During the authentication process, the authentication system U then requests the device (representing subject H) to sign some dynamic information (e.g. random number) with its private key, using the synchronization channels SFC and SRC. The signed information provided through the authentication submission channel ASC can then be verified using the complementary information C (the associated public key) from the reference storage R. For this commonly known process of digital signatures can be achieved by public key cryptographic functions, see for example [Bish2003] or [Beut1994].

4.2.4   Knowledge-based Authentication

Authentication by knowledge implies that among all potential users of an authentication system, the sub-group of authorized persons have some knowledge, which is undisclosed to the remaining subjects. In this case, the confidentiality of the information representing the knowledge needs to be assumed. In the decision phase of the authentication system U, information based on the user's knowledge will be read from the Authentication Submission Channel ASC and compared with information associated with the user identifier ID, read from the Reference Submission Channel RSC. If the two values are identical, the authentication system will respond with a positive result, otherwise, the authentication will fail. In this category, knowledge is mostly represented by textual information (e.g. password, passphrase or question and secret answer). However, different alternative approaches exist, for example, in the area of visual authentication by replacing text strings with structured images [DhPe2000].

Signal Modeling

Knowledge-based user authentication is based on the capability of human beings to memorize and reproduce semantic information. Typically this information can be reproduced as text, speech, but also, for example, by pointing to recognized visual objects. In all cases, the subject H needs to provide the memorized knowledge to the authentication system U, which requires interfaces. For this purpose, the typical human-to computer interfaces are commonly used, including keyboard, pointing devices (e.g. computer mouse), touch-screen and speech recognition technology. Signals, which eventually are available for the authentication process U via the authentication submission channel *ASC* are all of type captured signals $a(x,y,z)$ and can be typically interpreted as one-dimensional textual character sequences $a_{Character}(x)$ for typed and spoken text, where x denotes the character position index within the text. Alternatively, the captured signals may be interpreted as position sequences $a_{Position}(x,y)$ for information submitted by pointing devices, where x and y denote the spatial coordinates. The process of signal extraction is illustrated in Figure 4-4.

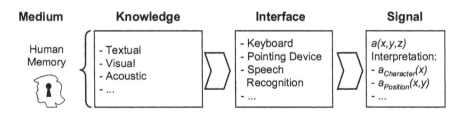

Figure 4-4. ASC signals based on knowledge-based authentication information

Reference Storage

For the storage of the complementary information C, two basic approaches can be taken; firstly, the complementary knowledge C associated with a subject H can be deposited as plain information modeled in an original signal representation in the reference storage or secondly, some kind of digest can be used. In practical knowledge-based authentication systems, the second possibility is usually preferred. For example, in the UNIX *crypt()* **password authentication mechanism**, knowledge is not explicitly stored in R, but rather some mathematical digest of it. In the particular case of the *crypt()* algorithm for example, the password of subject H is used as an encryption key for a Data Encryption Standard (DES) encryption of 64-bit runs of zeros, leading to non-reversible complementary information C (see [SiGa1996]).

From practice, it is commonly known that, in password-based authentication, the reproduction of knowledge for authentication by humans is rather unreliable, due to volatility errors. This is particularly the case, when passwords are chosen, which are computationally hard to guess [Bish2003], [Tann2001]. When typing passwords, subjects quite often make mistakes in keying the characters in right sequence. To compensate for this natural effect, practical knowledge-based authentication systems have implemented the recommended practice of requesting several entries during an enrollment and to verify the information among the multiple entries. This process of password re-confirmation during enrollment can be observed in password administrations of all modern operation systems.

Also, for this authentication method several verification retries have to be taken into account for each user case of rejection of a single authentication attempt. A premature disabling of authentication for affected users may lead to impractical solutions.

4.2.5 Biometric-based Authentication

Biometric-based authentication requires the presentation of some behavioral and/or physiological traits to the authentication system. Depending on the nature of such traits, the information will be propagated via different media, leading to the requirement of media-specific sensors in the information channel between the human subject H and the authentication system U.

Today, biometric traits can be classified into three categories of biometric modalities: behavioral modalities based on physical movement generated by the subject, audio produced by the subject (typically voice) and images representing physical characteristics of the individual. Each of the categories contains one or more biometric traits, each of which has one of the three specific representation media: physical movement, audio and image. For an automated authentication system, these traits need to be A/D converted into digital representations, which is done by measurement of the trait using sensors for sampling or capturing into discrete values. In the case of traits, which can be represented as discrete images, this conversion is performed by camera or scanning devices. For the digitization of continuous audio, microphones perform the conversion of modulated pressure information into analog electrical currencies, which are then quantized by an A/D converter (e.g. PC Audio device) into sequences of discrete values representing the amplitude of the original oscillation [StNa2004b]. For the A/D conversion of physical movement, special sampling devices provide signals representing the kinematics. Examples for such devices are data gloves for hand movement or digitizer tablets for handwriting dynamics.

Signal Modeling

In the domain of biometric traits based on physical movement, the type of information provided to the authentication system and thus the representative signals are dependent on the specific trait and the measurement method applied. In, for example, gait recognition, horizontal and vertical (x/y) positions of defined points of extremities of the human body are observed over a period of time. The measurement of the spatial movement of these points over time can be achieved in two ways: first, physical position sensors attached to the subject (e.g. data glove) can record the movement [EGGS+2003] and secondly, visual tracking can be used to extract the position of the points in a video representation [NiAd1994], see also Section 3.2.3 of the previous chapter. Audio-based biometric authentication also requires a continuous medium, see Section 3.2.1; therefore both categories can be modeled as sampled signals, while image-based modalities carry no temporal information and can thus be represented as captured signals. Further examples for behavioral and passive biometric modalities are discussed in Chapter 3.

Figure 4-5 provides an overview of various traits in the three categories mentioned, along with examples for sensors and resulting types of signals. In this illustration of the information channel, it becomes evident that all information for biometric-based authentication has to undergo two steps of media transition, the conversion from the physical medium to electrical signals, followed by the quantization process into digital representations. Both transitions are exposed to noise (sensor noise and quantization noise) and thus cause information loss. For our further discussion in the authentication model, we will assume that the two parameters of the quantization process, sampling rate and quantization levels, are reasonably configured to provide a sufficient digital representation of the traits in the authentication information signal A, which is provided at the destination of the channel ASC. In Figure 4-5, we have denoted each of the exemplary sampled signals $a(t)$ (as defined in Section 4.2.1) with an indicator of their physical origin, e.g. the pen tip force signal as $a_{Force}(t)$.

Reference Storage

The complimentary information C which is provided for comparison by U via the Reference Submission Channel RSC consists of a set of biometric information recorded during an earlier process of user registration, called enrollment (see Section 2.4.1 of Chapter 2), and has been transformed from the original signal representation into the complementary representation C by the complementary functions F. With respect to the corresponding functions F, it is necessary to distinguish between invertible (mathematically: bijective[4]) and non-invertible functions. For any invertible function f there exists one invertible function f^{-1} to allow any conversion between the two representation spaces fulfilling the following condition:

$$f^{-1}(f(A)) = A \qquad (4\text{-}4)$$

That is, any complementary representation of A can be losslessly converted into C and vice versa. In cryptography, non-invertible functions are used, for example, in hash functions such as Message Digest 5 (MD5), where the goal is to digest messages of arbitrary lengths into values of specified size, e.g. 128 Bit, in a non-invertible manner. Examples for invertible functions in cryptography are symmetric encryption methods like DES.

---

[4] Bijection is the mathematical term for a one-to-one and onto mapping between two sets and is a prerequisite to allow invertibility.

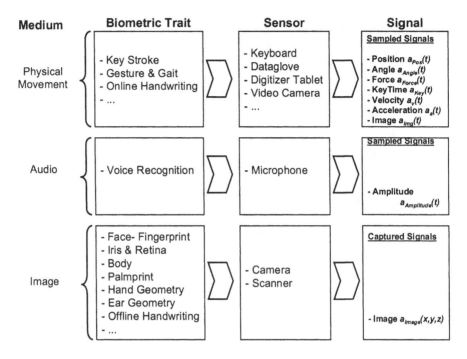

Figure 4-5. ASC signals derived from different traits and sensors for their acquisition

Practically, biometric authentication systems are either based on a non-invertible complementary function leading to complementary representations like the 2048-bit **Iriscode** [Daug1993] and fingerprint minutiae templates [MMJP2003], or the reference complementary information C is represented in exactly the same type of signal representation as A. This case can be modeled as a special case in our scenario by defining f as the identity function $C=f(A)=A$. The later approach of storing the complementary information C in exactly the same representation as the authentication information A is very common in behavioral biometrics such as online signature verification [Schm1999] and speaker recognition by voice, e.g. [TüSc2003].

4.2.6   Hybrid Systems

Specializations of combined authentication schemes are devices with integrated access control mechanisms based on combination of two or more of the three basic authentication schemes possession, knowledge and biometrics. Examples for this technology are chip-cards that need to be activated by PIN or memory devices with integrated fingerprint sensor and biometric user authentication. From a signal processing point-of view, these approaches can be modeled as two subsequent, conditional authentication steps and are therefore not considered in separate models. Such hybrid technologies, which are based on the combination of different authentication modalities, are also called **multifactor authentication schemes**. In our example of a memory device, which can be activated only by biometric fingerprint verification, the multi-factor authentication can be decomposed in a conjunction of two modalities: the biometric authentication of the user by the device and the possession-based authentication of the user by the authentication system A. Consequently, multi-factor authentication can be reduced to single-factor problems and we therefore focus our further views on single modalities.

4.3 Attacks to User Authentication Systems

Based on the introduced authentication model from Section 4.1 and the modeling of signals which are utilized for the transmission of information for authentication in Section 4.2, the goal of this section is to analyze potential attacks to user authentication systems. In our analysis, we proceed as follows: firstly, we refer to a general taxonomy for attacks to IT systems, which we have suggested in an earlier publication [ViSt2001]. Guided by this taxonomy we identify the most relevant goals of potential attackers and the types of actions, which may be performed in order to achieve these goals. For two particular goals, unauthorized access (in Section 4.3.1) and denial of service (in Section 4.3.2), we expand upon possible action methods, allocate points of attack in our general system model and present an extended action set to perform these attacks in Section 4.3.3.

Security attacks to computerized infrastructures are under scientific examination since many years and a number of organizations have been established for the observation and analysis of security incidents. One of the most active organizations in this area the **Computer Emergency Response Teams (CERT)**, established, for example, in the U.S.A. (US-CERT) and in several European counties (e.g. BSI-CERT in Germany). In a comprehensive research publication, 4299 incidents in the context of Internet-enabled computerized system have been analyzed [Howa1997] and one of the results was a general attack taxonomy. The taxonomy is to be interpreted as follows in brief: **attackers** apply **tools** to gain **access** to computerized systems resulting in an undesired **result** with malicious **objectives**.

In [ViSt2001], we have expanded this taxonomy in view of attacks to biometric systems; the following Figure 4-6 illustrates our taxonomy and provides examples for each of the attack actions.

In the context of discussion of attacks to authentication systems, the main concern is how potential attackers can make use of tools to exploit vulnerabilities, which kinds of actions are performed in these attacks and possible results. At this point, we can abstract from the nature of attackers and their objective. Furthermore, for the attack analysis of authentication systems, the result, which attackers seek, can be limited to one of two possible result states: **successful access** (without explicit specification of the further objectives, once success is authorized) or **denial of service**. Therefore, authentication aspects of attack analysis are mainly concentrated in the area covered by tool, the initial part of the access domain and the result of attacks, as drafted by the dashed line in Figure 4-6.

Given the two desired result categories and the signal representations presented earlier in this section, we can now analyze attack scenarios for the **three different authentication methods Possession, Knowledge and Biometrics**. For a methodical evaluation of different attack approaches, we use the technique of **thread analysis trees** [Schn1999], where the root node defines one specific goal of an attacker; the underlying nodes define alternative conditions and each of the leaves one specific method to achieve this goal. As we have already identified two goals of potential attackers, successful access and denial of service, we firstly develop one general attack tree representation for each of our two considerable results, which are then matched against each of the three authentication methods. Although in the modeling of the thread analysis trees, we consider the most relevant attack methods to authentication systems, it needs to be stated that completeness with respect to all considerable attack activities cannot be achieved in the context of this book chapter. Furthermore, we do not address the problem of securing the data channels pointed out in Section 4.1. Consequently, we assume secure communication, excluding the possibility of an attacker to intercept any of the channels of our authentication system model. With respect to the attacker's capabilities, the thread analysis assumes that she or he has access of a physical and/or logical nature to one or more of the system components H (Human Subject), U (Authentication System) or R (Reference Storage).

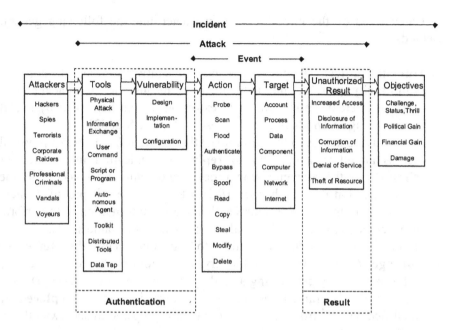

Figure 4-6. Attack taxonomy based on CERT [Howa1997] and [ViSt2001]

4.3.1 Unauthorized Access: Thread Analysis Tree

The thread analysis tree, which we have developed, is presented in the following Figure 4-7 for the scenario of an attacker seeking successful authentication.

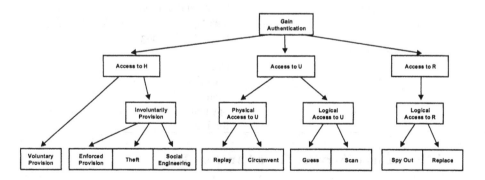

Figure 4-7. Thread analysis tree for unauthorized access

The tree leaves represent alternative methods to achieve authentication and thus comprise the action set extended from the original action column of the attack model in Figure 4-6.

Categorized by the three modules, we determine the following general methods:

- **Human Subject** *H* may either be cooperative to the attacker and **voluntarily provide** the authentication means, or an attacker may attempt to **steal, enforce** (e.g. by extortion) or get hold of it by **social engineering methods** like those presented in [MiSi2002].
- When having access to the **Authentication System** *U*, in case of physical access an attacker may try to **replay** authentication information or **circumvent** the authentication process and gain direct access to the Authentication Result Channel *ARC*. If logical access is provided, there is the possibility to either **guess** authentication information or to perform a systematic **scan** of possible values of *A* within the value space.
- If an attacker has the possibility to logically access the **Reference Storage** *R*, he or she may either try to get hold of the complementary information *C* by performing a read operation (**spy out, intercept**), or if write access is granted, the reference information may be **replaced** by modified data C^* from the attacker, which is prepared in such way that it will allow authentication of the attacker at a later authentication process.

Table 4-3 summarizes the most significant attack methods to our model of a general authentication system.

Table 4-3. Most relevant attack methods to attain access

Attacked Component	Method
H	Voluntary Provision
	Enforced Provision
	Stealing
	Social Engineering
U	Replay
	Circumvent
	Guess
	Scan
R	Spy Out
	Replace

4.3.2   Denial of Service: Thread Analysis Tree

For the scenario of an attacker seeking denial of service, i.e. to modify an authentication system in such way, that the authentication result yields negative, even for authorized and registered users, Figure 4-8 presents the thread analysis.

For the three components *H*, *U* and *R* as entry points for possible attacks to an authentication system, we can identify the following attack methods:

- the authentication means may be taken away from the authorized subject *H* by **stealing** or **looting**, disabling *H* to present the authentication information *A* to *U*.
- Potential attackers having access to *U* might **destroy** or **disable** the authentication system *U* by physical manipulations or, in case of logical access, may suppress services by data **flooding** or **confusion**.
- When having access to the reference storage *R*, attackers may also attempt to **destroy** complementary information *C* or **replace** it by modified information C^*, so that authorized users may not be authenticated anymore.

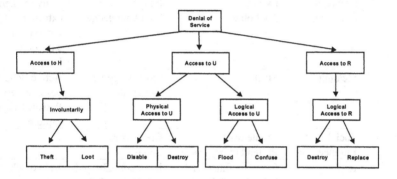

Figure 4-8. Thread analysis tree for denial of service

We summarize the most relevant attack methods with the goal to bring authentication systems in a denial of service state in Table 4-4.

Table 4-4. Most relevant attack methods to achieve denial of service

Attacked Component	Method
H	Theft
	Loot
U	Disable
	Destroy
	Flood
	Confuse
R	Destroy
	Replace

4.3.3   Actions: Possession, Knowledge and Biometrics

The previous two sections have determined extended methods, or action sets, for the two attack goals of unauthorized access and denial of service. In Table 4-5, we exemplify some specific actions, which have to be considered.

Table 4-5. Examples for extended actions, attack goal unauthorized access

Attacked Component	Method	Action Examples		
		Possession	**Knowledge**	**Biometrics**
H	Voluntary Provision	Lend object Make duplicate	Inform attacker	
	Enforced Provision	Extort, Loot object	Extort, Loot knowledge	Active Schemes: extortion difficult Passive schemes: extortion or looting
	Stealing	Steal	Eavesdropping Observation	Active Schemes: observe, record Passive Schemes: capture
	Social Engineering	Create trust Pretend to be trustee	Create trust Spoof	
U	Replay	Simulate functional behavior of object	Intercept ASC and record knowledge	Active Schemes: imitate record & replay Passive Schemes: capture & replay
	Circumvent	Corrupt authentication code Corrupt I/O	Corrupt authentication code Corrupt I/O	Corrupt authentication code Corrupt I/O
	Guess		Manual guessing	
	Scan		Exhaustive scan Dictionary scan Random scan	
R	Spy Out			Read templates Simulate authentication signal
	Replace			Replace by attacker's template

The attack actions are presented for both attack goals and are categorized by the attacked system components and the three different modalities possession, knowledge and biometrics.

Blank cells in Table 4-5 denote areas, where action paradigms cannot be determined. For example, it is infeasible to voluntarily provide biometric authentication information to a potential attacker or to gain it via social engineering due to the fact that biometric features are intrinsically linked the subject. The examples given have the supporting character to assist in our discussion on existing challenges in biometric user authentication in the following section.

4.4 Challenges in Biometric User Authentication

So far in this chapter, we have developed a generic view of user authentication systems, starting from a component-based architecture model to a channel-based information exchange between components. For the representation of information, we have defined three categories of signals, which are suitable for all three authentication modalities of possession, knowledge and biometrics. Furthermore, we have determined potential actions, which an attacker could perform in the two objective scenarios unauthorized access and denial of service. So far, we have explicitly included all three authentication modalities and have shown, that attack methods for all of them can be generalized, whereas the attack actions are specific to each modality.

In this section we now focus on the domain of **biometric user authentication**, and derive challenges in this area for the particular modality of handwriting biometrics. We show that some of the problems, which have already been solved for the other two authentication schemes, are still open areas for biometrics. The motivation and explanation of the challenges we present will be founded on the model and analysis earlier in this chapter.

First, we discuss the requirements for comparative **signal modeling** in Section 4.4.1, describing criteria for reproducible tests. There are two problems observed in the usage of signatures for biometric authentication due to their overt characteristics: the risk of **loss of anonymity** and **exposure to skilled forgeries**. These problems motivate the challenge of usage of alternative **semantic classes**, which we present in Section 4.4.2, followed by a discussion on the requirements to simulate different levels of knowledge of potential attackers in **test environments** by modeling **multi-level attack strengths** in Section 4.4.3. Physical characteristics of sensor devices used for sampling of handwriting vary very widely, and we discuss open questions in biometric authentication involving such different **sensor characteristics** of hardware devices in Section 4.4.4, which also influence signal modeling aspects of the first category. All these four open areas motivate our later discussions in Chapters 5, 6 and 7, which will then be focused on the biometric modality of handwriting. Open problems also exist in the area of protection of reference data, where **biometrics for generation of cryptographic keys** is of interest, wherever biometric references need to be encrypted, as we will show in Section 4.4.5 or alternative storage representations are required, which fulfill **security demands** with respect to confidentiality and at the same time possess low **complexity and capacity** requirements, as we show in Section 4.4.6. The later two aspects will be addressed in subsequent Chapters 6 and 7 of this book and we conclude this chapter by examples of **additional open research problems** in Section 4.4.7, which leave room for future contributions.

4.4.1   Signal Modeling

As shown earlier, all authentication systems provide authentication information from the user H to the authentication system U in form of signals transmitted via channels. These signals are converted from the analog world and are required to be digitally represented. For many biometric systems, these digital signal representations are proprietary to the sensor in use, the analog-digital conversion method and the verification algorithm. For many biometric methods, standards have been suggested (for example in [BioA2001] and [CBEF2001]), however, the purpose of these standards is interoperability of systems rather than the reproducibility of particular biometric signals for evaluation purposes. In comparison to biometrics, the problem of interoperability does not constitute a problem for the two other authentication schemes. Knowledge can be presented to the authentication system independently of the input device and for possession-based methods, well established standards exist (e.g. ISO 7816 interface standard for smart cards, [Citi2000]).

In order to ensure comparable evaluations of biometric systems, signal representations have to be determined that allow collection of test data signals at a level as close as possible to the sensor device. Furthermore, signals need to be attributed by their physical origin, i.e. the device type used for sampling, the origin of the recorded semantic and temporal information.

Such biometric test signals are qualified for evaluation of different authentication algorithms as they allow a precise reproduction of the signals transmitted via the Authentication Submission Channel ASC at any time later than the recording of test samples. The modeling of digital representations and the provision of test sets of reasonable size is a prerequisite for system evaluations independent of sensor-hardware, semantics of behavioral traits or matching algorithm specifics.

For passive biometric methods, which quite often are based on image data, an independent modeling of the biometric authentication information is given in a straightforward manner by standardized digital image formats such as bitmap (BMP) or Tagged Image File Format (TIFF). For such biometric methods, test databases of significant size have been published and are basis for contests like the Fingerprint Verification Contests (FVC) 2000, 2002 and 2004 [MMJP2003]. Bailly-Baillière et al. have recently presented the multi-modal protocol BANCA [BBBH2003], but this does not yet include handwriting semantics.

Device Independent Signal Model

Only very recently the first approaches for device independent signal modeling can be observed, like within the call for participation in the first international signature verification contest [SVC2004]. Thus the definition and implementation of independent handwriting signal representations for multiple semantics, tablet categories and attack strengths is an open research area, which will be addressed within this book in Chapter 5.

4.4.2   Evaluation of Writing Semantics

Usage of signature as authentication information A implies potential problems, if the image of writing is visible to others. Firstly, from an intercepted image, conclusions with respect to the identity can be drawn either by reading the textual content of the signature or by comparison to other signature references. Consequently, anonymity may be limited, when signatures are used for user authentication purposes. Secondly, possession of a visual copy of the signature can help to produce skilled forgeries, thus making the authentication system vulnerable for forgeries. A possible solution to this problem is the utilization of other writing semantics than signatures.

A number of methods for the use of active, behavioral biometrics for user authentication schemes have been presented and it has been shown in principle, that these systems are capable of supporting different categories of semantics. For the modality of online handwriting, for example, Schmidt has presented a new verification system and evaluated semantics of two categories: signature and the German word "Grünschnabel" [Schm1999] and Kato et al. have evaluated writer verification, based on handwritten symbol objects [KaHH2002] in addition to signature.

An analysis to which degree additional semantic classes, which are either based on individual knowledge or are systematically pre-defined, are suitable for biometric user authentication in comparison to the typically used semantics, the signature, have not yet been investigated scientifically. In particular, it will be of interest how biometric systems respond to identical writing semantic input for all users, i.e. to which degree such systems can differentiate users solely by the writing style rather than the writing content.

Secondly, with respect to application of behavioral biometrics for authentication by knowledge and being, it will be of interest, to which degree of accuracy users can be verified by private, individual writing semantics.

Evaluation of Handwriting Semantics

In an earlier publication [Viel2000], we have motivated the investigation of an initial set of five different semantic classes (*Signature*, identical German word *"Sauerstoffgefäß"*, identical number sequence *"8710"*, user-defined *Passphrase* and user-defined *Symbol*), representing user-specific semantics as well as system-wide well-defined writing semantics. This semantic set will be the basis for an evaluation of handwriting semantics, within Chapter 5 of this book.

4.4.3   Multi-Level Attack Strength

Closely related to the problem of multiple semantics is the question, to which extent authentication algorithms are capable of differentiating between different users (Inter-Class discriminatory power) and to which degree they are capable of robustly separating authentication attempts by forgers from authentic subjects (imposter discriminatory power). This aspect is of particular interest for the alternative semantic classes, where two options exist: semantic classes including explicit individual knowledge (such us passwords) or semantics without knowledge components (e.g. all users write the same text).

So far, almost exclusively the capabilities of Inter-Class discriminatory power have been investigated. Exceptions for passive biometric authentication schemes are initial work on skilled fingerprint forgeries by Matsumoto et al. ([MMYH2002]), and more recently for iris counterfeits ([MaHi2004] and [MaHS2004]). However, purposed forging needs to be investigated more deeply for active biometric traits due to their behavioral nature. For such analysis, it is necessary to consider that active biometric authentication traits, like those based on handwriting components, may include knowledge components as well as behavioral capabilities of the subjects. Thus, in the analysis of active biometric authentication systems, different security levels have to be considered, depending on the knowledge of forgers about the authentication information A used by authentic subjects.

Different Levels of Knowledge of Forgers

Here, one of the scientific challenges is to point out, which security level can be achieved by such bi-factorial authentication (i.e. combination of knowledge and biometrics) and to classify the achievable security level in relation to uni-factorial biometric authentication. Within this book, we will address this aspect by analysis of attacks to a biometric system with respect to different levels of knowledge of forgers about the original semantic. This aspect is considered by the overall evaluation methodology introduced in Chapter 5.

4.4.4 Sensor Characteristics of Digitizer Devices

It has been shown earlier in this section, that signals need to be recorded in all three categories of authentication systems and we have pointed out the two basic methods for this: capturing and sampling. For possession and knowledge-based authentication systems, it has been shown, that these recording processes typically result in low-noise signals and the resulting signals show little or no dependency on the sensor device used, due to their discrete nature. A computer keyboard, for example, does not reflect hardware-specific characteristics in the resulting text signal, which might have influence on a knowledge-based authentication process. However, the keyboard characteristics used for a biometric, keystroke-based authentication significantly affects the resulting sampled signal due to physical properties like attenuation, pressure sensitivity and others. Especially for continuous media, a wide variety of sensors with significantly differing characteristics can be found. Variations can be found in temporal and spatial resolutions of sensors, but also with respect to dimensionality (especially for movement sensors). For large-scale deployment, it is important to examine the dependencies between biometric authentication algorithms and sensors. Unlike in possession and knowledge-based systems, biometric signals are exposed to distortions based on the sensor characteristics, which may cause problems if some complementary information C has been generated from a sensor having different specifications than the sensor used to obtain the actual authentication information A. This problem is relevant especially for applications in large areas, where sensors with identical characteristics might not be available in every location, as well as in long-term considerations, where specific hardware might no longer be available after some time.

For the great majority of biometric authentication systems that can be found today, there are very few statements to their robustness with respect to cross-sensor verification. Although many of the algorithms presented in the literature perform normalization and extract non-dimensional features, such as minutiae diagrams [MMJP2003] or Iris Codes [Daug1993] and should therefore be capable of an inter-sensor verification, this specific aspect has not been sufficiently explored yet. Such characteristics require rather high stability of features derived from the sensor and a low dependency on sensor-intrinsic characteristics.

For a formalized description of the requirement of inter-sensor authentication, we refer to the two subsets of Select Functions, S_{Enroll} and S_{Verify}, defined at the beginning of this chapter and assume a scenario of two different sensor devices, *1* and *2*. $S_{Enroll,1}$ and $S_{Verify,1}$ denote Select Functions performed on device *1* and $S_{Enroll,2}$ and $S_{Verify,2}$ those on device *2*. With the further assumption of an argument-free *S*, as also introduced at the beginning of this chapter, and the definition of A_1, A_2, C_1 and C_2 denoting Authentication and Complementary Information from the first and second device respectively, we postulate the following condition for sensor independent authentication in algebra notation:

$$\left(l(A_1,C_1) = l(A_2,C_2)\right) \quad \wedge \quad \left(l(A_1,C_2) = l(A_2,C_1)\right) \quad \forall l \in L$$
$$with:$$
$$C_1 = f(S_{Enroll,1}()) \tag{4-5}$$
$$C_2 = f(S_{Enroll,2}())$$
$$A_1 = S_{Verify,1}$$
$$A_2 = S_{Verify,2}$$

That is, authentication of *A* obtained from one device by complementary information *C* from the other yields the same result of *l(A,C)* as for information *A* and *C* obtained from an identical device.

Inter-Sensor Authentication

During the remaining course of this book, one of the focuses will be to determine features in biometric raw signals for handwriting, allowing us to construct select functions having such characteristics. We do so by a fundamental assessment of the impact of utilizing different categories of tablets in the context of our evaluation of alternative semantic classes under differently scaled attack strengths in Chapter 5 and we will maintain the hardware categorization in the test methodology for our new algorithms in Chapter 6 and Chapter 7.

4.4.5   Key Generation from Handwriting Biometrics

Protection of reference data is required for authentication systems to ensure confidentiality. If reference samples of the entire original authentication signals need to be stored, these need to be protected from unauthorized access. Many of these security demands can be satisfied by cryptographic techniques, which generally are based on encryption using digital keys. As cryptographically strong keys are rather large, it is certainly not feasible to let users memorize their personal keys. Thus, in practical scenarios today, digital keys are typically stored on smart cards, protected by a special kind of password, the personal identification number (PIN). Due to the difficulties in using knowledge and possession as shown earlier in Section 4.3, some initial methods to apply biometrics for solving key management problems have been investigated in the past. We find approaches for the biometric modalities of fingerprint ([Nich1999], [UPPJ2004]) and voice [MRLW2001] but yet today, approaches for the modality of online handwriting are missing.

Key Generation

In Chapter 6, we will introduce a new method for the generation of an individually unique data representation from online handwriting signals, called Biometric Hash, which can be utilized for the generation of cryptographic keys. These cryptographic keys, which are derived directly from the biometric signals, can be utilized for encryption of complete reference signals or other type of information. Based on a large test database we will empirically show, to which degree these keys can be reproduced reliably and to which extent they may be reproduced by non-authentic persons.

4.4.6   Reference Storage

The reference storage components R of authentication systems based on possession and knowledge do not constitute problem areas with respect to **storage capacity**. Possession-based approaches typically only need to store some object identifiers along with user attribute data, representing the complementary information C and in case of smart devices additional information for cryptographic functions (e.g. cryptographic keys). Knowledge-based systems either store the explicit knowledge (encrypted or not encrypted) or some digest of the reference knowledge as complementary information C, as shown earlier in our discussions in Section 4.2.4. A good example for such mathematical non-reversible functions is the UNIX *crypt()* method for password authentication ([SiGa1996]), where a mathematical digest of the password is generated and stored by using the individual password together with a salt value as key for a symmetric encryption of a blank string of fixed length. This proceeding allows verification of passwords without having the necessity to explicitly keep the plain text passwords in the reference storage R.

In either cases, the size of the complementary information C is rather small and can range from of a few bytes (e.g. 64 bit cipher for UNIX *crypt()*) to a few hundred bytes (e.g. smart card including certificates and cryptographic key pairs). This rather compact size of the reference allows the design of authentication systems, where all or part of the references are stored on objects that remain in possession of the human subject rather than centralized at some other location.

Examples for such authentication devices, which remain in possession of users, are signature cards, which are based on smart chip cards and can only be activated by entering a PIN code, which is compared to the locally stored reference. The deposition of references at the user's end is advantageous compared to a centralized storage.

Another positive side effect of a **low-complexity** representation of C is the possibility to implement computationally effective authentication functions L. Daugman's Iriscode for example, is a 2048-dimensional binary vector, allowing the utilization of the computationally simple Hamming Distance function as the basis for authentication functions L [Daug1993].

From a **security point of view**, it reduces the risk of a successful attack to the reference storage, potentially compromising a great number of references. Attacks can only be addressed to single individuals and must take place in the direct vicinity of the owner of the object. Using mathematical digest functions like in the UNIX *crypt()* authentication furthermore prevent attackers from getting access to plain text representation of secret knowledge. Another positive aspect in the distributed reference storage is the absence of requirement for a complex and extensive reference management.

For biometric-based authentication however, aspects of capacity requirements and security of reference information are a more problematic domain. Firstly, the size of reference data may become rather large. It may range from a few Bytes in keystroke recognition to Megabytes of high definition iris images or for video-based authentication, which is a limiting factor with respect to decentralized reference storage. Secondly, due to natural variability of biometric information, it is impossible to apply discrete mathematical techniques like cryptographic hashes [Schn1996] to secure the reference data. Due to the second aspect, biometric authentication systems very often store the complete reference signal (e.g. fingerprint image, audio or handwriting signal) as complementary information C, with the impact of making the references store R vulnerable to spy and interception attacks.

Obviously, it is desirable to find similar characteristics with respect to size and security of R for biometric authentication systems as those existing for possession- and knowledge-based systems. Today, research activities addressing aspects of biometric data compression and digest functions are still very limited compared to disciplines like optimization of verification algorithms, although some initial work can be found for implementation of different biometric modalities on small devices (e.g. voice in [MRLW2001], fingerprint in [Stru2001] or signature verification in [HeFr2003]). The question how to find compressed representations with good discriminatory power remains insufficiently explored. Research addressing the security of biometric reference data has been widely neglected so far, and only a few first approaches to this problem can be found, e.g. by exploring cryptographic methods for securing fingerprint templates ([ClKL2003], [Nich1999]) or related work to derive cryptographic keys from fingerprint biometrics for Digital Rights Management (DRM) applications in [UPPJ2004]. With the beginning of large-scale deployment of biometric techniques and the subsequent extensive collection of reference data, it will be necessary to address security issues for these data much more intensively, which requires determination of security functions as well as compression methods allowing decentralized storage of templates.

A third aspect in biometric reference storage is anonymity. In some fields of application, it may be desirable to authenticate users without obtaining explicit knowledge about their identity. Such systems require reference storage mechanisms that firstly do not explicitly link identity information with the biometric templates and secondly disallow implicit derivation of identity information from the biometric complementary information C. The first requirement can be fulfilled by a conformable design of reference data, not comprising any personal information. For the second aspect, reference representations for C are required, that do not permit reconstruction of the original biometric trait A. This aspect is of particular relevance for biometric characteristics, which are publicly ascertainable, such as facial images, fingerprints and also signatures. Here, a reconstruction of the original biometric may allow a straightforward way to identify the user of an authentication system. The protection of reference information can be postulated by the infeasibility, or at least very high computational complexity, to find an identification function allowing to determine identities ID of subjects H from C.

Reference Storage

In the following chapters of this book, we will contribute to these problems in the storage of biometric references for the discipline of handwriting authentication by introducing a new concept for user verification, based on Biometric Hashes in Chapter 7. This concept effectively leads to a feature representation, which makes the reconstruction of the original handwriting signals computationally difficult and thus practically infeasible for attackers having today's computational means.

4.4.7   Additional Challenges

In the previous subsections, and based on our extension to Bishop's model, we have emphasized actual open research areas that are consequences of the introduction of biometrics in authentication technology and appear to be of high significance for the near future. Besides these questions, which will be discussed in detail within the scope of this book, the domain of biometric user authentication opens a wide field of additional problems, some of which are intrinsic to biometric processes, some others arise from combinations of different modalities or are motivated by political and social aspects of biometrics. Without aiming at a complete problem statement, the following three aspects show further actually relevant research areas:

Optimization of Accuracy

All biometric authentication methods are subject to false classification errors, as shown earlier. One of the main targets in this discipline is the minimization of error rates of biometric verification algorithms. A continuous activity in publication of algorithmic improvements in signal processing and pattern recognition can be observed and this activity is not expected to decrease in the near future. Very recent work submitted for publication in this area indicate the template update strategies could be an approach to compensate aging effects of biometric features (see for example Uludag et al., [UlRJ2004]), improving accuracy in long-term applications.

Multi-Modal Authentication Schemes

Due to the intrinsic problem of erroneous results of biometric authentic systems it appears advantageous to make use of more than one biometric modality for an authentication decision. Research has been conducted to fuse different modalities and to determine classifiers that take into account results of multiple biometric matching algorithms. Besides the aspect of finding methods to increase the overall accuracy of such multi-modal authentication systems, there remain open questions, for example, with respect to the degree of correlation between different modalities, questions of finding meaningful sets of modalities and other questions. It can be expected that especially for application areas with high security levels, multi-modal approaches can achieve significantly higher accuracy as compared to uni-modal systems. Jain and Ross identify this area as a promising opportunity to make human authentication more effective [JaRo2004].

Social Acceptance and Large-Scale Deployment

In addition to technical discussions on biometric authentication technologies and in conjunction with the practical applications of them, problems with respect to acceptance and functionality in large populations need to be addressed. Questions here include discriminatory power of biometric features in practice, manageability of authentication systems, cultural implications and social attitudes towards such systems. Recent political activities indicate that biometric data might be collected on a very wide scope in the near future, e.g. by a mandatory inclusion in travel documents. Impacts of large-scale deployment of biometrics, involving great numbers of users with varying cultural and technical background, are hard to predict from laboratory tests and conclusions can be drawn only once empirical real-world data is made available to research.

4.5   Notations and Abbreviations

The following Table 4-6 summarizes notations and abbreviations introduced in this chapter in alphabetical order.

Table 4-6. Summary of notations and abbreviations introduced in this Chapter 4

Designator	Name	Description	Introduced in
A	Authentication Information	Set of specific information with which entities (here: H) prove their identities	Chapter 4, from [Bish2003]
$a(x,y,z)$	Captured Signal	Digital representation of an analog signal, captured and quantized into non-overlapping discrete, sub ranges at discrete coordinates: $x \in \overline{X}, y \in \overline{Y}, z \in \overline{Z}$	Section 4.2.1
$a(t)$	Sampled Signal	Digital representation of an analog signal, sampled and quantized into non-overlapping discrete, sub ranges at discrete time instances $t \in \overline{T}$	Section 4.2.1
ARC	Authentication Result Channel	Channel to provide the result of an authentication to the external world	Section 4.1
ASC	Authentication Submission Channel	Channel to transmit authentication information A from H to U	Section 4.1
C	Complementary Information	Set of information that the system stores and uses to validate authentication information A	Chapter 4, from [Bish2003]
$crypt()$	Password encryption function	Cryptographic hashing function for securing passwords in UNIX operating systems, for example, see [SiGa1996]	Section 4.2.4

Table 4-6 (cont.)

Designator	Name	Description	Introduced in
DES	Data Encryption Standard	Symmetric encryption algorithm see [SiGa1996]	Section 4.2.4
F	Complimentary Functions	Set of functions that generate the complementary information C from the authentication information A, i.e. $f \in F, f: A \rightarrow C$	Chapter 4, from [Bish2003]
H	Human Subject	Entity of one individual subject in an authentication system	Chapter 4, from [Bish2003]
ID	Identity of User H	Declared identity of a user H	Section 4.1
L	Authentication Functions	Set of functions that verify identity, i.e. $l \in L, l: A \times C \rightarrow \{true, false\}$	Chapter 4, from [Bish2003]
$M_{Authentication}$	Authentication Request Message	Message sent from H to U to initiate the authentication process by user H	Section 4.1
$M_{RequestAuthenticationInfo}$	Authentication Information Request Message	Message requesting H to present authentication information A to U	Section 4.1
$M_{RequestComplimentaryInfo}$	Complementary Information Request Message	Message of U requesting Complementary information C from R	Section 4.1
MD5	Message Digest 5	Cryptographic hash function, for example, see [Bish2003]	Section 4.2.5
R	Reference Storage	Entity that contains (stores) all C for all H in an authentication system: $C \in R$	Section 4.1
RCC	Reference Information Control Channel	Channel for transmission of control data between U and R	Section 4.1
RSC	Reference Information Submission Channel	Channel for the transmission of complementary information C from R to U	Section 4.1
S	Select Functions	Set of functions that enable an entity to create or alter A and C	Chapter 4, from [Bish2003]
S_{Enroll}	Set of Select Functions for user Enrollment	Subset of S for generation of A for subsequent applications of F to generate C as enrollment of an entity to an authentication system: $S_{Enroll} \subseteq S$	Chapter 4

Table 4-6 (cont.)

Designator	Name	Description	Introduced in
S_{Verify}	Set of Select Functions for user verification	Subset of S for generation of A for the purpose of identity Verification of an entity to an authentication system: $S_{Verify} \subseteq S$	Chapter 4
SFC	Synchronization Forward Channel	Forward-channel for Synchronization from User H to Authentication system U	Section 4.1
SRC	Synchronization Reverse Channel	Reverse-channel for Synchronization from Authentication system U to User H	Section 4.1
Switch(a)	Switched Signal	Function represents its argument, if *SwitchingCondition* equals *TRUE* and 0 otherwise: $$Switch(a) = \begin{cases} a, & \text{if } SwitchingCondition = TRUE \\ 0, & otherwise \end{cases}$$	Section 4.2.1
$t \in \overline{T}$	Set of discrete sampling instances	Discrete time arguments of sampled signal representation $a(t)$	Section 4.2.1
U	Authentication System	Entity that performs enrollment and authentication task	Section 4.2.1

PART II: HANDWRITING BIOMETRICS - OVERVIEW

Chapter 5

EVALUATING HANDWRITING BIOMETRICS
Analyzing the Effects of Handwriting Semantics and Digitizer Hardware

5. EVALUATING HANDWRITING BIOMETRICS

Many processes of senso-motoric phenomena generated by humans have been explored by scientists. In this area, intersecting disciplines of biology, psychology but also engineering, models have been developed for a better interpretation of behavior. Especially in the domain of man-machine interfaces, a discipline in the area of **Human-Computer Interaction (HCI)**, signal processing based modeling of such natural processes is a prerequisite to design methods allowing computer-based interpretation of human behavior.

The two main modalities utilized for man-machine interfaces today are gestures and speech. The later domain is a huge research area, which has been of interest to many researchers over the past decades. It addresses the problems of automated recognition of textual content of spoken languages (an overview can be found, for example, in [BeRi1999]), automated recognition of the speaker's identity (i.e. [Furu1994]) or other, more unusual goals like the detection of the speaker's emotional state [Zott2003].

As shown in Figure 5-1, the area of gesture-based HCI shows a higher diversity with respect to the modalities. We find approaches based on tracking of hand motion by either video-based tracking or data gloves, analysis of body movement or more specialized techniques based on well-defined gestures like those used in sign language. Some approaches also focus on special input devices like computer mouse. A comprehensive overview of various research activities is given by Cohen in [Cohe2003].

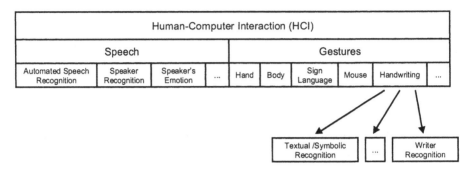

Figure 5-1. Human-to-machine modalities in HCI

It becomes plausible that the process of generating handwriting belongs to the category of gesture-based modalities for human-to-machine interfaces. Here, we find two major goals of the gesture interpretation: the recognition of written text or symbols and the recognition or verification of the writer's identity. The later discipline describes the positioning of the topic of the upcoming chapters of this book, handwriting biometrics for user authentication in the context of HCI. The usage of handwriting as an authentication gesture requires that the entire process can be represented in a time variant manner. This special discipline is called online handwriting due to the fact that physical measures of the writing process are accessible over time in a signal representation. In Chapter 4 we have shown that, although signal-based analysis of handwriting in the field of user authentication has been scientifically pursued over many years now, there exist a number of aspects, which have not been investigated to a sufficient degree today. In this chapter, we will contribute to the following three important open areas:

Alternative Semantic Classes

In the analog world, one specific writing semantic has been in favor for centuries for user authentication purposes: the signature. For many scientific and practical approaches to automated signature verification, this has been the fundamental motivation. However, as stated in the previous chapter, little work has been done to analyze alternative semantics for user authentication purposes. In this chapter, we will explore the usability of such semantics, differentiating on the aspects of individual knowledge and public knowledge.

Multi-Level Quality of Attacks

An assumption, which is widely accepted in this research discipline, is that the similarity between original handwriting samples and forgeries depends heavily on the forger's skills, knowledge and degree of training. As we have not found any empirical evaluation of this assumption yet, another aspect of the work discussed in this chapter will be effect analysis of forgeries of different qualities.

Hardware Dependency

Little knowledge exists on the effects of digitizer hardware with different physical characteristics to biometric authentication algorithms based on online handwriting. Here, we are interested in two aspects:

- to which degree does the **accuracy** of biometric authentication depend on spatial and/or temporal resolutions of sensor hardware?
- What is the impact of **cross-sensor authentication** if sensors possess different technical properties?

In order to be able to empirically evaluate these aspects, we define a methodology, which has implemented in our evaluation system, called PlataSign and a database of test samples. This **evaluation framework** is used for an **empirical analysis**, which we perform by applying the **test methodology** to an **exemplary verification algorithm** and we show **quantitative results** for all three aspects towards the end of this chapter. Furthermore, test methodology, evaluation system and categorization of tablets, semantic classes and attack strength levels will be the fundament for the further evaluations in Chapter 6 and Chapter 7 of this book.

The concept of our analysis is described in this chapter as follows. First, in Section 5.1, we summarize the most relevant previous theoretical work on handwriting generation. Based on this theoretical overview, we continue in Section 5.2 with an overview of the state-of-the-art in handwriting user authentication based on online signals from handwriting digitizer tablets. Requirements for the design of an evaluation system are postulated in Section 5.3, followed by a section on the technical implementation in our evaluation system in Section 5.4, resulting from these requirements. Section 5.5 describes the structure of evaluation samples in our database, which will be the basis for all our further evaluation scenarios in the context of this book. Our evaluation methodology for the experiments is described with respect to experimental setup, verification algorithm as metric and test environments as scenarios in Section 5.6. Evaluation results are presented in Section 5.7 for the aspect of suitability of alternative semantic classes and in Section 5.8 for the impact of hardware characteristic, differentiated by forgery quality. Finally, the last two sections summarize the most important findings of this chapter in Section 5.9 and resume the notations and abbreviations introduced in this chapter in Section 5.10.

5.1   Theoretical Models of Handwriting Generation

Besides for the generation of handwriting, modeling of human traits used for communication has also inspired theoretical work for other modalities as well, for example, in an early work on the generation of human speech by Rabiner and Schafer almost three decades ago [RaSc1978].

The theory on how the human handwriting is generated has been a research of high interest since approximately 4 decades and looking at scientific activities in the area, a bias can be observed roughly between 1960 and 1980. Theoretical models are not only of significance for the computerized production of cursive handwriting, but also for their analysis towards writing recognition and writer identification. Work in the area is based in the early scientific discipline of **Cybernetics**, defined by Wiener as [Wien1949]:

"... the study of control and communication in the machine or in the animal...".

In this initial approach, a system model based on a first-order feedback system was introduced, consisting of the components **comparator, effector, sensor** and **feedback loop** (see Figure 5-2).

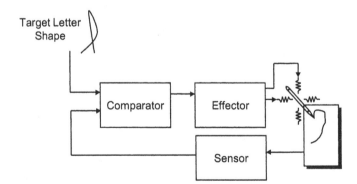

Figure 5-2. First-order feedback handwriting generation system based on [Scho1991]

Using this cybernetic system model, the handwriting process is described as follows [Scho1991]:

- a target letter shape enters the system at the **effector**, where muscles are activated thus generating output,
- the visual, proprioceptive and tactile **sensor** delivers a displacement or velocity **feedback** signal to
- the **comparator**, which in return continuously actives the effector muscles.

This initial model provided a first systematic explanation for the process of human handwriting. However, around 1970, it became evident that models purely based on cybernetics are not sufficient to describe the writing process because of timing constraints. In several biological experiments, it has been observed that effective basic reaction times of human beings are always above 100 milliseconds, mainly due to the delays in the biological process of muscle movement generation and runtimes of signals in the human neural system. Some typical reaction times presented in [Scho1991, pp. 7] lead to the conclusion that effective reaction times are typically 130 milliseconds. In parallel, it has been observed, that human beings can generate controlled frequencies with periods well below these boundaries. For example, skilled piano players can generate 16 strokes per second. These observations lead to the conclusion that human-controlled processes like handwriting are not continuously provided by a feedback signal and thus cannot be described sufficiently by a closed feedback loop model. For this reason, the concept of **cognitive motor theory** has been introduced, which is based in an open-loop approach. The main difference compared to the cybernetic explanation is the motor program component, biologically represented by the central nervous system, which determines an aimed movement in advance in terms of muscle activation ratios. This generation of programmed movement is limited to a short sequence, allowing the writing of only very basic shapes. These basic shapes are called strokes and they make out a specimen in human handwriting. As in this system layout, the feedback signal arrives too late to actually influence the production of an individual stroke, feedback information is used to influence the program for future strokes in the writing process, adjusting the motor program by learning. An example for such a feed-forward concept is the horizontal line orientation correction, which has been evaluated by Schomaker and van der Plaats, see [Scho1991, pp. 11], where the effect of blindfolding of cursive handwriting has been explored. In summary of the theoretical work, Schomaker and Van Galen point out two main tendencies in the theory of handwriting [ScGa1996]:

- **Signal Modeling**: to model the effects of the muscle movement on the pen tip movement during the writing process, it appears to be sufficient to abstract from the intricate anatomical and biomechanical processes and to concentrate on the effective pen tip movement. This view also encourages the usage of modern tablet digitizer devices, capable of sampling dynamic signals originating from pen movement.

- **Modularity**: motor processes to form letter formation, size and slant, as well as their anatomical and biomechanical implications can be modeled in separate modules interacting in a specific process flow. The basic process steps that have been determined for a modular process representation, are **grapheme** selection (i.e. letter code identification), allograph selection (i.e. letter form retrieval), overall size control and basic processes. Note that the number of modules to be defined for a writing system model may vary as additional factors like forces or pen orientation may or may not be included in a specific model. This view has been developed heuristically and does not necessarily reflect the anatomical organization of the human brain.

Based on these theoretical insights, a wide number of engineering models have been proposed for the artificial generation of handwriting. They started from very early electromechanical experiments based on a machine, driven by two electrically step motors to control horizontal and vertical diflections of a pen and led to models based on neurophysiologic knowledge. A comprehensive overview and discussion of computational models can be found in [ScGa1996]. As the focus of our work is the determination of writer dependent features in handwriting-based writing signals, the discussion of computer models at this point are limited to significant approaches taking into account the signals of recorded pen-tip movement.

Hollerbach [Holl1981] provides a signal-based theoretical model for the generation of human cursive handwriting. This model is based on the assumption, that the complexity of hand movement during handwriting can be reduced to two roughly orthogonal degrees of freedom, which are controlled by two oscillatory processes: one for the horizontal and one for the vertical generation of letter shapes. Both signals are modulated in amplitude and phase, combined and superimposed on a rightward hand movement of constant velocity over the writing surface. This process leads to the generation of one continuous sequence of cursive handwriting, as a basic element of written text. In this theory, a mass-spring model for the muscle movements, presented in earlier publications such as [GoTh1965], justifies the signal modulation in both dimensions and is represented by equations of motion for such a mechanical system.

The following Figure 5-3, originally reproduced from [Holl1981], illustrates Hollerbach's model, based on a dynamic subsystem for the effective pen movement of the hand (denoted as *"Subsystem Hand"* in

Figure 5-3) and a superimposed movement of the entire subsystem over the writing surface (denoted as *"superimposed horizontal hand movement on writing surface"*). Hollerbach's model is based on the assumption that the overall system is not exposed to any loss of dissipation energy due to viscous friction. Consequently, it does not involve damping components. This can be assumed as a reasonable assumption for the model due to the relative short duration and thus the limited number of oscillation periods during the process of writing a single stroke. With this simplification, the equations of motion for the subsystem hand can be derived in dependence of the horizontal pen position (x), vertical pen position (y), the vertical acceleration $\ddot{y}$ of pen mass m_y, being the second order temporal derivative of y, and the horizontal acceleration of the subsystem m_x, $\ddot{x}$ equal to the second order temporal derivative of x. Note x,y, $\ddot{x}$ and $\ddot{y}$ all denote continuous signals in this model, where an explicit temporal argument is omitted for the sake of clarity.

The two orthogonal pairs of springs represent the movement forces in directions of the agonist (x_g and y_g) and antagonist (x_n and y_n), having spring constants of $k_{g,x}$, $k_{n,x}$, $k_{g,y}$ and $k_{n,y}$ respectively. The forces are applied to pen mass m_y. For modeling of the horizontal pen oscillations, Hollerbach considers the entire vertical subsystem as mass m_x (see area bordered by a rectangle in Figure 5-3), which itself is attached to the horizontal springs.

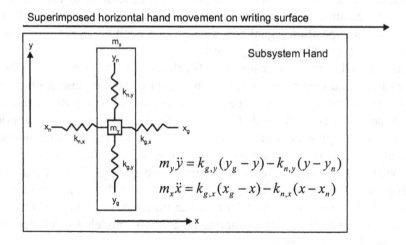

Superimposed horizontal hand movement on writing surface

$$m_y\ddot{y} = k_{g,y}(y_g - y) - k_{n,y}(y - y_n)$$
$$m_x\ddot{x} = k_{g,x}(x_g - x) - k_{n,x}(x - x_n)$$

Figure 5-3. Hollerbach's spring-mass model for handwriting generation, reproduced from [Holl1981]

Based on this model the equations of movement can be derived easily, as shown in Figure 5-3. In [Holl1981], it has been shown that an implementation of the model is suitable to generate cursive script, if modulated with the right parameter. The problem of how to control such an oscillatory system in order to generate reasonable semantics is not addressed in Hollerbach's work, however it is indicated that the required stimuli originates from the human motor system.

Schomaker et al. [ScTT1989] develop a more extensive model for the generation of cursive handwriting, which still makes use of Hollerbach's oscillatory theory at the level of stroke generation, being the smallest entity of the writing process. In addition to this, they develop a reactive control system, which is based on a five-level model: Initially, a writer starts with the intention to write a message, which takes place on a **semantic level**. At the **lexical and syntactical level**, the semantic information of the overall textual message is **decomposed into words**. The third stage translates these words into **graphemes**, as the representation of letters in cursive script. Based on these graphemes, the producer of cursive script then uses a grammar for the determination of abstract codes to connect basic components, called **allographs** to represent these graphemes. Finally, the translation of allograph primitives into a parameterized sequence of strokes is done in the fifth stage, called the **quantitative level**. These stroke parameters are fed into the stroke generation process, which is in charge of the pen tip displacement signals. Figure 5-4 illustrates the model of Schomaker et al., showing the entire process of generation of cursive script from the semantic level down to the process of pen movement signals (horizontal pen position signal $x(t)$, vertical pen position signal $y(t)$) and an exemplary image of handwriting result.

The model considers **cognitive feedback** of the writer by **lining observation** and **error correction** on the level of stroke generation. In the study, the authors present experimental results of computer generated cursive script based on three different sets of parameters and their numerical analysis of the generated script versus originals shows that the model is adequate to obtain a reasonable approximation of the human cursive handwriting. However, it has been observed that open problems exist in the generic modeling of inter-stroke connections (e.g. a "m-e" letter transition considered to be the same as a "n-e" letter transition) and in the horizontal progression model (horizontal progression could be modeled as a function of the horizontal stroke sizes).

The approach of Schomaker et al. shows the effect, that the modeling of curvature by only two orthogonal signals may become a difficult problem, as it is solely represented by phase shift. In order to simplify this problem, Bullock et al. introduce a third degree of freedom, the horizontal wrist rotation, to model the curve trajectory during the writing process [BuGM1993]. A justification for this approach is given by the anatomy of a wrist during the writing process, where the vertical wrist rotation accounts for the *x* movement, the horizontal rotation produces curvature and the finger extension generated movements of the pen tip in *y* direction.

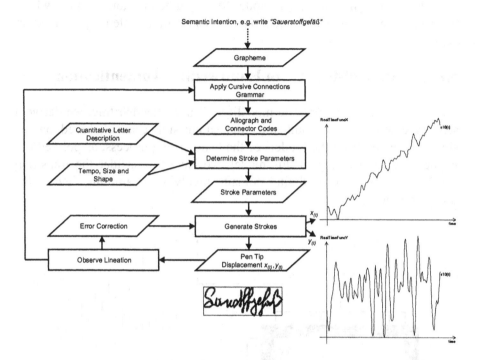

Figure 5-4. Computational model of cursive handwriting-based on [ScTT1989]

A statistical model has been presented in [StCh1994], which is based on the assumption, that the writing of a character by hand is the impulse response of a slowly time-varying second order system. For parameter estimation, the velocity curves of the writing samples have been partitioned into fixed-length non-overlapping frames and piece-wise linear functions within each frame have been defined. The model results in one parameter vector for each signal orientation (horizontal and vertical) for each stroke with a vector dimension proportional to the number of frames, which leads to a statistical model for writer-specific stroke generation. It has been shown that the model is adequate for writer imitation (cursive script generation) as well as for character recognition and writer identification.

The theoretical approaches for modeling of the human handwriting process given in this section provide an insight to selected work in the area and are at all not exhaustive. However, from the work presented, **we conclude** that for a **system representing the handwriting process**, we **require at least three signal dimensions: horizontal and vertical pen**

movements and pen-up / pen-down signals. Consequently, for an **analysis** of individual characteristics of writers in such writing processes, the same signals can be utilized. The following chapter will develop this observation towards the design of a system model for an authentication channel, which fits well into the general model for authentication systems presented in Section 4.2.

5.2   State-of-the-Art in Handwriting Authentication

For the particular biometric modality of online handwriting, we derive a schematic model of the authentication submission channel, based on the signals revealed from the models of the handwriting process, as pointed out in the previous section. In this model, we have to consider the transition from the physical to the digital domain, involving a sampling device, the digitizer tablet.

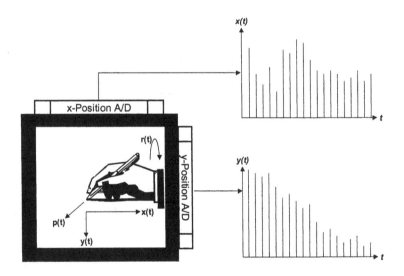

Figure 5-5. Physical movements and x/y position sampling in a handwriting process

As shown in Figure 5-5, we model the physical movement of the hand during the writing process by horizontal and vertical movement of the hand (*x(t)* and *y(t)*), rotation of the wrist *r(t)* and pressure applied to the pen tip *p(t)* over time. These physical movement characteristics are drafted in the center of the symbolized digitizer tablet.

Depending on the technical capabilities of the digitizer device, some or all of the physical phenomena, or derived quantities of them, are electronically registered, quantized and converted into a digital representation, namely sampled signals (see Section 4.2.1 of the previous chapter).

The model shown in Figure 5-5 shows a schematic digitizer tablet with a capability of sampling two signals: horizontal and vertical writing position signals, *x(t)* and *y(t)* respectively. Consequently, the signals, which model the authentication information *A* in our general model for an authentication system (see Chapter 4), are the results of an analog-digital (A/D) conversion process. Like all A/D transitions, we have to consider information loss in this process, mainly due to three reasons:

- **Insufficient Sampling Rates:** the sampling rate of the digitizer device needs to fulfill Nyquist's Theorem stipulated as follows: in order to represent the analog signal waveform without error from samples take at equal time intervals, the sampling rate must be at least double to the highest frequency component in the original signal. As discussed in Section 5.1, it has been shown that typical reaction times of human writers do not exceed 130 milliseconds, thus it is widely accepted that any components in handwriting signals above a frequency of approx. 10 Hz do not include any information significant for biometric analysis. Many signature verification approaches try to eliminate noise effects induced by higher frequencies by integration of a low-pass filter in the preprocessing of signals (e.g. 10 Hz Low-pass filter in [PlYB1992]). For the sampling devices, which will be used in context of our work, the sampling rates are well above 10 Hz (see Appendix A) and we can easily assume that Nyquist's theorem is fulfilled. Therefore we assume no significant information loss with respect to sampling rates.

- **Quantization Distortions**: the conversion from the continuous, analog signal to a digital representation by signal sampling implies the assignment of continuous ranges of analog signal values to discrete values (see previous chapter, Section 4.2.1). Because this assignment can only be performed by approximation, it always introduces quantization noise. The degree of distortion introduced by quantization is depending on the statistical characteristics of the original signal and the parameters of the sub range mapping of the quantization process. In principle, quantization noise is determined by the cardinality of the set of discrete values defined for representing the continuous value sub ranges in the continuous original signal. In the context of handwriting digitizer devices, this characteristic is also called resolution, where for a given spatial size, a higher resolution implies higher cardinality, thus reduction of quantization errors and a lower resolution will consequently increase the tendency for quantization errors. For the further evaluation of handwriting modalities, we will accommodate aspects of different quantization capabilities by categorizing digitizer devices based on their sampling resolution later in this chapter in Section 5.5.3.

- **Non-Ascertainability of Physical Measures:** as can be seen from the example in Figure 5-5, the digitizer device may not be able to reproduce all dimensions of the signals of the analog writing process. In this example, only $x(t)$ and $y(t)$ signals are recorded by the device, information about wrist rotation or pen pressure are omitted. As a consequence, only part of the dimensionality of the handwriting generation process as shown earlier, can be reproduced by the sampling interface. In practice, the dimensionality of signals provided by digitizer tablets may vary significantly. This factor will be considered as well as the quantization aspects in our tablet classification introduced later in this chapter (Section 5.5.3)

So far in this chapter, we have based our discussion on theoretical work for generation of handwritten script, where in most cases, the objective of the writing process is the generation of continuous text. Or goal however, is to discuss aspects of handwriting for authentication purposes. In order to justify our signal-based model and before presenting an state-of-the-art overview of user authentication algorithms published prior to this work in Section 5.2.3, we explain why we assume that the same models presented for generation of continuous text can be used for generation of authentication scripts. We do so by briefly comparing aspects of user intentions when writing continuous text (as implied by the theoretical work presented in this chapter so far) compared to writing for authentication purposes, e.g. signatures in Section 5.2.2. Further, we give on overview on signal types, which can be obtained from state-of-the-art digitizer hardware technology for handwriting sampling, such as used in the context of this book.

5.2.1   Human Domain: Semantic Selection and Intention

We have shown that the initialization of a writing process takes place by the intention of a human to write a specific semantic. In case of production of continuous text, this semantic is a sequence of words, which are related to each other by the forming of sentences by the human brain. In the model of Schomaker et al. [ScTT1989], these semantics are fed sequentially on a word-level to the handwriting generation system. In other words the semantics are controlled by the intention to write continuous text.

For authentication purposes, we assume that the writing process can be modeled in the same way. However, the intention in this case is slightly different. For example, when signing a document, it can be assumed that the user's intention is to generate a special writing specimen with a specific purpose related to an identity. This applies to both authentic persons as well as to forgers. Authentic persons can have two different intentions: either they want to confirm their identity by a precise reproduction of their typical signature, or they could attempt to deny their identity by disguising their writing style. For the authentication purpose, subjects may choose to use more than one specific writing sequence. The practice to use two and more different types of signatures is very common, for example, by using both initials and signatures in contract documents. Therefore, the writer has the arbitrary choice of which specific handwriting specimen he or she is planning to produce. In [Viel2000], we have motivated that this arbitrary choice of writing semantics[5] can be extended to the selection of semantic classes for handwriting-based user authentication as well and we expand on this aspect as one of the contributions by introducing a semantic class model in Section 5.5.2.

According to our interpretation, both processes of generating handwritten continuous text and authentication semantics are initiated by the intention of subjects to create script with a specific content and a determined characteristic. The physiological writing processes in either cases are identical. Consequently, we find it safe to assume that the signal-based model, as developed in this chapter so far, can be used for modeling both categories of handwriting.

5.2.2 Interface Domain: Signal Sampling

Sampling devices for recording of handwriting signals vary widely in view of the physical modalities, which are measured. Looking into sampling technology for handwriting, which are based on other than contact-free approaches[6], two main categories of sampling devices can be identified

---

[5] In the context of our work, we use the term semantic in a sense that a particular semantic implies a specific syntax (spelling) as well as writing style (biometrics). We are aware that a wide range of differing definitions of the term semantics exist, depending on the various disciplines in the context of computer sciences, for example, in Multimedia Semantics, see [FaSt2002]. An extensive discussion on terminology is not required for the understanding of the term in our user authentication concept and would be beyond the scope of this book.

[6] An example for a contact-free signature sampling and verification approach is the system of Munich and Perona [MuPe1998], based on real-time pen-tip tracking by video. Although it has been conceptionally shown that vision based sampling technology is adequate for tracking the horizontal and vertical pen tip, the spatial accuracy of such approaches is well below contact-based digitizer tablets. Furthermore, a precise reconstruction of pressure or

today: tablet-based and pen-based digitizers. Devices of the first category record at least one signal from the writing surface, whereas the second category of digitizers can be used on arbitrary surfaces, as the signals are exclusively sampled in the pen. In practice, a great number of digitizers combine both techniques by recording some types of signals on a digitizer surface and others by sensors in the pen.

We have identified the following typical physical measurements signals, which can be provided by industrial digitizer tablets today and which are made available to software programming interfaces by the device drivers as sampled signals of category $a(t)$ (see also our definition of sampled signals in Chapter 4, Section 4.2.1 and tablet device characteristics of our test set in Appendix A):

- Horizontal pen position signal $x(t)$,
- Vertical pen position signal $y(t)$,
- Pen tip pressure signal $p(t)$,
- Pen azimuth signal $\Theta(t)$,
- Pen altitude signal $\Phi(t)$.

Additional physical measurements have been presented for special, force-sensitive pens, which are not included in the set of hardware devices used in the context of this book. However, for the sake of completeness, we want to mention the device used by Martens and Claesen [MaCl1996], allowing the reconstruction of acceleration signals:

- Horizontal pen acceleration signal $a_x(t)$ (via horizontal pen force),
- Vertical pen acceleration signal $a_y(t)$ (via vertical pen force).

As such force-sensitive pens were not used in the context of our work, we focus our model for the representation of handwriting processes on the five signals $x(t)$, $y(t)$, $p(t)$, $\Theta(t)$ and $\Phi(t)$.

From technical specifications of the variety of commercially available pen-based sampling devices, it can be observed that devices show a high variation in the resolution of the physical measurements and also in the dimensionality of the recorded signals. A classification of the selection of industrial sampling devices, which has been included in the context of our work will be given in a later part of this chapter, Section 5.5.3.

---

wrist angle signals has not been achieved today. Therefore, we limit our further views to contact-based digitizer technology.

Due to the historical development and the different stages of expansion of our evaluation system, not all physically supported signals have been recorded for each of the tablets in the database. Details about the actually collected signals will be provided in a later section discussing the evaluation procedure.

5.2.3   Algorithms for Writer Authentication

Biometric authentication based on handwriting dynamics has been a research area since many decades with a wide variety of approaches that have been published. In an early state-of-the-art report, Plamondon and Lorette summarize the most relevant work in the domain until the late 1980's [PlLo1989]. They identify a total of 180 references to scientific work, roughly half of which is allocated in static (offline) and half in dynamic (online) signature verification. This initial overview categorizes into two concepts for the comparison techniques: parameter-based (statistical approach) and function-based techniques. A supplementary article on the state-of-the-art in signature verification until 1993 was published by Leclerc and Plamondon a few years later, now including an overview on signature verification approaches based on Neural Networks [LePl1994]. Detailed references of work until the mid 1990's can be found in both articles, as well as in the technical report of Gupta and McCabe [GuCa1997]. We therefore limit our views to more **recent activities** related to our work in **online verification of handwriting**, which we have observed since then.

For the sake of clarity, we have structured the related work into five categories. The first four concepts comprise approaches which are based on new technical concepts (Dynamic Time Warping (DTW), Hidden-Markov-Models (HMM), Neural Networks and Multi-Level Approaches), which were presented to contribute to this research domain. The last category provides an overview on activities on biometric user authentication based on handwriting semantics other than signatures.

Dynamic Time Warping (DTW)
Wirtz takes up the **dynamic programming** concept for time warping, known from speech recognition, utilizing it for a **stroke-based alignment** of the two signal representations during the functional comparison. Tests based on 644 original signatures from six signers and 669 forgery signatures from 11 forgers have been conducted with and without the time warping concept for an adopted verification algorithm [SaKo1982]. Test results indicate accuracy improvements between factor 2 and 43 [Wirt1995].

Martens and Claesen [MaCl1996] present a system, which is based on a special sampling device, a force-sensitive special pen, providing five dimensions of writing signals. By applying an alternative **DTW algorithm to form and motion signals**, they report an improvement of EER from 6.7% to 3.3% for their database of 360 signatures from 18 subjects. In [MaCl1997], the authors have extended their discussion towards the **trade-off problem** between **computational effort** for time warping and the **expected achievements** with respect to accuracy.

Hidden-Markov-Models (HMM)

Kashi et al. present a signature verification system based on 23 statistical features of global characteristics of the writing process, improved by an additional model of **local features as HMM chains**, known from speech recognition [KHNT1997]. By combining the two approaches, they observe a decrease in EER from 4.5% to 2.5% for their test set of 542 genuine and 325 forgery signatures of 59 persons.

Ly Van et al. present a method in [VaGD2004], that is based on the fusion of two complementary scores descended from a Hidden Markov Model (HMM) for on-line signature verification. The decision is based on the **arithmetic mean of two HMM similarity scores**, obtained on one single input signature, which is compared to a threshold value. The approach was evaluated based on two different databases, one containing 1266 genuine signatures from 87 individuals, the other one containing 1530 signatures from 51 individuals. They report EER of 2.84% for the first and 3.54% for the second database database, after fusion of both scores.

Gaussian Mixture Models (GMM)

Richiardi and Drygajlo evaluate the use of **GMM for online signature verification** in [RiDr2003] **in comparison to a HMM-based approach**. They observed an almost identical accuracy in their tests based on a database collected from 50 users, with a number of 25 original signatures, plus 25 forgeries of 5 other subjects each. The EER observed in their experiments was around 5%.

Neural Networks

Since the report of Leclerc and Plamondon [LePl1994], little activities can be observed in the area of Neural Networks for signature verification problems. Besides multi-level approaches, which use neural networks as one classifier in combination with other methods, Wu et al. [WuJL1997], introduce a single-algorithmic system, using **Linear Prediction Coding (LPC)** for a **Multilayer Perceptron (MLP) neural network**. With different settings of frame sizes and a test set of 810 original signatures and 638 forgery signatures from 27 individuals, they report an optimum EER of 4%.

Multi Level / Multialgorithmic Approaches

Xiao and Dai present a signature verification system, which is based on **three levels** of features: a **global statistical** analysis, a **string representation** derived from stroke information **and a stroke template matcher** [XiDa1995]. They report a significant improvement by synthesizing the three measures, leading to an FMR of 1.7% at a FNMR of 0.9%, based on a test set generated by 30 persons, consisting of 100 original signatures in Chinese language and 200 forgeries.

Hangai et al. introduce **two new signal types** to online signature verification: **pen altitude and pen azimuth signals** [HaYH2000]. They report a maximum EER improvement from 14.2% to 1.8% for 480 original and 480 forged signatures of 24 subjects.

Kim et al. suggest to utilize **personalized feature sets** of statistical parameters and report an improvement in EER from 5.5% to 4.28% for a data set originated from nine persons with 120 originals and 120 forgeries each [KiPK1995].

The **combination of spatial and temporal features** is explored by Jain et al., using a string matching algorithm for the temporal alignment of local features [JaGC2002]. In their results, based on test of signatures of 102 individuals, comprising of 1232 original signatures and 60 forgeries, they report an observation of FNMR of 2.8% at a FMR level of 1.6%.

Fuentes et al. suggest the **combination of a HMM-based** approach with a **neural network** in [FuGD2002]. The fusion of the complementary experts is based on a support vector machine and the authors report a significant improvement by this fusion, as compared the results of each single expert.

Ly-Van et al. [LBR+2004] **combine signature verification** (based on HMM's) with **text dependent (based on DTW) and text independent (based on Gaussian Mixture Model) speech verification,** at a time. They report that fusion increases the performance by a factor 2 relatively to the best individual system. Their test data set contains 5 genuine bimodal values and 12 impostor bimodal values for each of 68 individuals.

An method for **on card biometric authentication** by means of handwriting signatures is presented in [HeFr2004]. The reference data are stored on the smart card. By on card matching they do not have to leave the safe environment of the smart card. The matching algorithm used is a **variant of dynamic time warping.** The test database contains 50 genuine signatures and 69 forgeries of 5 persons. The authors determine an EER of 8% and a computing time about 25 seconds on a Java card and about 8.5 seconds on a native code card.

Non-Signature Semantics

From the point of view of feature selection, Schmidt pursues a Multi-Level approach of combining statistical, structural and time frequency analysis [Schm1999]. In difference to other related work, the approach has been tested in a database containing also **writing samples of the same textual content** (German word *"Grünschnabel"*) in addition to the handwriting category of signatures. Results have been published, for example, on the discriminatory power of Signatures versus this additional category. Schmidt reports error rates at several operating points, e.g. FNMR rates of 5.4% at a FMR level of 0.6% for a test set of 2383 originals and 1638 forgeries for a total of 116 persons.

Kato et al. utilize the system concept of [HaYH2000] and extent it by pen inclination difference features on stroke levels. They investigate the possibility to apply user-specific, more or less complex **drawings as authentication information**. Based on first tests, they report FRR for different writing symbols such as circle and figures (e.g. squares), with minima in the range of 8%, without explicit mention of number of test subjects and samples.

In retrospective to these recent publications, a number of areas arise, which have not been investigated to a sufficient degree today.

Firstly, a large **heterogeneity in the test sets** can be observed: literally all approaches have been tested for disjoint test data. Although the absolute result figures in terms of EER suggest comparability at first sight, for a more objective comparison, a **unified modeling of the handwriting signals** is mandatory, allowing the reproduction of tests for different algorithms and under different parameterizations.

Secondly, the application of handwriting **semantics other than signatures** appears interesting, as it allows for individual selection of writing content by each user. We have shown that rudimentary approaches to this have been published; a systematic differentiation of such semantics and their evaluation on a significantly large data set is still missing.

The third and fourth categories of open problems denote the definition of dedicated attack strength and hardware characteristics of the sampling devices. The evaluation results reported in the literature very often do not mention under which conditions forgeries are generated and it can be assumed that **forger success rates significantly depend on the quality of the counterfeits**. Also, we were unable to identify scientific work addressing the problem of **cross-sensor verification**, which can be an important aspect in practical applications. In order to find conclusions on these two aspects, a systematic modeling of attack strength and hardware categories is required.

Many practical applications for user authentication based on handwriting are imaginable in the area of IT security, but among the literature studied, we were unable to find work addressing important questions for cryptographic solutions, two of which are how to apply this authentication scheme for key management or how to ensure security for reference templates.

5.3　Design Requirements for Evaluation Systems

The detailed analysis of handwriting modalities for user authentication requires a tool, which allows efficient realization of tests under various parameterizations and moreover ensures the reproducibility of results derived from these tests. In order to meet these requirements, a number of design aspects have been elaborated, formalized and implemented into our evaluation system, called PlataSign. In this section of the book, we will discuss the most relevant of these technical system design requirements. A description of how these requirements are fulfilled by our evaluation system will be given in the following Section 5.4, further implementation details of the system can be found in [ZoVi2003] and in Appendix B.

In the following subsections, the design requirements of Reproducibility, Compatibility, Modularity and Test Parameterization by System Parameters will be discussed.

5.3.1　Reproducibility

The evaluation system has to ensure that signals received from the sampling device can be identically reproduced and made available for subsequent tests from the evaluation database. Furthermore, the consistency between the signal annotation and the digital signal representation needs to be ensured, i.e. the link between data representing the physical signal and any associated metadata. Formulated from the point of view of a test controller, first each single signal taken from the evaluation database needs to be identifiable, classifiable and obtainable for other components of the evaluation system. Secondly, no two requested signals having the same identity must have a difference other than zero. Further, to provide a full reproducibility, no lossy compression may be applied during the progression from the original recording by the data recorder to the test controller. Therefore, we require for an evaluation system that no signal pre-processing or feature extraction is applied by any component in the system other than the authentication algorithm.

For repetitions of processes in both modes of an authentication system, Enrollment and Verification (see Chapter 2, Section 2.41), we postulate this requirement of reproducibility for signals of both categories. The evaluation system needs to be capable to reproduce the handwriting-based signals of enrollments, as well as in authentication mode in different evaluation environments.

5.3.2   Compatibility

Looking at the various types of different digitizer devices with very different physical characteristics, which are available today, one important aspect is to design the device interface of the data recorder in such way, that it is compatible to a wide number of different sensor devices and also to be open to inclusion of future generations of hardware devices.

5.3.3   Modularity

For the design of the evaluation system, the demand of independency between the evaluation procedure and the authentication algorithm is of essential nature. If the evaluation methodology would be enabled to adopt processes to the results of the authentication algorithm, or vice versa, results of evaluations have to be seen under the special situation of local optimization, leading to non-representative conclusions in comparison to alternative approaches.

Consequently, the authentication algorithm should not have any information about the empirical knowledge, which is aggregated at the evaluation system level during the course of a test run in order to disallow any adoption of the biometric algorithms, specifically to a given test set.

5.3.4   Modeling of System Parameters

Both the specifications of test profiles and the test database need to be structured in a way that allows definitions of meaningful test sets. This implies that along with the requirement for reproducibility of signals, a systematic annotation of the test signals is required with respect to the nature of sampled signals. More precisely, this includes situational information about the context of the handwriting process with respect to intention (enrollment, verification, attack), type of semantic used for the intention (*Signature*, others) and the type of the physical sensor used for this process (digitizer hardware characteristics).

Besides the basic parameter for practically all biometric authentication systems, the decision threshold, most algorithms allow for additional parameterizations. In order to perform tests under different configurations, for these cases, different predefined sets have to be stored the test profiles as well.

5.4   PlataSign Evaluation System: Architecture

In this section, we present our concept of implementation of an evaluation environment fulfilling the requirements postulated in the previous Section 5.3. In an abstract representation, the main components of our evaluation system can be seen from Figure 5-6.

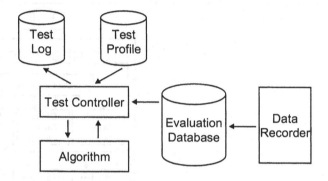

Figure 5-6. Scheme of the basic components of our evaluation system

An evaluation database stores all signals together with annotation data, which is generated by the data recorder. Here, it is important, that the data recorder component abstracts from the actual physical sampling device, from which the evaluation datasets originate. However, details of the physical characteristics of the sensors are also part of the annotation data, thus they are known to the system. The test controller is the central component in this architecture, which implements the function of reading specific test profiles from a profile database, performing tests according to the test profile on specific algorithms and logging the test results into a test log file.

Figure 5-7 presents a more detailed architectural layout of our PlataSign evaluation system, which can be subdivided in three main functional components: The Recorder module, Evaluator and a Database component. The modules are linked by the central Database component, where the recorder has read and write access to data and the evaluator may only access the database in read mode. In this section, only a brief structural overview of the system can be given, abstracting from many functional details in the software implementation. More details of the PlataSign evaluation system implementation are given in Appendix B.

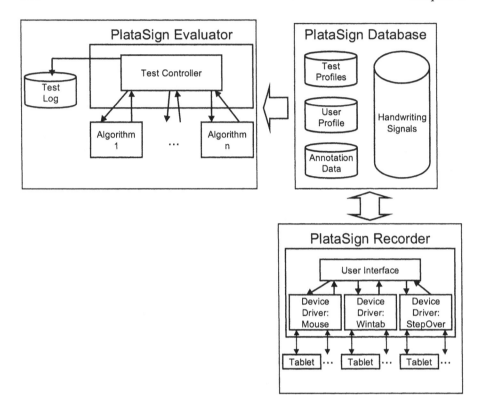

Figure 5-7. Schematic system architecture of the PlataSign evaluation system

PlataSign Database

In the database, additionally to all the data sampled from recorder components, information about the evaluator component is stored centrally. The implementation of this component supports network database server configurations, thus the database service can be run on a dedicated server system within a network setup as well as on a local system. For the implementation, a freely available database server software has been chosen (MySQL, [mySQ2005]) and a data model has been defined and implemented [Rama2000], in accordance to the requirements for evaluation of handwriting-based biometric authentication data.

In the following Section 5.5, we will explain how we have laid out the structure of PlataSign Database in order to fulfill the requirements of modeling the **System Parameters** (see Section 5.3.4).

PlataSign Recorder

This component implements all functions to digitally sample online handwriting signals using different digitizer tablets, visualize the signals in a user interface and to provide means to classify, attribute and store the signals in the PlataSign Database.

In order to fulfill the design requirement of **Compatibility**, as postulated in Section 5.3.2, we have implemented support of three different types of device driver interfaces, thus ensuring compatibility to a very wide range of digitizer tablets:

- **Mouse Driver Emulation Support**: this interface is the most generic way to record writing signals from a digitizer tablet, as almost all such devices provide drivers emulating the movement control of the mouse cursor of the graphical interface of an operating system by movement of the pen over the digitizer surface. However, recorded signals from this interface are generally only two dimensional (*x*/*y* position over time), limited to the actual computer display resolution of the recording system and the continuity of the digitized signal is distorted to the event handling of the inter process messaging of the operating system.

- **WinTab Driver**: this is a generalized digitizer tablet API specification for Microsoft Windows™ operating systems and is the interface, which is most commonly supported by tablet devices. Besides the possibility to sample the *x*/*y* position signals in the physical spatial resolution of the tablet device (typically a magnitude higher than in mouse emulation mode), the interface also defines higher dimensions of signals including pressure, and pen angle signals. Synchronization between the software system and the driver is established via defined messaging events of the operating system.

- **"Tablet-B" Driver** is a proprietary device driver provided by one of the tablet manufacturers. The driver can be accessed by a run-time library, which communicates directly with the hardware via a serial interface, providing *x*/*y* position signals as well as pressure signals in the physical resolution of the sensor. Synchronization between the system software and the driver is achieved by call-back functions.

Practically all digitizer tablets available on the market at time of publication of this work can be used for data recording thus a very high degree of compatibility has been reached with respect to this component of the system.

PlataSign Evaluator

The Evaluator component mainly implements the two requirements of Reproducibility (see Section 5.3.1) and Modularity (Section 5.3.3). **Reproducibility** is provided by a test controller functionality, which reads test profiles from the database, builds test programs from these profiles and executes them by controlling the authentication algorithms, feeding them with original signals from the database and logging the results to test logs.

To make allowance for the other design goal for our PlataSign evaluation system, **Modularity**, it is required that a replacement of the biometric authentication algorithm is possible without changing any other components of the system. Technically, this demand has been realized by separation of the test controlling task and the verification process in two software layers, where the controlling layer is integrated in the program context of the evaluation system and the biometric algorithm is encapsulated into runtime libraries (Dynamic Link Libraries, DLL). The interface between the two layers is defined by the functional specification of the DLL interface, details of which can be found in Appendix B.

5.5   Data Structuring of Evaluation Samples

In Sections 4.4.1 to 4.4.6 of Chapter 4, we have emphasized six main challenges which we are addressing in this book. These challenges require the definition of compatible system parameters and attributes, which are included in the data model of the PlataSign database. In this Section 5.5, we explain how we have realized the aspects of signal modeling (Section 5.5.1), alternative writing semantics (Section 5.5.2), sensor characteristics (Section 5.5.3) and different levels of attack strength (Section 5.5.4). Section 5.5.5 presents some statistical figures with respect to the quantitative structure of the collected data.

5.5.1   Signal Representation

Each writing process is sampled and quantized at discrete times by the PlataSign Recorder module, resulting in a *Sampled Signal* representation of type $a(t)$ for each signal provided by the digitizer tablet. These entire sampled signals, without any preprocessing or filtering, are stored as sets of sequential sampling points. Each of the sampling points in one signal set includes values for each of the five different, quantized physical measurements (as shown in Section 5.2.2), where the sequential order is maintained by a continuous index and the discrete time of recording of each particular sampling point is stored as a time stamp relative to the first pen-down event of each set. Table 5-1 specifies the field names in the structure of the corresponding database table for the values of sequence index (*indx*), timestamp (*tsint*) and the five physical measurements *x*, *y*, *press*, *alti* and *azim*.

Table 5-1. Data fields in database structure for a single sampling point

Field Name	Description
sampleid	Unique sample ID
indx	Continuous sequence index, starting with 0
x	Quantized horizontal position of actual sampling point
y	Quantized vertical position of actual sampling point
oldx	Quantized horizontal position of preceding sampling point
oldy	Quantized vertical position of preceding sampling point
tsint	Time stamp in milliseconds, starting with 0 for first sample of a signal
press	Quantized press value
alti	Quantized altitude signal
azim	Quantized azimuth signal

Each of such sets of sampled signals, also denoted as samples, represent signals of one writing process either for one enrollment or one verification event. One or more of these sampled signals are joined together to sets of *Enrollment Samples (ES)* or *Verification Samples (VS)*, see Chapter 2, Section 2.4.1.

5.5.2   Semantic Class Modeling

Until recently, techniques for verifying a writer based on handwriting dynamics have been almost exclusively studied for one specific handwriting semantic, the *Signature*. Although the use of this particular semantic appears to be reasonable mainly due to its social and legal acceptance and a typically high degree in practicing (see also the case study discussed in Chapter 3, Section 3.5.2), there exist no reasons not to extent the application of algorithms to additional semantic classes. In [Viel2000], we have introduced the concept of semantic class modeling, allowing the users of a biometric authentication to select a writing semantic other than the signature for the writing process. A straightforward approach is the usage of passphrases, passwords or personal identification numbers (PIN), but also hand-drawn sketches or symbols were considered for this purpose in the initial publication. Usage of sketches is particularly interesting for online handwriting verification, because the online methods can be designed in such way that they are sensitive with respect to the writing sequence, which is not the possible for offline methods.

To exemplify this, we refer to the following Figure 5-8, adopted from [Viel2000]. It illustrates two possible ways for a writer to generate a simple sketch "house". While in this example, the visual result of both writing processes are identical, some discriminatory power can be derived by the different writing sequences. The concept of using dedicated knowledge about the generation process of hand-drawn sketches has been further studied in later publications, for examples some sketch authentication algorithms have been presented in [KaHH2002] and [BrZu2003] and a graphical user authentication system for a pen-based PDA has been published in [KaSt2001]. However, results of these approaches are presented for one isolated semantic class, unrelated to other categories of semantics.

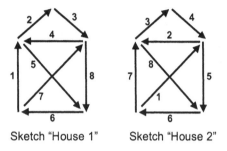

Sketch "House 1"   Sketch "House 2"

Figure 5-8. Example for two different writing sequences for semantic class *Symbol*

Another motivation for our selection of semantics is the possibility of evaluation to which degree writers can be differentiated, which use identical writing semantics. In order to meet these aspects, the semantic class structuring of the PlataSign evaluation system has been designed to explore the behavior of authentication algorithms exposed to different semantic classes. For our evaluation system, we have chosen a selection of five representative semantic classes as follows:

1. **Signature**: the users were asked to use their typical signature for the recording of the authentication writing process.
2. Individual **Passphrase**: an individual combination of letters, numbers and words was asked from each user, where the selection of the actual textual content was entirely left at the user's choice.
3. Individual **Symbol**: in correspondence to passphrases, users were asked to use simple sketches of symbols for authentication purposes. No predefined symbols were suggested, the drawing content was entirely freely chosen by the subjects.
4. Identical handwriting samples of the word *"Sauerstoffgefäß"* were asked from the users. This German word was selected mainly because of two reasons: firstly, it has a reasonable size in terms of visual size and writing duration for sampling on all digitizer tablets. Secondly, it has a rather high complexity for the cursive writing process, as it includes a

number of significant up and down sweeps, especially in the letters "f"
and "ß" plus dynamics due to the double point on the Umlaut "ä", as can
be seen from Figure 5-9:

Figure 5-9. Images of writing samples for semantic class *"Sauerstoffgefäß"* from two
different writers

5. Identical PIN *"8710"* for all users. Here, handwriting samples of one
    identical number code *"8710"* were asked from all users. In comparison to
    the semantic *"Sauerstoffgefäß"*, we have chosen a short writing sequence
    based on a limited alphabet of numbers.

In summary, we have defined three categories of semantics with user-
specific writing content, including the *Signature*, plus two semantics based
on identical text for all writers.

5.5.3   Classification of Digitizer Tablets

As stated earlier in this section, the physical parameters of digitizer
hardware are quite different, which is also reflected by the fact that our
PlataSign evaluation system currently supports three different device drivers.
As one of our main goals is the analysis of handwriting-based authentication
algorithms on different hardware platforms, a classification of tablets by
their physical characteristics and the sampling method is required.
    The classification which we apply in the context of this book is based on
the two aspects of spatial resolution and signal dimensionality.

Spatial Resolution: depending on the physical characteristics of the
digitizer hardware and the implementation of device drivers, we introduce a
classification depending on the resolution of the horizontal and vertical pen
position signal. Here, two categories of interfaces can be found: firstly, many
of the digitizer tablets can be operated in a mouse-emulation mode, where
the digitizer pen is used as a pointing device, replacing the computer mouse.
In this mode, the spatial resolution is limited by the screen resolution of the
display and may be independent from the physical resolution of the digitizer.
For some digitizers, especially those used in Personal Digital Assistants
(PDA), this resolution is a consequence of the physical design of the device,

where the digitizer resolution is identical to the screen resolution and the digitizer surfaces are affixed directly above the screen surface of the device. Other digitizers implement mouse emulation by mapping of the x/y signals in the original resolution of the tablet onto the actual screen resolution of the display. This mapping is performed by the device driver. Effectively, the spatial resolution of mouse driver emulations and PDAs are in the range of app. 100 lines per inch (lpi), whereas today device drivers providing the full resolution of external digitizer tablets can achieve spatial resolutions in the range of 500 to 3000 lpi.

Signal Dimensionality: all digitizer tablets provide at least three dimensions of signals: a horizontal and a vertical position signal ($x(t)$ and $y(t)$) plus a signal for the pen pressure $p(t)$ (see Section 5.2.2). The later may, in the trivial case, be a binary pen-up/pen-down signal $p_{PenDown}(t)$, denoting if the pen at a specific point in time has applied a sufficient amount of pressure to the tablet surface to consider that the user intents to generate a writing sequence. More sophisticated devices provide the pressure signal in a higher quantization resolution, e.g. up to 1024 quantization steps for some of the devices considered in this work. Above these three dimensions of signals, some devices provide additional measurements of the angle of the pen above the writing plane (altitude angle) and in the heading direction of the writing plane (azimuth angle).

Considering the different characteristics, we have determined a classification scheme, which allows grouping of the tablets in to categories of similar physical characteristics. The classification attributes are:

- **Spatial Signal Resolution**: 3 categories: Low (Screen Resolution, less than 100 lpi), Medium Resolution (at least 100 lpi, but less than 2000 lpi) and High Resolution (higher than 2000 lpi),
- **Pressure Signal Quantization**: 2 categories: Binary Signal (PenUp/PenDown) or Quantization Steps higher than 2,
- **Pen Angle Signals**: two categories: Azimuth and Altitude signals are available (yes/no).

The following Table 5-2 classifies all tablets used for the evaluation task in the context of this book. We have chosen to consider only test data of tablets having a significant number of samples in the database, representing a specific category. Therefore for all further evaluations, we refer to subsets of tablets as shown in the following tables, whereas a description of technical details of the entire set of digitizer tablets used in the context of the evaluation system will be given in Appendix A.

Table 5-2. Tablet classification by physical characteristics, X denotes an applicable property

Tablet ID	Spatial Signal Resolution			Pressure Signal Resolution		Pen Angle Signal	
	Screen *	Medium *	High *	Binary	Q>2	Azimuth	Altitude
2	X			X			
5	X			X			
6	X			X			
21	X			X			
22	X			X			
24	X			X			
26	X			X			
7		X			X		
9		X			X		
16		X			X		
17		X			X		
19		X			X		
28		X		X			
27		X		X			
1			X		X	X	X
4			X		X	X	X
8			X		X	X	X
12			X		X	X	X
11			X		X		
23			X		X		
25			X		X		
29			X	X		X	X

* Resolutions: Screen < 100 lpi, 100 lpi ≤ Medium < 2000 lpi, High: ≥ 2000 lpi

This classification scheme will be used for all tests discussed later in this book. It allows the evaluation of methods across different individual tablet types and between groups of tablets having similar properties, in order to draw conclusions regarding hardware-dependency of authentication algorithms. Photographs of some of the devices listed in Table 5-2 are shown in Figure 5-10.

Figure 5-10. Selection of digitizer tablets used in the evaluation environment

5.5.4   Scaling of Attack Strength

Besides optimistic situations, where biometric authentication systems are exposed to authentication data of cooperative, authentic users, with a positive intention to achieve a minimum-error recognition result, scenarios of malicious users attempting to gain positive authentication results have to be considered. The capability to distinguish authentic users from non authentic users is one of the key measures for the quality of biometric authentication systems and is typically constituted in form of False-Match and False-Non-Match trade-off function (see Chapter 2, Section 2.4.4). However, when looking at False-Match characteristics of biometric authentication systems, it is important to consider the circumstances under which authentication information has been generated. In an earlier publication [ZoVi2003], we have already addressed this question and have introduced a general taxonomy for the origin of biometric authentication information. This taxonomy, as shown in Figure 5-11, differentiates intentions of users, based on the position of the user into authentic and non-authentic persons. For authentic users, it further distinguishes between three intentions: **Declarers of Intention** (DoI, denoting cooperative users seeking authentication), **Deniers** (authentic users that do not want to be authenticated) and **Compelled Users** (who are forced mentally or physically by a third party to gain authentication).

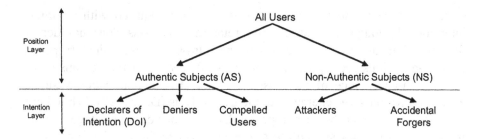

Figure 5-11. Taxonomy for the generation of biometric authentication information
([ZoVi2003])

For the part of non-authentic subjects, we have determined two sub-categories: Attackers, who purposely and with malicious aims want to gain authentication as a different person and secondly accidental forgers, which are either exposed to the authentication system under declaration of an incorrect identity (for verification-based authentication) or which are wrongly identified by the authentication system.

For the design of the evaluation system, our goal was to provide a model to cover the cases of cooperative users (DoI), simulation of accidental forgeries as well as intended attacks. As handwriting-based biometrics belongs to the class of active modalities, requiring user cooperation, the simulation of users denying their biometric characteristics is trivial, as the process of the handwriting can easily be disguised by a writer. Thus we do not consider these scenarios in our evaluation. Furthermore, the simulation of compelled users appears to be a non straightforward task, as it is quite difficult to simulate psychological and/or physical stress and it can be assumed to be hard to estimate behavior of subjects, exposed to a situation where she or he is forced to present the biometric behavior.

For the remaining category of attacks to the biometric authentication system which are simulated in our evaluation system, we classify into the following types of forgeries [ViSt2001], [ZoVi2003]:

- **Random Forgeries,**
- **Blind Forgeries,**
- **Low-Force Forgeries,**
- **Brute-Force Forgeries**.

Accidental forgeries are simulated within the evaluation environment by comparison of enrollment information of single users to verification data of all other user, in a specific semantic class and tablet category. Consequently, this class of biometric authentication information is based on a random selection strategy and the samples have not been acquired with a forgery intention. Although in a strict interpretation, this class does not denote forgeries, but rather data to determine the Intra-Class discriminatory power for non-malicious users [Waym1999], it is often used for the demonstration of the non-acceptance of false users by biometric authentication systems, especially for passive schemes like the iris analysis [Daug1993]. While here, it is often used under the term imposter data, we consider this category as the lowest level of attack strength to a biometric system in our classification of four forgery strengths, as introduced in [ZoVi2003]. Thus we refer to this category of forgeries as **Random Forgeries**.

The second category of forgeries, the **Blind Forgeries**, are writing samples that have been generated by non-authentic subjects having a descriptive or textual knowledge about the original writing sequence they counterfeit. For example, for the generation of such forgeries, users have been provided with the precise spelling of *Signatures* and *Passphrases* of the counterfeited person. In case of the semantic class *Symbol*, a verbal description of the original symbol was made available to the forgers. Obviously, this proceeding is only meaningful in case of covert semantics. For writing samples, which are based on the same textual content ("*8710*","*Sauerstoffgefäß*"), the generation of Blind Forgeries does not make sense, as the textual knowledge is known to all subjects in any case; the result of Blind Forgeries is identical to Random Forgeries.

We have denoted the third category of forgeries as **Low-Force Forgeries**, due to the fact that they are generated with rather low effort, but with a higher knowledge about the visual image of the result of the handwriting process of the authentic person. In order to produce such forgeries, test subjects have been provided with analog or digital copies of the original writing in its offline representation. For active displays combining digitizer tablet and computer screen, this has been achieved by a projection of the original writing image in the background of the writing plane, allowing the forger to draw a digital blueprint of the original image. For the tablets not equipped with a display, this has been achieved by paper copies placed between the surface of the tablet and the pen, also allowing to generate a blueprint. It is noticeable however, that for the generation of these forgeries, no knowledge about the dynamic context of the generation of the original was available to the forgers. For the *Symbol* sample shown in Figure 5-8, for example, a potential forger would have had no information about the stroke sequences. Figure 5-12 shows a user generating Low-Force forgeries based on a digital blueprint on an active screen (left image) and the process on an inactive, external device (right image).

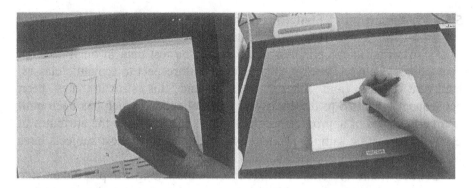

Figure 5-12. Forger generating Low-Force forgeries on two different digitizer tablets

This additional knowledge about the handwriting dynamics is introduced in the class, which contains forgeries which have been generated with the highest level of effort: **Brute-Force Forgeries**. Here, the forger has all the knowledge available for Low-Force Forgeries and in addition, he or she gets the opportunity to observe the writing process of the original several times and thus to train the handwriting dynamics. For active displays, this observation can be done without presence of the original writer by automated replay functionality, presented in [ZoVi2003]. This function simulates the writing by animating a cursor in real time on the screen, reproducing the writing trace. Examples for such real-time writing projection are given in Figure 5-13, outlining the replay process on active displays of the PlatsSign user interfaces for Microsoft Windows™ (left) and Palm OS™(right).

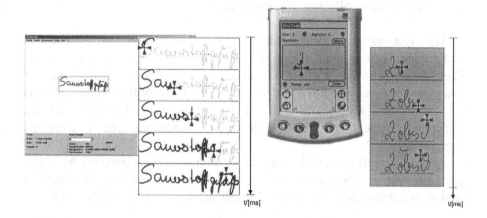

Figure 5-13. Real-time writing process projection in our PlataSign evaluation system for Windows™ and Palm OS™

5.5.5   Quantitative Structure of the Data Collection

As specified in the previous subsections, the test data in our PlataSign evaluation system has been well structured with respect to semantic classes, hardware devices and forgery strength and this structure has been consequently applied to the entire test data collection, which has been built up over a period of approximately four years. In addition to the attributes of each of the writing samples, some basic attributes of the test subjects have been registered:

- **Gender** (male or female) - among all handwriting samples taken into account for evaluation 4932 where generated by female subjects (32.9%) and 10073 by male persons (67.1%). Out of the total numbers of persons contributing to the test database (106), 23 were female, 77 were male and 6 persons contributed anonymously, without providing information about gender, handedness or age.

- **Right/Left Hander** - all of the 23 female test subjects were right handers, whereas 7 of the 77 male persons were left handed, accounting for a total of 1809 handwriting samples (8264 for right-handed males and 4932 for right-handed females).

- **Age** - in order to classify the age of the subjects, the birth year was registered for each of the testers. Figure 5-14 illustrates the relative distribution of number of users and handwriting samples by the year of birth. Two accumulations of users can be observed: the main peak in terms of number of users around the birth year 1979 and a secondary peak with respect to number of samples around the years 1983. This distribution reflects quite well the age structure of the environments, in which the data collection was performed.

The test subjects origin almost exclusively from an educational background, where most users were in the field of computer science, electrical engineering or closely related. Also, some graduate students and senior researchers have been included in the test. Recording of the data has been performed at three different university locations[7], two of which are associated to the department of computer science and one to electrical engineering.

All test samples were obtained in an environment supervised by a test operator, who in most cases was a senior student working on a project related to handwriting evaluation. All test persons were mentally motivated

---

[7] Due to accommodate privacy requirements of test subjects, we have obliged ourselves not to disclose precise locations and times of recording of test samples.

to provide stable and typical writing samples for enrollment and verification, with the goal to get correctly authenticated as often as possible. With respect to forgeries, they have been asked to attempt to generate them as good as possible for each of the attack levels. However, besides this physical motivation, no other means like reward money or other neuter benefits were utilized neither for accomplishments of authentic verifications nor for successful false acceptances by the authentication system.

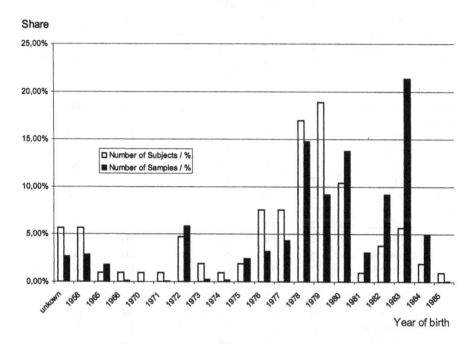

Figure 5-14. Test subjects and handwriting sample distribution over age

One major criterion for our data collection was a reproduction of a heterogeneous structure with respect to semantics, hardware devices, attack scenarios and users. From the design aspects for the evaluation environment opened in this section, it becomes obvious that a great degree of freedom exists in the structure of the test set. Thus it is necessary to mention that due to this high complexity, neither exhaustive nor homogeneous distribution of test samples can be achieved and this has not been aspired.

The following Table 5-3 summarizes the quantitative structure of the data in our evaluation database, separately for each of the tablet categories, semantic classes and recorded action types.

Table 5-3. Quantitative database structure of our evaluation database

Tablet Category	Semantic Class	No. of Persons	Enrollments	Verification	Blind Forgeries	Low-Force Forgeries	Brute-Force Forgeries
			Number of Samples				
All	Signature	97	3474	1796	339	1228	1110
	"Sauerstoffgefäß"	99	1901	1506	168	656	623
	"8710"	99	1701	1517	228	950	605
	Passphrase	101	1638	1429	901	760	570
	Symbol	102	1689	1374	982	774	607
Tablet-A	Signature	22	984	600	223	233	271
	"Sauerstoffgefäß"	16	262	200	0	101	40
	"8710"	16	154	141	0	140	40
	Passphrase	20	169	80	539	70	40
	Symbol	17	193	80	558	100	40
HIRES-PQ-Angle	Signature	36	633	294	0	260	300
	"Sauerstoffgefäß"	37	291	230	0	0	80
	"8710"	39	234	250	0	41	80
	Passphrase	42	209	235	162	40	70
	Symbol	37	232	244	204	40	70
MIDRES-PQ	Signature	32	2264	851	339	360	307
	"Sauerstoffgefäß"	32	957	564	88	241	40
	"8710"	32	840	552	148	284	40
	Passphrase	36	725	461	659	230	40
	Symbol	34	783	470	698	244	40
Tablet-B	Signature	12	545	211	80	80	0
	"Sauerstoffgefäß"	16	570	324	84	140	0
	"8710"	16	618	371	140	140	0
	Passphrase	15	489	351	120	156	0
	Symbol	15	522	360	140	140	0

5.6   Evaluation Methodology

The PlataSign evaluation system introduces a number of new aspects for the evaluation of biometric authentication based on handwriting, as it introduces a systematic classification of handwriting semantics and digitizer tablets, as introduced in the previous sections. Some first results of initial evaluations of the usability of semantic classes on the accuracy of biometric user verification systems have been published in [Viel2000], [ZoVi2003], [KaHH2002] and [BrZu2003] and have indicated, that semantic classes beyond the handwritten *Signature* appear to be appropriate for user verification in general. However, a systematic comparison between verification results originated by signatures versus other semantic classes could not be found in the literature.

Our methodology for evaluation of online-handwriting-based authentication system, as well as the general application of semantic classes beyond the *Signature*, requires a conceptional proof that these semantic classes are applicable for handwriting-based authentication in general. In order to produce comparable results for the evaluation of specific algorithms later in this book, we define our test methodology in the following subsections as follows: we firstly describe our experimental setup (Section 5.6.1) and secondly, a basic verification algorithm is introduced in Section 5.6.2. This algorithm is intended as a first evaluation metrics, which has been designed and implemented for initial validation of our test methodology. In Section 5.6.3, we define scenarios of 25 test cases, depending on different tablet categories and semantic classes. These scenarios are the basis for the experimental results presented later in this chapter, as well as for all other evaluations in later chapters (Chapters 6 and 7). Note that for those later tests, the experimental setup and the test scenarios remain exactly as defined here for all further experiments in this book, whereas the metrics, i.e. the algorithms, will be redefined for the evaluations in later chapters (see Section 5.6.2).

5.6.1 Experimental Setup

Each experiment is based on structured test sets, built by selection of Enrollment and Verification samples having specific characteristics with respect to different hardware categories and semantic classes (see experimental scenarios in Section 5.6.3). These sets describe **test entities, also called test environments (*te*)**, which have been defined as groups of data subsets to be evaluated.

All these test environments can be further categorized into five action types: *Enrollment, Verification, Blind Forgery, Low-Force Forgery* and *Brute-Force Forgery* (see Section 5.5.4). Based on these action types and for each test environment, one experiment consists of the following verification tests:

- *Verification* **Test (Test A, Intra-Class Test)**: Verify all authentic writing samples (Verification Samples) within the test environment against all enrollments build from the Enrollment Samples of identical persons. Result of this test is the False-Non-Match-Rate (FNMR) characteristics, representing the **Intra-Class misclassification.**
- *Random Forgery* **Test (Test B, Inter-Class Test)**: Verify all writing samples of subjects **other than the originator** of each enrollment set. Again, this test considers only those samples defined in the actual test environment. This test yields the **False-Match-Rate for *Random***

Forgeries, FMR_{Random} , which is an error term for the **Inter-Class discriminatory power** of a verification algorithm.

- *Blind Forgery* **Test (Test C1)**: Verifies all forgeries having a Blind-Force attack level (see Section 5.5.4) against all enrollments samples of the attacked person. This test results in the **FMR for** *Blind Forgeries*, FMR_{Blind} and can be considered as a measure for the misclassification error characteristic, if the verification algorithm is exposed to **intended attacks** with rather **low attack strength**.
- *Low-Force Forgery* **Test (Test C2)**: Analogous to C1 but for *Low-Force* **Attacks, results in** $FMR_{Low\text{-}Force}$. Like FMR_{Blind} , it is a measure for misclassification in case of **intended attacks**, in this case for **medium-level attack strength**.
- *Brute-Force Forgery* **Test (Test C3)**: Analogous to C1 but for *Brute-Force* **Attacks, results in** $FMR_{Brute\text{-}Force}$. Like FMR_{Blind} and $FMR_{Low\text{-}Force}$, this test yields a characteristic for **intended attacks**, in this case for **high-level attack strength**.

5.6.2   Experimental Metric: MQED Verification Algorithm

Due to the generic Layout of our PlataSign evaluator module, as outlined in Section 5.4, the test controller can make use of several verification kernels, which are made available to the evaluation system in form of dynamic link libraries (DLLs). A further configuration option for the test environments is the selection of the verification algorithm. All test environments are persistently stored as test profiles in the PlataSign database and can be configured by a graphical interface, which is described in detail in Appendix B.

As stated in the introduction to this section, we use one fundamental metric in this chapter: the Minimum Quadratic Envelope Distance (MQED) verification algorithm. Our goal is to conceptionally prove our semantic class model and the effects of different sensor devices. Before applying the same test methodology with different metrics regarding authentication algorithms for cryptographic key generation (Chapter 6) and user verification (Chapter 7), the usability of semantic classes is quantitatively validated by applying this rather simpe authentication algorithm to the different semantic classes under various test scenarios, using the experimental setup as described in the previous Section 5.6.1.

In the context of this conceptional evaluation, the authentication algorithm was motivated by two main design goals:

- **Self-Parameterization**: besides a set of reference samples, one verification sample and an adaptive threshold parameter, no external parameters should be required for a verification process. Thus, no means of a local optimization with respect to the hardware or semantic characteristics exist and the test results can be considered as unbiased.
- **Hardware Independency**: the technique should allow verification between any two tablets.

In order to meet these requirements, the Minimum Quadratic Envelope Distance (MQED) Verification Algorithm, as a basic function-based approach has been designed by us according to the following formalization:

Feature Set

The feature set chosen is simply a two-dimensional, cumulated distance vector of the horizontal and vertical writing signals $x(t)$ and $y(t)$, based on the distance measure metric defined in the following paragraph.

Distance Measure

As for all function-based features, the general result of the Minimum Quadratic Envelope Distance (MQED) feature shall be to find a **scalar distance measure** to describe the **dissimilarity** between **one verification signal** and a **set of reference signals**, where all signals are represented as sampled signals, as per definition in Section 4.2.1 of the previous chapter.

Our approach, to define a measure **between one single verification signal** *vs* and a **set of (multiple) reference** *signals es* $\in$ **ES** can be reduced to a **minimization problem** of a set of distance measures between one verification signal and each of the reference signals. While we expand on the minimization aspects later in this section, we now discuss a method to determine such a distance measure between two sampled signals. For the sake of clarity, we start by giving some definitions of relevant terms and functions:

- *Normalize(a(t), $N_{Samples}$, a_{Min} , a_{Max})* normalizes, i.e. re-samples the sampled signal given in argument $a(t)$ to countable set of $\{1, ..., N_{Samples}\}$ sampling values in a non-negative integer range of $[a_{Min}, a_{Max}]$, at temporal equally distanced times $\{t_1, ..., t_{NSamples}\}$. Results of the function *Normalize* are called **normalized signals** and are denoted by tilted letters, e.g.:

$$\tilde{a} = Normalize(a(t), N_{Samples}, a_{Min}, a_{Max}), with \ \tilde{a} = (\tilde{a}_1, ..., \tilde{a}_{N_{Samples}}) \ (5\text{-}1)$$

- δ denotes a **generic distance function** and takes **two arguments**. Both arguments are **either scalars, sampled or normalized signals** and the function returns a scalar in both cases, denoting a distance between the two arguments.
- with δ_{Scalar} denoting the distance function between two scalar values and defined as the absolute difference of the two values, e.g.:

$$\delta_{Scalar}(x_1, x_2) = |x_1 - x_2|, \tag{5-2}$$

we can develop a normalized distance function δ for two sampled and signals $a_1(t)$ and $a_2(t)$ as follows:

$$\tilde{a}_1 = Normalize(a_1(t), N_{Samples}, a_{Min}, a_{Max})$$
$$\tilde{a}_2 = Normalize(a_2(t), N_{Samples}, a_{Min}, a_{Max})$$
$$\delta(a_1(t), a_2(t)) = \frac{1}{N_{Samples}(a_{Max} - a_{Min})} \sum_{i=1}^{N_{Samples}} \delta_{Scalar}(\tilde{a}_{1,i}, \tilde{a}_{2,i}) \tag{5-3}$$

That is, the cumulated distance of each of the $i \in \{1, ..., N_{Samples}\}$ **reference points** t_i at discrete scalar distances of normalized signal values, $\delta_{Scalar}(\tilde{a}_{1,i}, \tilde{a}_{2,i})$, is normalized to the number of samples, $N_{Samples}$ and Interval length of the scale $[a_{Min}, a_{Max}]$. This general distance function for two sampled signals $a_1(t)$ and $a_2(t)$ has the property $0 \leq \delta(a_1(t), a_2(t)) \leq 1$.

An example for the determination of δ is illustrated in the following Figure 5-15. We present two exemplary normalized signals $\tilde{y}_1$ and $\tilde{y}_2$, based on the sampled signals of the vertical writing positions during the writing process, $y_1(t)$ and $y_2(t)$ and a normalization to the value range $[y_{Min}, y_{Max}]$. While in the chart, the graphs for $\tilde{y}_1$ and $\tilde{y}_2$ are displayed as continuous waveforms, the discrete normalized values are represented by the ordinate values of the intersections of the graphs at the doted vertical lines denoting each of the $i \in \{1, ..., N_{Samples}\}$ indices, also denoted as reference points, of the normalized signals. The example further illustrates the first and the last distances δ_{Scalar} for indices $i=1$ and $i=N_{Samples}$.

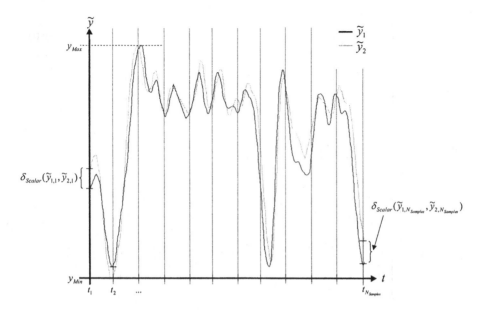

Figure 5-15. Example for signal distance measures δ_{Scalar} in normalized domain

While for the example from Figure 5-15, a rather small distance measure for δ can be expected as the reference points appear visually well aligned on the abscissa, practical handwriting signals typically do not show such a good temporal alignment, requiring some method for time shift compensation.

Time Offset Compensation

A major problem in the determination of similarity using functional distance measures in handwriting signals is their natural variability in the time domain and the rather large amplitudes, especially in the vertical writing signal. This effect can result in a steep increase of the distance measure, even of two identical signals with a small time shift.

Figure 5-16 illustrates this problem of time shift by determining the distance of two non-normalized vertical writing signals $y_{1(t)}$ and $y_{2(t)}$, where signal $y_{1(t)}$ is identical to $y_{2(t)}$, except for a time offset $\Delta_{TimeOffset}$: $y_2(t) == y_1(t+\Delta_{TimeOffset})$. Note that in this example, we refer to the representation as sampled signals, which are graphically interpolated in Figure 5-16.

Despite the identical curve progression, and due to the high gradient of both signals y_1 and y_2 at a given reference time t_i , we observe a rather large difference $y_1(t_i)-y_2(t_i)$, which obviously will result in a great distance measure for δ. However, in this example, δ can be minimized by introducing a linear time shift of $\Delta_{TimeOffset}$, shifting either y_1 to the right or y_2 to the left.

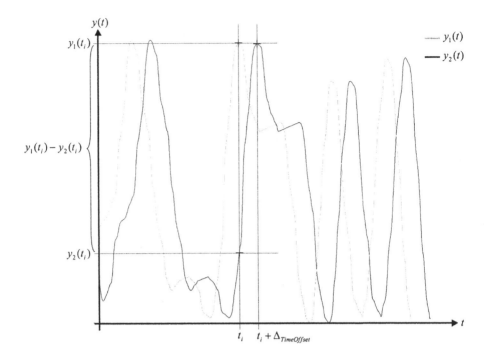

Figure 5-16. Time shift problem example in non-normalized domain

The example presented in Figure 5-16 is a simplified view to the time shift problem, as it simply assumes a linear time offset in the handwriting signals. In practice, it has been observed that the temporal variability in handwriting dynamics is more complex, with typically a global offset component (caused by delays in the beginning of the writing process) and an additional non-linear time-shift.

In order to overcome the non-linear deviations, the **Dynamic Time Warping (DTW)** technique has been suggested as a method to optimize the signal alignment. An early theoretical approach to this has already been introduced as early as 1977 by Yasuhara and Oka [YaOk1977], and the problem of time alignment in on-line handwriting has been followed by many other researchers. Wirtz suggests to use **Dynamic Programming technique (DP)** with a third index based on strokes [Wirt1995], Martens and Claesen adopt a DTW algorithm known from spoken word recognition [MaCl1996] and further develop their approach to a method waiving the requirement of equal sample rates between the two signals [MaCl1997]. Schmidt introduces a DTW technique based on a combination of DP and an extremism-based time alignment [Schm1999]. All researchers report significant improvements in recognition accuracy for function-based verification algorithms.

Due to our intention to apply function-based MQED algorithm as a first evaluation technique for our three goals of **analyzing effects** of **semantic classes, hardware characteristics** and different **attack levels,** we simplify our evaluation methodology by utilizing the perception of previous research, that non-linear time warping can optimize the recognition accuracy on a global scope. Thus we limit the time alignment to an offset alignment prior to calculation of the distance measures and refrain from implementing sophisticated non-linearity compensation.

For our MQED algorithm, temporal offset compensation is achieved by the following heuristic approach, which minimizes the distance measure δ between two sampled signals $y_1(t)$ and $y_2(t)$:

an iterative process applies a 10% neighborhood of the total writing time T_{Total} $(y_1(t))$ of a vertical position signal $y_1(t)$, represented by N_{Offset} absolute time offsets Δ_j, $j \in \{1, ..., N_{Offset}\}$ to the vertical position signal $y_1(t)$ in positive as well as in negative direction. The offset $\Delta_{j,Min}$, minimizing the following equation will be considered as the time alignment constant:

$$\Delta_{j,Min} = \arg\min(\delta(y_1(t + \Delta_j), y_2)), \forall j \in \left\{1, ..., N_{Offset}\right\} \qquad (5\text{-}4)$$

i.e. the value of $\Delta_{j,Min}$ is defined by the positive or negative time offset value minimizing the neighborhood, with $\delta(y_1, y_2)$ being the distance function between two sampled signals $y_1(t)$ and $y_2(t)$.

Classifier

As clarified earlier, our goal in this part of the book is to give a conceptional proof for our evaluation methodology presented in Sections 5.4 to 5.6 by testing a fundamental, threshold-based verification algorithm. The classification of the verification result is implemented based on separate distance measurements of δ_x and δ_y for the horizontal $(x(t))$ and vertical $(y(t))$ writing position signals of an actual verification sample *vs* and each of the x- and y-reference sample signals $es_{x,j}$ and $es_{y,j}$ of the $j=[1, ... ,e]$ samples within a set of x- and y-signals in enrollment samples $ES_x=\{es_{x,1}, ... es_{x,e}\}$ and $ES_y=\{es_{y,1}, ... es_{y,e}\}$ respectively. With $\Delta_{j,Min}$ denoting the time offset as determined above, the effective distance measure $\delta_{Effective}$ is then given by the minor of the two values δ_x and δ_y, implementing a nearest neighbor classifier:

$$\delta_x = Min(\delta(x(t_i + \Delta_{i,Min}), es_{x,j}) \ \forall \ es_{x,j} \in \{es_{x,1}, ..., es_{x,e}\} = ES_x)$$

$$\delta_y = Min(\delta(y(t_i + \Delta_{i,Min}), es_{y,j}) \ \forall \ es_{y,j} \in \{es_{y,1}, ..., es_{y,e}\} = ES_y) \qquad (5-5)$$

$$\delta_{Effective} = Min(\delta_x, \delta_y)$$

The condition for a positive authentication decision is met, if $\delta_{Effective} \leq T$, with T being the decision threshold parameter. Otherwise, if $\delta_{Effective} > T$, the authentication results yields negative.

In a figurative explanation of the MQED algorithm, the distance measure can be described as the lower of the two cumulated distances between $x(t)$ from the **envelope formed by the enrollment signals** ES_x and $y(t)$ and the envelope formed by the enrollment signals ES_y, respectively. This graphical perspective motivates the algorithm's name.

5.6.3   Test Scenarios: Tablets and Semantic Classes

For the semantic classes, all five categories: *Signature, Passphrase, Symbol, "Sauerstoffgefäß"* and *"8710"*, as defined in Section 5.5.2, are applied separately as a grouping criterion. For the tablet categorization, five classes have been defined, as can be seen from the following Table 5-4, where the structure of the each of the tablet classes can be described as follows:

- **Tablet-A**: this class consists of writing samples collected on one single type of tablet device (Medium Resolution according to classification Section 5.5.3, active display with visual feedback of the writing process on the computer screen). For this single tablet category, the greatest number of writing samples (5265) on one single device have been recorded. Also, above all samples, the practice of collecting test samples has shown that this device is most effective in for the generation of forgeries.
- **Tablet-B**: this category also reflects one specific type of digitizer tablet, which is based on a pressure-sensitive surface sensor, independently of the pen used. Here, both samples generated by an inking ball-pint pen and writing generated by a non-inking pointing device have been considered.
- **MIDRES-PQ**: this group contains the joint set of all tablet types, which provide the pen position signal at a medium resolution (according to the classification in Section 5.5.3), plus a pressure signal at a quantization level higher than two.

- **HIRES-PQ-Angle**: groups all samples, which have been collected on devices with a high spatial resolution as defined in Section 5.5.3, plus signals of the pen angles (azimuth $\Theta(t)$ and altitude $\Phi(t)$) during the writing process.
- **All**: this group is defined by the union set of all above groups.

Table 5-4. Tablet groups for the test environment definition, X denoting a specific tablet type belonging to a particular group

Tablet ID	Test-Environment ID				
	Tablet-A	Tablet-B	MIDRES-PQ	HIRES-PQ-Angle	All
2					X
5					X
6					X
21					X
22					X
24					X
26					X
28					X
7	X		X		X
9			X		X
16		X	X		X
17		X	X		X
19		X	X		X
27		X			X
1				X	X
4				X	X
8				X	X
12				X	X
11					X
23					X
25					X
29					X

This tablet categorization leads to two categories of samples: those recorded only on their respective types of digitizer tablets (homogeneous sets, *Tablet-A* and *Tablet-B*), and those samples sampled from sets of mixed sensor types (heterogeneous sets).

Consequently, the entire set of test scenarios consist of five tablet categories by five semantic classes, thus 25 experimental scenarios for the setup as described in Section 5.6.1 exist. Table 5-5 summarizes the entire number of writing samples in the test database (enrollments, verifications, all attacks) for each of these 25 scenarios.

Table 5-5. Total number of writing samples in each test scenario

| | Tablet Category | | | | |
Semantic Class	Tablet-A	Tablet-B	MIDRES-PO	HIRES-PO-Angle	All
Signature	2333	928	4153	1523	8044
Passphrase	918	1131	2151	758	5399
Symbol	988	1177	2269	827	5528
"Sauerstoffgefäß"	619	1134	1922	638	4953
"8710"	491	1285	1896	644	5100

In the context of this book, we also refer to each of these scenarios as **one test environment** *te*, from the **set of all test environments,** *te* ∈*TE*.

5.7 Experimental Results: Suitability of Semantic Classes

For the evaluation, if and to which extent semantic classes beyond signature are appropriate for biometric authentication purposes, we have defined the following criteria:

Handwriting samples of a specific semantic class are **applicable for biometric user authentication,** if the Error-Rate-Diagram (functions False-Match Rate FMR and False-Non-Match-Rate FNMR of threshold *T,* see Chapter 2, Section 2.4.3) has the following basic properties:

- **Boundedness**:

$$0 \leq FNMR(T) \leq 1 \ \forall \ T \text{ and } 0 \leq FMR(T) \leq 1 \ \forall \ T \qquad (5\text{-}6)$$

- **Monotony**:

$$FNMR(T_1) \leq FNMR(T_2) \ \forall \ T_1 \geq T_2 \qquad \text{and} \qquad (5\text{-}7)$$

$$FMR(T_1) \geq FNMR(T_2) \ \forall \ T_1 \geq T_2 \qquad (5\text{-}8)$$

That is, both value ranges of FMR and FNMR have a limited value space of *[0,1]* and FMR is a monotonic increasing function of *T*, whereas FNMR is a monotonic decreasing function of *T*.

In order to quantify the suitability of each of the four non-signature semantic classes, we define an **Empiric Suitability Factor** (*ESF*) in relation to the Equal-Error-Rate (EER) graphically determined from the Error-Rate-Diagrams of the reference semantic class, the *Signature*. The factor is determined simply by the ratio between the EER of the actual semantic class $sc \in SC = \{Signature, Passphrase, Symbol, "Sauerstoffgefäß", "8710"\}$ and the EER of semantic class *Signature*:

$$ESF := \frac{EER_{sc}}{EER_{Signature}} \tag{5-9}$$

Thus, while *ESF=1* indicates an identical EER as the reference semantic class, values greater than 1 indicate a lower suitability, since the EER is higher than for the reference class whereas a value of less than 1 indicates a better suitability than the semantic *Signature*.

Figure 5-17 illustrates the method of graphical determination of EER from an error rate diagram (in this case tablet category *Tablet-A*, semantic class *"Sauerstoffgefäß"*). The ordinate value at the intersection points of the FNMR graph and each of the three FMR graphs yields the respective values of $EER_{Random}=0.22$, $EER_{Low\text{-}Force}=0.35$ and $EER_{Brute\text{-}Force}=0.32$ for this example.

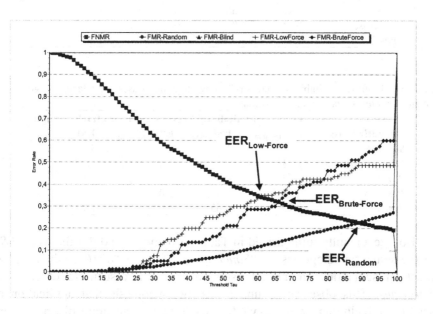

Figure 5-17. Graphical EER determination, tablet category *Tablet-A*, semantic class "Sauerstoffgefäß"

A comprehensive comparison between the error function graphs would obviously require a more detailed comparison method than the *ESF* presented here, by only comparing two specific operation points in the error rate characteristics. However, as the purpose of work presented in this section is purely the axiomatic analysis of semantic classes and the EER comparison is a widely accepted first order estimate for accuracy of biometric user authentication by verification, this proceeding appears to be a reasonable method to find a quantitative ranking of the five semantic classes.

We have performed verification tests at different threshold settings for all four semantic classes additional to *Signature* and all five tablet categoriesand the following tables (Tables 5-6 and 5-7) summarize the *ESF* results observed for the most relevant observations. These are based on two representative table category settings, *All* (as a proxy for maximum heterogeneity of tablets) and *Tablet-A* (as proxy for a single table type, minimum heterogeneity).

Table 5-6. Empirical Suitability Factors (*ESF*) by semantic classes and attack strength, tablet category *All*, n/a denotes not available

Semantic Class	Empirical Suitability Factor (ESF) per attack strength			
	ESF_{Random}	ESF_{Blind}	$ESF_{Low-Force}$	$ESF_{Brute-Force}$
Signature	1	1	1	1
"Sauerstoffgefäß"	1.78	n/a	1.05	1.05
"8710"	1.45	n/a	0.7	0.71
Passphrase	0.11	0	0	0
Symbol	1.11	0.93	0.75	0.95

Table 5-7. Empirical Suitability Factors (*ESF*) by semantic classes and attack strength, tablet category *Tablet-A*, n/a denotes not available

Semantic Class	Empirical Suitability Factor (ESF) per attack strength			
	ESF_{Random}	ESF_{Blind}	$ESF_{Low-Force}$	$ESF_{Brute-Force}$
Signature	1	1	1	1
"Sauerstoffgefäß"	1.83	n/a	1.03	0.84
"8710"	1.92	n/a	1.09	0.84
Passphrase	0.75	1.5	1.06	0.89
Symbol	0.75	0.65	0.64	n/a

Both test results summarized in Tables 5-6 and 5-7 exhibit the worst *ESF* in the semantic categories of *"Sauerstoffgefäß"* and *"8710"*, which utilize identical semantics among all users, in the attack scenario of *Random Forgeries*. This observation underlines the hypothesis that application of semantics including zero-knowledge, leads to less accurate discriminatory power by the algorithm. However, with a maximum *ESF* of 1.92, the utilization of these semantic classes appears still acceptable in cases, where a degradation in accuracy of a maximum factor of two is acceptable. When exposing the user authentication algorithm to indented forgeries, the accuracy degradation appears less severe. The worst ESF observed in this scenario yields to 1.09, indicating an overall reduction of the verification accuracy of less than 10% (see row *"8710"*, column $ESF_{Low-Force}$ in Table 5-7). In case of tablet category *All*, even an improved accuracy can be observed for semantic class *"8710"*, with *ESF* of 0.7 for *Low-Force* and *Brute-Force Forgeries (*see row *"8710"* in Table 5-6*)*.

While the usage of identical semantic content for all users appears to degrade the overall accuracy of the verification algorithm in almost all attack scenarios, we observe improvement by introduction of knowledge. The performance of semantic *Passphrase* shows a drastic improvement of verification results when applied to a heterogeneous set of tablets compared to the semantic class of *Signatures*, with all *ESF* equal to zero, except for the scenario of *Random Forgeries*, where we observe *ESF*=0.11 (see row *Passphrase* in Table 5-6). Although not as outstanding as in tablet category *All*, the tendency of improvement is confirmed for the *Tablet-A* category, as far as *Random* and *Brute-Force Forgeries* are concerned. In the later tablet category, we also observe an *ESF*=1.5 for *Blind Forgeries* (see row *Passphrase*, column ESF_{Blind} in Table 5-7*)*, which indicates that *Passphrases* can be easier successfully counterfeited in case of textual knowledge alone than *signatures*. This finding confirms the intuitive assumption, that in comparison to other semantic classes, user verification based on the handwritten *Signature* depends more on behavioral and structural information in addition to textual knowledge.

An interesting aspect is the ranking of semantic class *Symbol*. In all cases except Random Forgeries for tablet category *All*, this semantic class outperforms *Signatures (*see rows *Symbol* in Tables 5.6 and 5.7). In summary, we can state that all semantic classes are adequate for the biometric user authentication process. All our tests confirm the tendency of an expected degradation in system accuracy by a maximum of factor 2 for semantic classes of identical textual semantic (zero-knowledge) for all users of an authentication system and a potential improvement in system accuracy up to 35% by utilizing semantics involving individualized knowledge (*Passphrase* and *Symbol*).

5.8 Experimental Results: Hardware Dependency Effects

In this section, we want to evaluate, to which degree the accuracy of a biometric authentication algorithm for handwriting verification is dependent on the tablet category. To discuss this aspect, we analyze the graphs in Figures 5-18 to 5-21, representing the error rate characteristics of the same semantic, *Signature*, in tests of the MQED algorithm, for four different tablet categories: a) *Tablet-A*, b) *Tablet-B*, c) *All* and d) *Midres-PQ*.

The Equal Error Rates graphically obtained from the error rate diagrams in Figures 5-18 to 5-21 are shown in Table 5-8.

Table 5-8. Equal Error Rates for different tablet categories, semantic class Signature

Tablet Category	Equal Error Rate (EER)			
	EER_{Random}	EER_{Blind}	$EER_{Low\text{-}Force}$	$EER_{Brute\text{-}}$
Tablet_B	0.1	0.26	n/a	0.34
Tablet_A	0,12	0,2	0,34	0,38
All	0,18	0,3	0,4	0,42
Midres-PQ	0.15	0.25	0.4	0.42

From the graphically determined EER for all three tablet categories, as given in Table 5-8, we conclude the following: from the EER_{Random} of *Random Forgeries*, as a measure for the Inter-Class discriminatory power, we observe that the tablet category comprising digitizer devices of greatest inhomogeneity shows the lowest accuracy with an EER_{Random} of 18% (see row *All*, column EER_{Random} in Table 5-8).

The best tablet set in this category is *Tablet-B*, containing only one type of digitizer tablets with an EER_{Random} of 10% (see row *Tablet-B*, column EER_{Random} in Table 5-8). The other table category consisting only of one specific device type, *Tablet-A*, shows a similar EER_{Random} of 12% (see row *Tablet-A*, column EER_{Random} in Table 5-8), whereas the tablet set consisting of tablets of medium spatial resolution with respect to the classification in Section 5.5.3, *Midres-PQ*, with an EER_{Random} of 15% is closer to category *All* (see row *Midres-PQ*, column EER_{Random} in Table 5-8). Thus, the highest degradation between homogeneous and heterogeneous sets yields to 80% increase in EER (from 10% increase to 18% EER_{Random}) between tablet categories *Tablet-B* and *All,* and the lowest to 25% (from 12% to 15% EER_{Random}) from *Tablet-A* to *Midres-PQ*.

On the other end of the attack strength scale, we observe an increase in error rates between 9,5% ($EER_{Brute\text{-}Force}$ for *Tablet-B* vs. *All*) and 17% ($EER_{Brute\text{-}Force}$ for *Tablet-A* vs. *All*), when the MQED algorithm is exposed to skilled forgeries.

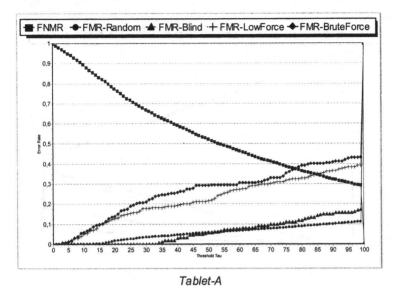

Figure 5-18. Error rate diagrams for tablet category *Tablet-A*

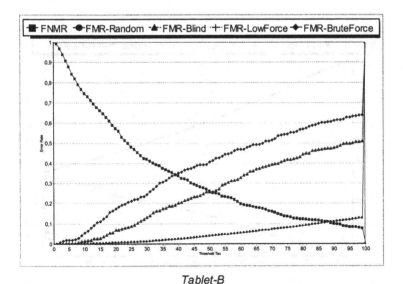

Figure 5-19. Error rate diagrams for tablet category *Tablet-B*

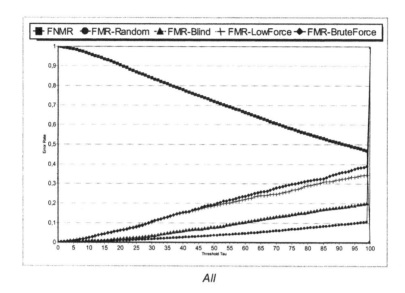

All

Figure 5-20. Error rate diagrams for categories *All*

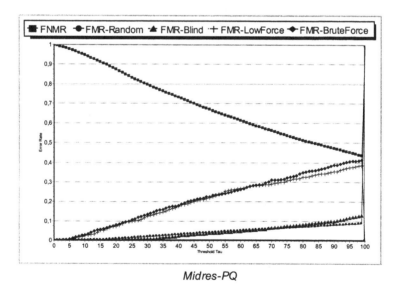

Midres-PQ

Figure 5-21. Error rate diagrams for categories *Midres-PQ*

Although at this point, we will limit our discussions on the effect of different tablet categories to one specific semantic class, the *Signature*, we can state that the tendency of an in increasing loss in accuracy with an increasing degree of heterogeneity of hardware characteristics has been confirmed by the tests of other semantic classes as well. With respect to the hardware dependency, which has been exemplarily analyzed in this section, we can summarize as follows:

- Increasing heterogeneity of physical characteristics of tablet set leads to decrease of accuracy.
- This degradation is **more distinctive for Random Forgeries** than for the classes of indented forgeries.

5.9 Summary

In this chapter, we have introduced an evaluation methodology, which is based on conclusions of theoretic models of cognitive motor theory with respect to adequate signal models for the handwriting generation process of humans. We have presented a theoretical, signal-based model for **generation of handwriting,** which is modeled by the four **signal dimensions** horizontal/vertical writing position, pen pressure and wrist angle. From the practical viewpoint of physical capabilities of handwriting digitizer **sampling devices,** as used in the context of our evaluations, we have identified a maximum of **five different independent handwriting signals,** which can be provided by such devices. These signals are horizontal/vertical pen positions, pressure and two types of angles, which can be utilized for the biometric authentication process. Two signal types (horizontal/vertical position) are identical in the theoretical model and practical sampling devices and we assume that a correlation exists between the theoretical wrist angle and the practical pen angle signals. Consequently, we have performed our analysis of authentication aspects based on these five signals.

From this signal model, we have derived **design criteria for an evaluation system,** mainly ensuring **lossless and reproducible signal data representation,** the possibility to model **digitizer tablet categories, semantic classes** and **attack strengths.** From these requirements, we have developed the **structural model of the database component** of our system implementation, PlataSign. Other components of our evaluation system presented in this chapter are the Recorder module, as input interface for the test subjects and the Evaluator component, implementing the test methodology for a test controller. Our experimental scenarios are based on the following categorization of the test data collection:

- **Semantic class modeling**: three overt plus two covert semantic classes are introduced.

- **Tablet category modeling**: from our collection of digitizer hardware, we define five representative categories.
- **Attack strength modeling**: four levels of attack strength are introduced, where three of these are based on intentional counterfeits produced with different effort and one describing the scenario of Inter-Class tests.

This evaluation concept is designed for further utilization by additional algorithms in Chapters 6 and 7of this book, but it is entirely intuitively motivated. Thus we need to empirically prove our evaluation concept. We do so by various experiments based on the metric of a **basic verification algorithm, Minimum Quadratic Envelope Distance (MQED)**. The results of these experiments can be recapitulated as follows:

- **Semantic classes involving individual knowledge** (e.g. *Passphrase* and *Symbol*) possess a degree of **suitability for the authentication process** based on handwriting biometrics, which can be ranked **at the same level as *Signatures***. A more detailed view of these semantics further unveils a slightly higher discriminatory power in case of exposure to indented forgeries for these knowledge-based semantics.
- Using the same semantic content (e.g. *"Sauerstoffgefäß"*, *"8710"*) and **thus zero-knowledge components** for all users of an biometric authentication system appears acceptable, if an **accuracy decrease by a factor of two** can be taken into account.
- **Increasing heterogeneity** of digitizer tablet with respect to their physical characteristics **leads to increasing error rates**. If cross-tablet verification is desired in authentication scenarios, an accuracy decrease of up to 80% needs to be accepted.
- Attack strength of forgeries does have an significant impact on the false acceptance probabilities. Chances of a **skilled forger increase to be wrongly authenticated** by the biometric verification **increase by factor two to three**, if Low-Force or Brute-Force attack strength is applied, as **compared to the commonly known Inter-Class False Match Rates** (FMR_{Random}).

These fundamental observations justify our evaluation methodology. We therefore will re-use this implementation of our evaluation methodology for further experiments in Chapters 6 and 7 of this book.

5.10   Notations and Abbreviations

Table 5-9 summarizes all notations and abbreviations introduced in this chapter in alphabetical order.

Table 5-9. Summary of notations and abbreviations introduced in Chapter 5

Designator	Name	Description	Introduced in
$a_x(t)$, $a_y(t)$	Pen acceleration signals	Horizontal ($a_x(t)$) and vertical ($a_y(t)$) pen acceleration of special pen from [MaCl1996]	Section 5.2.2
DTW	Dynamic Time Warping	Method for time alignment of two signals, known from speech recognition [SaKo1982]	Section 5.2.3
δ	Generic Distance Function	Denotes a generic distance function and takes two arguments. Both arguments are either scalars, sampled or normalized signals and the function returns a scalar in both cases, denoting a distance measure between the two arguments	Section 5.2.3
δ_{Scalar}	Scalar Distance function	Denotes the distance function between two scalar values and is defined in this chapter as the absolute difference of the two values, e.g.: $$\delta_{Scalar}(x_1, x_2) = |x_1 - x_2|$$	Section 5.2.3
$\Delta_{TimeOffset}$	Time Offset between two signals	Time Offset between two signals, for example: $y_2(t) := y_1(t + \Delta_{TimeOffset})$	Section 5.2.3
e	Cardinality of Enrollment sets ES_x and ES_y	Number of samples in an Enrollment Set ES_x and ES_y	Section 5.6.2
ESF	Empiric Suitability Factor	Determined by the ratio between the EER of the actual semantic class $sc \in SC = \{Signature, Passphrase, Symbol, "Sauerstoffgefäß", "8710"\}$ and the EER of semantic class *Signature*: $$ESF := \frac{EER_{sc}}{EER_{Signature}}$$	Section 5.8
ES_x, ES_y	Sets of pen position signals in enrollment set	Sets of x- and y-signals in enrollment samples $ES_x = \{es_{x,1}, \dots es_{x,e}\}$ and $ES_y = \{es_{y,1}, \dots es_{y,e}\}$ respectively.	Section 5.6.2
GMM	Gaussian Mixture Models	Probabilistic classification method, often used for speech recognition	Section 5.2.3

Table 5-9 (cont.)

Designator	Name	Description	Introduced in
HMM	Hidden-Markov-Models	Probabilistic method, often used for speech recognition [KHNT1997]	Section 5.2.3
$k_{g,x}$, $k_{n,x}$, $k_{g,y}$, $k_{n,y}$	Spring constants	Spring constants for horizontal and vertical agonist $(k_{g,x}$, $k_{g,y})$ and antagonist $(k_{n,x}$, $k_{n,y})$ springs in Hollerbach's system of equations for handwriting generation	Section 5.1
lpi	Lines per inch	Unit for spatial resolution of digitizer tablets	Section 5.5.3
m_x	Horizontal mass	Horizontal mass in Hollerbach's system of equations for handwriting generation	Section 5.1
m_y	Vertical mass	Vertical mass in Hollerbach's system of equations for handwriting generation	Section 5.1
Normalize()	Normalization function	Normalizes, i.e. re-samples the sampled signal given in argument $a(t)$ to countable set of $\{1, ..., N_{Samples}\}$ sampling values in a non-negative range of $[aMin, aMax]$, at temporal equally distanced times. Results of the function *Normalize* are called normalized signals are denoted by tilted letters, e.g.: $\tilde{a} := Normalize(a(t), N_{Samples}, a_{Min}, a_{Max})$, with $\tilde{a} = (\tilde{a}_1, ..., \tilde{a}_{N_{Samples}})$	Section 5.6.2
p(t)	Pen tip pressure signal	Sampled signal of the pressure applied to the pen tip as provided by digitizer tablets	Section 5.2.2
Θ(t)	Pen azimuth signal	Sampled signal of the pen azimuth in view from above, as provided by digitizer tablets	Section 5.2.2
Φ(t)	Pen altitude signal	Sampled signal of the pen altitude, i.e. the gradient angle of the pen relative to the tablet surface, as provided by digitizer tablets	Section 5.2.2

Table 5-9 (cont.)

Designator	Name	Description	Introduced in
$sc \in SC$	Semantic class	One semantic class out of the set of all semantic classes SC as defined in Section 5.5.2: $sc \in SC = \{Signature, Passphrase, Symbol, "Sauerstoffgefäß", "8710"\}$	Section 5.8
T	Decision Threshold	Decision threshold value of a verification algorithm (see Chapter 2, Section 2.4.4)	Section 5.8
te	Test Environment	One test environment te, from the set of all test environments, $te \in TE$. Describes the experimental scenarios	Section 5.6.3
t_i	Reference Point	Discrete time of a reference point i in a normalized signal $\tilde{a}(t)$: $\tilde{a}_i = \tilde{a}(t_i)$	Section 5.6.2
x	Horizontal writing position (Continuous)	Variable for the horizontal writing position in Hollerbach's system of equations for handwriting generation	Section 5.1
$\ddot{x}$	Horizontal writing acceleration (Continuous)	Variable for the horizontal writing acceleration in Hollerbach's system of equations for handwriting generation	Section 5.1
$x(t)$	Horizontal pen position signal	Sampled signal of the horizontal writing position as provided by digitizer tablets	Section 5.2.2
y	Vertical writing position (Continuous)	Variable for the vertical writing position in Hollerbach's system of equations for handwriting generation	Section 5.1
$\ddot{y}$	Vertical writing acceleration (Continuous)	Variable for the vertical writing acceleration in Hollerbach's system of equations for handwriting generation	Section 5.1
$y(t)$	Vertical pen position signal	Sampled signal of the vertical writing position as provided by digitizer tablets	Section 5.2.2

Chapter 6

BIOMETRIC HASH
How to derive Cryptographic Keys from Handwriting

6. BIOMETRIC HASH

As motivated in Chapter 4, the generation of cryptographic keys from biometric features for the encryption of stored references is a challenging problem in handwriting biometrics. This chapter will contribute to this challenge by introducing a new biometric authentication algorithm, the Biometric Hash function, capable of generating individually unique feature vectors, based on handwriting input, which are suitable to derive cryptographic keys as well as for a non-reversible representation of biometric reference data. Before we introduce our algorithm in detail, we want to summarize the idea and applications of hash functions in general.

A definition of **cryptographic hash functions** by the American National Standard for Telecommunications [ANT2000] emphasizes their significant properties:

"A mathematical function that maps values from a large (or even very large) domain into a smaller range, and is (a) one-way in that it is computationally infeasible to find any input which maps to any pre-specified output; and (b) collision-free in that it is computationally infeasible to find any two distinct inputs which map to the same output. "

Hash functions have been introduced in signal processing in the early 1950's, with the purpose of mapping large collections of messages into a smaller set of message digests known as hash values [Nich1999]. Their original purpose was error detection in communication in case of randomly occurring transmission errors. With the progress in the scientific discipline of cryptography, the specific category of cryptographic hash functions has been introduced.

One very common example for application of cryptographic hash functions can be found in the context of digital signatures for message authentication, based on asymmetric encryption schemes like RSA, introduced by Rivest, Shamir and Adleman in [RiSA1978], which is discussed in this section, to motivate our work on hashes based on biometric features.

The generation of a digital, cryptographic signature of a message and their verification require the following data: a cryptographic asymmetric key pair of a signatory subject *H*: *PrivateKey$_H$* and *PublicKey$_H$* and the message to be signed, *Msg*. Further, cryptographic functions for signature, *CryptoSign* and for Verification, *CryptoVerify* are used as well as a concatenation operator, denoted by "||". Given this notation and three helper variables *Hash, Sig* and *Hash**, the processes of generating a signed message *Msg$_{Signed}$* (i.e. the signature process) and the complementary process of verification can be formulated into the following functional description:

Cryptographic Signature:

Hash = CryptoHash(Msg)
Sig = CryptoSign(Hash, PrivateKey$_H$)
Msg$_{Signed}$ = Msg || Sig

Cryptographic Verification:

(Msg || Sig) = Msg$_{Signed}$
Hash = CryptoVerify(Sig, PublicKey$_H$)
Hash* = CryptoHash(Msg)
Verification Result = TRUE, if (Hash*==Hash) , FALSE otherwise

That is, during the **cryptographic signature process**, a cryptographic *Hash* is generated from the message to be signed, *Msg*, and this *Hash*, representing digest information of *Msg*, is then signed with the private key *PrivateKey$_H$* , resulting in the cryptographic signature *Sig*. *Sig* and *Msg* are finally concatenated to build the signed message: *Msg$_{Signed}$ = Msg || Sig*.

In the complementary process of **cryptographic verification**, the message *Msg* and signature *Sig* are retrieved by truncation of *Msg$_{Signed}$* and the originally signed *Hash* value is retrieved from the cryptographic verification function, using the public key of the signer, *PublicKey$_H$*: *Hash = CryptoVerify(Sig, PublicKey$_H$)*. Furthermore a second *Hash** value is determined from message *Msg* by applying the cryptographic hash function, $Hash^* = CryptoHash(Msg)$, and the verification of the cryptographic signature yields *TRUE*, if $Hash = Hash^*$, *FALSE* otherwise.

In this method, asymmetric cryptography is used to authenticate the origin of a signature, assuming that only the authentic sender is in possession of the private part of the asymmetric key pair, $PrivateKey_H$. Instead of signing the entire message, which may result in performance problems for asymmetric schemes and also cause a significant increase of size of the signed message, it has become good practice to sign a digest of the original message. Cryptographic hash functions have advantageous properties for generating such digests and a variety of different algorithms implementing cryptographic hash functions, such as Message Digest 2,4 and 5 (MD2, MD4, MD5) or Secure Hash Algorithm (SHA) exist. An overview of algorithms for cryptographic hash functions can be found, for example, in [Schn1996].

Message Authentication Codes (MAC) possess identical properties as cryptographic hash function with the only difference that they are dependent on an additional key parameter. Consequently, Schneier [Schn1996] defines MAC as *"key-dependent hash functions"*.

Challenges

Motivated by the function of cryptographic hashes and related work on fingerprint ([Nich1999], [UPPJ2004]) and voice ([MRLW2001]), the goal of the Biometric Hash function presented in this chapter is to find a function for mapping biometric features into a value space of defined dimensionality, adopting three of the key properties of cryptographic hashes:

- **mapping** from a (very) **large value domain** to a **smaller value space**,
- **infeasibility** to **find input** that **maps pre-specified output**,
- **infeasibility** to find any **two distinct biometric signal inputs** originating from any two **different users**, which **map to the same output**.

The third property, the infeasibility of finding any two distinct inputs which map to the same output, thus the requirement for a collision-free mapping, cannot be guaranteed[8]. However, it may be ensured to a specific degree for Biometric Hashes as well as for cryptographic hashes, as the distribution of information in the source value space (the biometric features)

---

[8] Note in this context, the term of computational infeasibility describes the property of a complex mathematical problem, which cannot be solved by state-of-the-art computational devices within reasonable time.

are a-priori unknown and can only be estimated based on empiric evaluations. Furthermore, the design of the Biometric Hash needs to take into account the intra-personal fuzziness of biometric signals from identical users, with the consequence, that virtually no pair of biometric signals from the same user are identical. While cryptographic hash functions often are chosen in a bit-sensitive manner, in such way that a small change in the source value result in a significantly large alteration of the hash value, for the purpose of the Biometric Hash function, this property is reformulated to the requirement for an Intra-Class stability and Inter-Class sensitivity (see Section 2.4.2).

Formally, using the general algebra notation for authentication systems as adopted from [Bish2003] and introduced in Chapter 4, Section 4.1, Biometric Hash functions can be defined as follows:

let B be the **set of all Biometric Hash vectors** $b \in B$, where each b is a vector of dimensionality k: $b=(b_1, \dots ,b_k)$.

Then the **set of Biometric Hash functions** $m \in M$ **map** two arguments from the set of **authentication information** A **and complementary information** C **to** the **set of Biometric Hash vectors** $b \in B$, as per the following equation:

$$m \in M, m : A \times C \to B \tag{6-1}$$

That is, the goal of the Biometric Hash function is not to yield a binary authentication result *{TRUE, FALSE}*, like defined earlier for the set of authentication functions L in Chapter 4. Rather than that, a set of Biometric Hash functions M is searched for, that map arguments A and C to a set of robustly generated, identical Biometric Hash vectors, with individual values for each user H of the biometric system. Formally, with A_{H1} and A_{H2} denoting Authentication Information and C_{H1} and C_{H2} the Complementary Information of any non-identical subjects H_1 and H_2 respectively, we postulate:

$$m : A_{H1} \times C_{H1} \to b_{H1}$$
$$m : A_{H2} \times C_{H2} \to b_{H2} \tag{6-2}$$
$$b_{H1} \neq b_{H2}$$

That is, **any Biometric Hash generated** from A and C of the **same person** yields **one specific, individual Biometric Hash vector** value b. Any **Biometric Hash vectors from two different subjects** H_1 and H_2 shall yield **non-identical Biometric Hash** vectors b_{H1} and b_{H2} respectively.

It needs to be annotated that today, neither for cryptographic nor for Biometric Hashes algorithms have been found, that fulfill strictly all of the above requirements. For example, it is easy to prove that due to the mapping from a large value space onto a significantly smaller space, a collision-free mapping cannot be achieved for any possible input value of a hashing function. As in cryptography, it has become good practice to accept some degree of collision likelihood for given real-world input value spaces, the possibility of collisions can also not be excluded for Biometric Hashes.

Additional Characteristics of the Biometric Hash

Cryptographic hashes provide means to verify integrity of digital messages and MAC can additionally verify the authenticity by a key component, representable by knowledge and/or possession. An innovative characteristic of the Biometric Hash is the extension of these properties for biometric user authentication. In preview to Section 6.3 we can state, that depending on the operational mode, the Biometric Hash can be configured in such way, that it either includes an individual knowledge component or not, by use of alternative semantic classes.

Approach/Concept

The basic idea of the Biometric Hash for online handwriting is to extract a set, or vector, of statistical feature values from actual handwriting samples and to find a parameterized transform function for mapping of these values to a stable hash value space. Since the statistical features are extracted from the global representation (see Section 3.2 of Chapter 3) of the writing sample, the dimensionalities of both feature and hash vectors reamin static and equal to the number of different statistical parameters.

Originally, the new concept of Biometric Hash was introduced in [ViSM2002], along with a first proof of concept based on a limited number of statistical features (24 features) and a small test population (10 subjects). Motivated by this work, an extension of the feature space for the hash calculation has been presented in [ViSt2004], along with an integration of the Biometric Hash algorithm in a new concept for feature analysis. Here, the feature set size has been extended to a 50-dimensional feature vector and a significantly extended test set has been used to evaluate the contribution of each of the individual components.

We pursue the requirement to reveal additional features from the biometric signals and to evaluate the impact of an extension of parameter dimensionality for the Biometric Hash algorithm in this book. Basis for the discussion in this chapter will be the actual status of our system implementation at time of publication, which is based on 69 features, having extended the feature set described in [ViSt2004] by additional parameters derived from aspects of handwriting forensics, see [ViSS2004]. As all other biometric techniques, the Biometric Hash function is based on fuzzy features of natural measurements, which are subject to noticeable Intra-Class statistical variability. For parameterization of the Biometric Hash, as we have no deterministic means for the definition of the system parameters, we investigate two different estimation approaches involving different categories of empirical system knowledge along with a trivial, unparameterized (zero-knowledge) setting.

Our hypothesis, that a Biometric Hash functionality can be achieved by this approach will be evaluated in tests, where we revert to the test methodology based on tablet classification and forgery strength modeling, as introduced in the previous Chapter 5, see Section 5.6. We will present and discuss terms of system accuracy as well as collision probabilities at distinctive operation points and will identify optimization possibilities.

This Chapter 6 is organized as follows. Based on the motivation given here, the following Section 6.1 defines the main design goals for the Biometric Hash algorithm, followed by a section describing the algorithm implementing the Biometric Hash function set M in detail (Section 6.2). Due to the fact that we are looking at an authentication method with an entirely different result category than other biometric systems, we have to define a specific evaluation metric, which is given in Section 6.3. The following two sections address the problem of system parameterization, by suggesting heuristic approaches for parameter estimation in three scenarios (Section 6.4) and a technique for the treatment of features subject to statistical outliers (Section 6.5). Significant test results will be discussed in Section 6.6 and the chapter will be recapitulated by a summary in Section 6.7. An overview of the notations and abbreviations introduced is provided at the end of this chapter in Section 6.8.

6.1   Objectives for a Biometric Hash based on Handwriting

From the discussions in Chapter 4, Section 4.4, significant open problems in the area of biometric authentication have been revealed, some of which can be solved with the approach presented in this chapter. The **general objectives of the Biometric Hash** target **four problem categories**, which have been exposed: **security, storage capacity and complexity issues of reference** storage (see Section 4.4.6 of Chapter 4), as well as the **key generation problem** (Section 4.4.5 of Chapter 4). Before introducing the algorithm of the Biometric Hash in detail, we summarize these design objectives of the Biometric Hash for online handwriting and motivate them from the general authentication problem.

Anonymity, Irreproducibility: Non-Invertible Reference

It has been shown in Chapter 2 that one of the important security goals may be the preservation of privacy, and one major condition necessary for this is the ensuring of anonymity by protection of the biometric templates. In this particular case of handwriting biometrics, especially when semantic of *Signatures* is used for authentication, the identity of the writer can easily be derived from the biometric authentication information in many cases. The visual result of the writing process, which is recorded in the biometric signal, unveils the real name of the writer in many cases to other readers. The identity may be determined in two ways: either the textual content of the writing sample is legible for the reader, or the reader may compare the actual sample to a collection of other signature samples, which may have been collected from sources external to the authentication system. Similar problems arise from other biometric methods, where overt physical or behavioral information may be derived from complementary information in the references. Other examples for such modalities, not related to handwriting, are storage of facial images in face recognition systems or audio sequences in speaker verification.

Apparently handwriting semantics, especially the handwritten signature, are overt biometric features to some degree for those environments, where attackers have access to other writing samples with known origin or where identities can be directly read from some representation of the authentication information. If in these cases, references are stored as complete original signals, an attacker may analyze the authentication information and determine the identity only based on the biometric signals, even if he or she does not get any information on the identity related to the data.

Besides the problem of providing anonymity, access to the full biometric signals may generate the problem of replay attacks. Once in possession of the complete signal representation, an attacker may use the information to attempt replay attacks. For example, the handwriting positioning signal could be used to control an automaton, which simulates the pen movements on a digitizer tablet.

Consequently, in analogy to the problems of the storage of references in a knowledge-based authentication system, the deposition of references in the original representation makes the full authentication information available to everyone having logical access to the storage facility and causes problems with respect to anonymity and reproducibility. Thus, storage of reference data in its original representation should be avoided.

Similar problems are known from knowledge-based authentication: On the example of the password authentication in UNIX operating systems, it has been shown in Chapter 4, Section 4.2, that mathematical digest functions like the *crypt()* function (see Section 4.2.4) can be utilized to overcome this problem. We have seen that, from a mathematical point of view, such cryptographic hash functions implement a non-invertible transformation from the domain of Authentication information A onto the complementary information domain C, if applied to the formalization introduced in Chapter 4. In order to secure the stored reference information, a function with similar properties of a cryptographic hash function is desirable for biometric user authentication systems.

Capacity limitations, Dimensionality

As shown in the section on modeling of authentication signals in Chapter 4, information based on sampled biometric measurement may become large. Besides the security problem in storing full reference information, there may be additional capacity limitations in the reference storage R. Especially in application scenarios, where references are stored locally, e.g. in personal devices like smart cards, there may be insufficient space to store the entire original reference data. In this respect, a Biometric Hash function with the property of mapping the original data into a significantly smaller domain in an irreversible way, providing a collision-free mapping to the original data may overcome capacity limitations.

Furthermore, another design goal is to find a mapping function that does not only reduce the size of complementary information C, but additionally allows the projection of original biometric signals of arbitrary size onto a value space of pre-defined dimensionality. Besides the benefit of limiting capacity requirements, a fixed dimensionality has the advantage to apply computationally simple distance measures and comparison functions, such as the Hamming Distance function, which is utilized in other biometric modalities, for example Daugman's Iris Code [Daug1993], for verification and particularly identification purposes.

Cryptographic Key Generation from Biometrics

The purpose of any authentication system is the authorization or rejection of subjects gaining physical or logical access to a specific application. In many cases, such applications of authentication systems are the handling of digital key management problems for cryptographic security mechanisms. Here, we find two categories of keys: keys for symmetric systems, where all participants of the secret communication share the same secret key and asymmetric systems, with key pairs of a private (and thus secret) and a publicly available keys. In either category, we have the requirement to protect the secret or private keys from unauthorized access. As cryptographically strong keys are rather large, it is certainly not feasible to let users memorize their personal keys. As a consequence of this, in real world scenarios today, digital keys are typically stored on smart cards, protected by a special kind of password, the personal identification number (PIN). However, there are problems with PIN, e.g. they may be lost, passed on to other persons accidentally or purposely or they may be reverse-engineered by brute-force attacks.

These difficulties in using pass-code-based storage of cryptographic keys motivate the use of biometric authentication for key management, which are based on biometric measures of subject's traits rather than on their knowledge alone. Various methods to apply biometrics to solve key management problems have been presented in the past [Nich1999]:

- **Secure Server Systems**, which release the key upon successful verification of the biometric features of the owner.
- **Embedding of the digital key** within the biometric reference data by a trusted algorithm, e.g. bit-replacement.
- **Combination of digital key and biometric image** into a so-called Bioscrypt™ in such a way that neither information can be retrieved independently of the other.
- **Deriving** the **digital key** directly **from a biometric** image or feature.

There are problems with all of these approaches. In the first scenario, a secured and trusted environment is required for the server and further, all communication channels need to be secured, which is not possible in all application scenarios. Embedding secret information in a publicly available data set like in the second suggestion will allow an attacker to retrieve secret information for all users, once the algorithm gets compromised. The idea of linking both digital key and biometric feature into a Bioscrypt™ can result in a good protection of both data sets, but it is rather demanding with regard to the infrastructure required. Approaches of the fourth category face problems due to the fact that biometric features typically show a high degree of intra-personal variability due to natural and physiological reasons. A key that is composed directly from the biometric feature values might not show stability over a large number of verifications. Secondly, if the derivation of the key is based on passive traits like the fingerprint, the key is lost forever, once the biometric traits are compromised.

To overcome the problems of approaches of the last category, it is desirable to **derive a robust key** value **directly from an active biometric trait**, which includes an **expression of intention** by the user. A voice-based approach for such a system can be found in [MRLW2001], where cryptographic keys are generated from spoken telephone number sequences. However, as for all biometric techniques based on voice, there are security problems in replay attacks, which can easily be performed by audio recording.

Low computational complexity

Biometric authentication on low-performance computational devices such as PDA's or smart cards may become a problem, if the underlying algorithms are computationally complex. Particularly signal processing in time-frequency domain, involving transformations between time and frequency representations may be mathematically too complex to be processed on such small devices. The challenge here is to find methods which can be used to derive features from the original biometric signals with low computational complexity and which still have the property of providing discriminatory power between the users of an authentication system. Furthermore, efficient implementation of authentication functions $l \in L$ are desirable for authentication systems with limited resources or with the requirement to compare authentication input A of users with a very large database (e.g. for identification purposes).

Related work in the area of handwriting has addressed this aspect in [DDN+1995], with the motivation of studying the technical feasibility of implementation of a dynamic signature verification system in a digital signal processor (DSP) device. With a set of nine statistical features, which can be computed in runtime linear to the sample numbers of the biometric signals, it has been shown that a verification process can be executed in approximately 0.5 seconds on a state-of-the-art DSP.

The Biometric Hash function is designed in a way that it enables features that can be efficiently extracted from the biometric raw data, although it does not generally limit the type of features to be included. Further, it allows the usage of computationally very efficient distance measures and comparison methods in the authentication mode.

6.2   Description of the Biometric Hash Algorithm

In this section, we provide a detailed description of our Biometric Hash algorithm. The goal is to find a **function *m* (called Biometric Hash function)** having **two arguments** A (Authentication Information) **and** C (Complementary Information), which **yields an individual Biometric Hash vector *b*** of dimensionality k: $b=(b_1, \ldots ,b_k)$. A and C in our algorithm are represented by sets of k-dimensional statistical features extracted from the sampled handwriting signals and represented by a feature vector n. The goal of this section is to successively develop the algorithm in the following subsections.

We start with a description, how and which statistical parameters are extracted from the sampled biometric authentication signals in Section 6.2.1, followed by an overview of the algorithm in Section 6.2.2. Algorithm details for determination of the **Interval Matrix parameter** representing the complementary information C in the Biometric Hash algorithm m, are given in Section 6.2.3. This generation of C, which implements a Complementary function f as defined in Chapter 4, requires an additional parameter, the **Tolerance Vector *tv*.** In Section 6.2.4 we present a discussion on the impact of this parameter. Finally, the **Biometric Hash function** is introduced as an **interval mapping operation** in Section 6.2.5.

6.2.1 Statistical Features from Online Handwriting Signals

From the objectives for Biometric Hashes, given in the previous subsection, as well as from the features classes introduced in Chapter 5, it becomes obvious that features from the class of statistical measures of the sampled signals qualify for the determination of Biometric Hashes. Firstly, statistical features can easily be chosen in such way, that a reverse projection from feature space to signal space becomes computationally difficult, which is a non-straightforward problem for functional or structural representations, especially under consideration that even lossy reverse projection may result in compromised biometric signals. As outlined in Figure 6-1 on the example of a horizontal writing position signal $x(t)$, statistical features loose their explicit reference to spatial or temporal position with the originating signal, unlike structural or functional features.

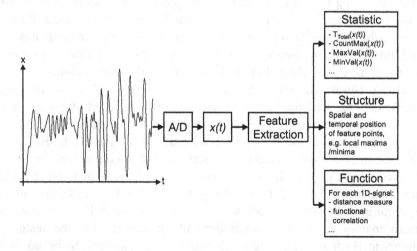

Figure 6-1. Example for a feature taxonomy (statistic, structure and function) extracted from an exemplary biometric signal $x(t)$

Structural features are based on the coding of occurrences of predefined points in the original signal. These special points can be defined in the temporal domain (e.g. zero-crossings in velocity signals) as well as spatial (e.g. line crossings), whereas functional features use the original functional representations directly, or re-sampled signals from those, as characteristics [PlLo1989]. Intrinsic to both structural and functional features is the possibility to estimate an original signal due to the fact that discrete values are associated with the temporal and/or spatial sequence, which is an important difference to statistical features. Here, statistical analysis of the entire original signal is performed with respect to different characteristics. For example, as shown in Figure 6-1, the total writing time $T_{Total}(x(t))$, number of local maxima ($CountMax(x(t))$) and minimum and maximum amplitudes values ($MinVal(x(t))$, $MaxVal(x(t))$) could be extracted from an horizontal writing position signal. Although these parameters allow the **construction** of some **arbitrary signal** having the same statistical properties, it will be **computationally difficult** to re-construct a signal, which shows a great structural similarity to the original signal.

Another characteristic differentiating statistical from structural and functional features is their dimensionality. While for the later two categories, the feature dimensionality cannot be predicted without a-priori knowledge of the original signal, the first category of **statistical feature vectors** obviously **have a predefined dimensionality**, if determined globally, i.e. over the entire signal duration. This property avoids processing steps of signal concatenation (see, for example, [JaGC2002]) or segmentation (e.g. [HKCF1992] and [GuCa1997]). Thus the objective of static dimensionality for the resulting Biometric Hash value, as postulated in Section 6.1, can also easily be met by choosing global statistical features, provided that these are based either on entire writing samples, or by applying segmentation into predefined segment numbers. Thus **the number of features chosen at design time** of an algorithm will **determine the dimensionality of the resulting Biometric Hash** values. Thirdly, compared to digital signal representations, statistical features typically are composed of a single scalar value, making them rather compact with respect to storage requirements.

For the design of the Biometric Hash algorithm presented in this section, some assumptions with respect to the statistical characteristics of features are required. In Chapter 2, it has been pointed out, that all biometric measurements adequate for biometric authentication have to fulfill a number of requirements with respect to intra-personal variability, inter-personal discriminatory power, ascertainability and permanence. For the design of a Biometric Hash function, there are two aspects that need to be taken into consideration. One aspect is the necessary requirement of possessing an **inter-personal discriminatory power** that is, they are suitable **to**

distinguish classes of different subjects. The other consideration is that it has been shown that all biometric measurements are subject to a **natural intra-personal variability** due to their non-deterministic origin. In Chapter 5, the observation has been stated with respect to the original biometric raw data, whereas at this point characteristics of statistic parameters based on these signals are discussed. Feature extraction for online handwriting biometrics can be considered as a lossy mapping from a multi-dimensional space of signal values to a value space of lower dimensionality. This is especially true for extraction of statistical features, as here information of an arbitrary dimensionality is mapped onto a one-dimensional space.

Consequently, we make the following assumptions:

Discriminatory Power

It is assumed that each of the statistical features used as parameters to the biometric hash function preserves some discriminatory power from the original signals. As a minimum requirement, it can be formulated that none of the statistical features values show a constant value over the set of all users of the authentication system, i.e. each feature can differentiate the set of all users into at least two disjoint classes.

Intra-Personal Variability

It is assumed that the statistical feature derived from the original biometric signal sustains the intra-personal variability. If statistical features can be found, which do not reflect this variability and additionally possess the characteristics of a discriminatory power, they either do not require any further mapping, as the statistical value itself already contains the properties necessary for a Biometric Hash value component. Or, if the discriminatory power is zero, in any case the property contains no significant information and the feature can be omitted.

Therefore, the requirements for statistical features to be considered for the design of a Biometric Hash algorithm can be summarized in **necessary requirement for discriminatory power** and a **sufficient requirement for intra-personal variability**. Note that the later aspect focuses on biometric data of one single individual only (Intra-Class), whereas the first condition is based on the entire set of users of a biometric authentication system (Inter-Class). As these features characterize non-deterministic terms and thus need to be evaluated in empirical evaluations, we have chosen the following methodology for the Biometric Hash: for the forthcoming discussion of statistical features for the Biometric Hash, rather than evaluating the condition a-priori for each of the suggested parameters, we present a **design**

for the system, including an **initial large set of features** along with an **a-posteriori analysis** with respect to the above conditions.

The proceeding of **obtaining a hash vector by interval mapping,** as presented in the following subsections, requires the utilization of a fixed number of scalar feature values, which are computed by statistical analysis of the sampled physical signals. Statistical analysis of handwriting signals has been a research topic since many years and a large set of statistical functions has been applied to online handwriting signals. A comprehensive overview of relevant features used in publications on signature verification can be found in [PlLo1989] and [LePl1994]. From these enormous degrees of freedom, we determine a characteristic subset of features, allowing to empirically prove the concept of our new method. An exhaustive itemization of all possible statistical features is neither necessary nor required for a general evaluation. In this work, we base the selection of our set on features known to be adequate from the literature, complemented by new statistical terms determined by us, for example, on the basis of forensic analysis of handwriting (see [ViSS2004]). In the following Table 6-1, the entire set of statistical features is summarized in an indexed order.

We **denote this set of statistical features as feature vector *n*,** where *n* consists of $i \in \{1, \dots, k\}$, *k=69* **single scalar** values n_i: $n=(n_1, \dots, n_k)$.

Each of parameter names in Table 6-1 denotes a short identifier for the quantity and a brief description is given in the column parameter description. In addition to the statistical parameters, which have been used also in earlier work, we have contributed **additional features** in the following categories:

- Centroid-based statistics: these terms relate temporal information to the spatial centroid of the writing sample (features n_{11}, n_{12}, n_{13}, n_{15}, n_{16}, n_{17} and n_{18} in Table 6-1).
- **Extremum and average values** of **pressure and pen angle signals** (features n_{19} to n_{25} in Table 6-1).
- **Spatial segmentation** in four columns and three rows of equal-sized areas and determination of number of pixels in each spatial segment, as shown in the example in Figure 6-2 (features n_{32} to n_{43} in Table 6-1 refer to rectangular blocks 1 to 12 in Figure 6-2).

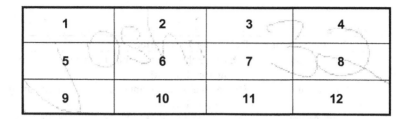

1	2	3	4
5	6	7	8
9	10	11	12

Figure 6-2. Example of the 4-by-3 spatial segmentation

- **Temporal Segmentation** into five time intervals of equal length (features n_{46} to n_{55} in Table 6-1)
- **Forensically motivated** features, which have been elaborated from publications by forensic handwriting analysts and have been transformed into technical parameters in [ViSS2004], see features n_{56} to n_{69} in Table 6-1. This feature category considers properties like baseline angle and pressure dynamics in very beginning and end of the writing process

Table 6-1. Summary of statistical feature parameters for the Biometric Hash calculation

Feature	Parameter Name	Parameter Description
n_1	TTotal	Total writing time in ms
n_2	SampleCount	Total number of event pixels
n_3	AspectRatio	Image Width * 1000 DIV Height
n_4	VxAbsolute	Average velocity in x direction in 1000 * pixels / ms
n_5	VyAbsolute	Average velocity in y direction in 1000 * pixels / ms
n_6	SegmentCount	Number of consecutive pen-down segments
n_7	VxMin	Minimum absolute x-velocity during sample
n_8	VxMax	Maximum absolute x-velocity during sample
n_9	VyMin	Minimum absolute y-velocity during sample
n_{10}	VyMax	Maximum absolute y-velocity during sample
n_{11}	CentroidX	Centroid of horizontal pen position in bounding box
n_{12}	CentroidY	Centroid of vertical pen position in bounding box
n_{13}	CentroidDist	Distance of Centroid from origin
n_{14}	MaxPressure	Maximum absolute pressure occurred during writing (or -1, if n/a)
n_{15}	CentroidX_SN	Centroid of horizontal pen position normalized to bounding box width * 1000
n_{16}	CentroidY_SN	Centroid of vertical pen position normalized to bounding box height * 1000
n_{17}	CentroidDist_SN	Distance of Centroid from origin normalized to bounding box diameter * 1000
n_{18}	CentroidAzimuth _SN	Horizontal azimuth of centroid from origin normalized to PI/2 * 1000
n_{19}	MaxAltitude	Maximum absolute altitude of pen occurred during writing (or -1, if n/a)
n_{20}	MinAltitude	Minimum absolute altitude of pen occurred during writing (or -1, if n/a)

Table 6-1 (cont.)

Feature	Parameter Name	Parameter Description
n_{21}	MaxAzimuth	Maximum absolute azimuth of pen occurred during writing (or -1, if n/a)
n_{22}	MinAzimuth	Minimum absolute azimuth of pen occurred during writing (or -1, if n/a)
n_{23}	AvgPressure	Average Writing Pressure relative to MaxPressure * 1000
n_{24}	AverageAzimuth	Average Azimuth of pen projected on writing plane
n_{25}	AverageAltitude	Average Altitude of pen above the writing plane
n_{26}	Vx_TN	Normalized Average velocity in x direction in pixels / VxMax * 1000
n_{27}	Vy_TN	Normalized Average velocity in y direction in pixels / VyMax * 1000
n_{28}	TPenUp	Absolute cumulated Pen-up time in ms
n_{29}	RatioTPenUpPEn Down	Ratio of TPenUp by TTotal * 1000
n_{30}	NoSamples	Total Number of Sample Values
n_{31}	PathLength	Total absolute Path Length in Pixels
n_{32}	PixelCountR1C1	Number of pixels in first row, first column
n_{33}	PixelCountR1C2	Number of pixels in first row, second column
n_{34}	PixelCountR1C3	Number of pixels in first row, third column
n_{35}	PixelCountR1C4	Number of pixels in first row, fourth column
n_{36}	PixelCountR2C1	Number of pixels in second row, first column
n_{37}	PixelCountR2C2	Number of pixels in second row, second column
n_{38}	PixelCountR2C3	Number of pixels in second row, third column
n_{39}	PixelCountR2C4	Number of pixels in second row, fourth column
n_{40}	PixelCountR3C1	Number of pixels in third row, first column
n_{41}	PixelCountR3C2	Number of pixels in third row, second column
n_{42}	PixelCountR3C3	Number of pixels in third row, third column
n_{43}	PixelCountR3C4	Number of pixels in third row, fourth column
n_{44}	IntegralX	Numeric Integration of normalized X values
n_{45}	IntegralY	Numeric Integration of normalized Y values
n_{46}	AreaX1	Numeric Integration of X values for 1st one-fifth time period
n_{47}	AreaX2	Numeric Integration of X values for 2nd one-fifth time period
n_{48}	AreaX3	Numeric Integration of X values for 3rd one-fifth time period
n_{49}	AreaX4	Numeric Integration of X values for 4th one-fifth time period
n_{50}	AreaX5	Numeric Integration of X values for 4th one-fifth time period
n_{51}	AreaY1	Numeric Integration of Y values for 1st one-fifth time period
n_{52}	AreaY2	Numeric Integration of Y values for 2nd one-fifth time period
n_{53}	AreaY3	Numeric Integration of Y values for 3rd one-fifth

Table 6-1 (cont.)

Feature	Parameter Name	Parameter Description
		time period
n_{54}	AreaY4	Numeric Integration of Y values for 4th one-fifth time period
n_{55}	AreaY5	Numeric Integration of Y values for 4th one-fifth time period
n_{56}	PenDPress	Average Pen Down Pressure normalized to 1 * 1000
n_{57}	PenUPress	Average PenUp Pressure normalized to 1 * 1000
n_{58}	BaselineAngle	Baseline Angle of the Sample
n_{59}	HistYZone1	Histogram of Y for Zone 1 in % * 100
n_{60}	HistYZone2	Histogram of Y for Zone 2 in % * 100
n_{61}	HistYZone3	Histogram of Y for Zone 3 in % * 100
n_{62}	AreaRatio1	Area(ConvexHull) vs. Area(BoundingBox) * 1000
n_{63}	AreaRatio2	Area(ConvexHull(Segments)) vs. Area(ConvexHull(Sample)) * 1000
n_{64}	AreaRatio3	Area(ConvexHull(Segments)) vs. Area(BoundingBox) * 1000
n_{65}	PathRatio1	PathLength(ConvexHull) vs. PathLength(BoundingBox) * 1000
n_{66}	PathRatio2	PathLength(ConvexHull(Segments)) vs. PathLength(ConvexHull(Sample)) * 1000
n_{67}	PathRatio3	PathLength(ConvexHull(Segments)) vs. PathLength(BoundingBox) * 1000
n_{68}	HistXLeft	Histogram of X for left in % * 100
n_{69}	HistXRight	Histogram of X for right in % * 100

The set of statistical parameters has historically grown with the system development and the initial selection was oriented on the computational limitations on small hand-held computers (Palm PDA). In the initial publication of the Biometric Hash algorithm, a basic set of 24 parameters has been used for the proof of concept [ViSM2002]. In subsequent research on the Biometric Hash ([ViSt2004], [ViSS2004]), the number of features considered has been developed to the current set of 69 features, presented in Table 6-1, at the time of publication of this book. In comparison to the number of features taken into account by other statistical approaches (e.g. Schmidt: 13 [Schm1999], Dullink et al.: 9 [DDN+1995]), this set size appears to be relatively large for an algorithm analysis. Thus we refrain from implementing additional statistical functions, although the algorithm does not have any intrinsic limitations with respect to the dimensionality k of the feature vector.

6.2.2 Algorithm Overview

Figure 6-3 illustrates the general process of the Biometric Hash calculation, consisting of the two modes of **Interval Matrix (*IM*)** determination and the **Biometric Hash function *m* to generate a Biometric Hash vector *b*.** The diagram in Figure 6-3 shows the process of Interval Matrix (*IM*) determination in the upper area, whereas the generation of the Biometric Hash is shown in the lower part. In view of the two general modes of a biometric authentication system, *Enrollment* and *Authentication* (see Chapter 2, Section 2.4.1), the first process can be considered as the enrollment stage, which is the prerequisite for any later user authentication. Authentication in this case is represented by the process in the lower part of Figure 6-3, in the Biometric Hash generation. The initial process steps are identical in both cases. In the data acquisition phase, the pen position signals *x(t), y(t),* the pressure signal *p(t)*, the pen altitude signal *Φ(t)* and the pen azimuth signal *θ(t)* are recorded from the input device. These signals are then made available to the feature extraction both in as normalized (*x/y/p* normalization for determination of time variant features) and an unfiltered sampled signals. The following feature extraction process is configured by the definition of the set of *k* statistical features *{n₁ , ..., nₖ}*, representing feature vector *n*, to be calculated for the Biometric Hash determination, and calculates the parameter values for the actual sample.

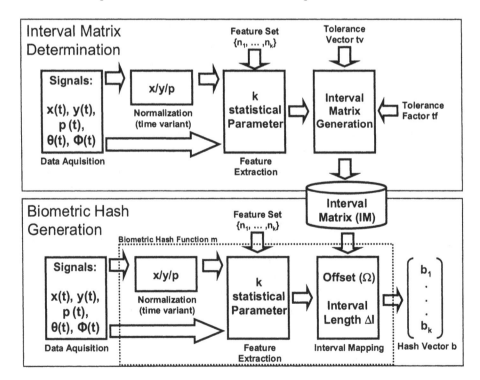

Figure 6-3. General model of Biometric Hash generation

After feature extraction of the k parameters, the further processing depends on the operation mode. In Interval Matrix generation mode (***Enrollment***), the actual features are processed into an **Interval Matrix *IM***, constisting of an an **Interval Length vector** ΔI and an **Interval Offset vector** Ω: ***IM=(ΔI, Ω)***. *IM* is determined individually for each subject under consideration of two parameters: a **Tolerance Vector** *tv*, also of dimensionality k: $tv=(tv_1, ..., tv_k)$, introducing individual weights for each of the respective feature vector components $(n_1, ..., n_k)$ and a **Tolerance Factor** *tf*, implementing a global weighting of all features. A detailed discussion on how to obtain these parameters will follow in Section 6.4. The *IM* is determined during enrollment as outlined above and the algorithm for this will be presented in detail in Section 6.2.3. After determination, the *IM* is attributed by the user's identity, persistently stored and **represents the complementary information** C in the system for reference by subsequent authentication processes.

In Biometric Hash generation mode, an feature vector $(n_1, ..., n_k)$ is mapped to the Biometric Hash vector b by the interval mapping process, making use of a persistently stored user-specific Interval Matrix (*IM*).

At time of Biometric Hash generation, the actual statistical feature vector, together with the *IM* assigned to the claimed identity, is made available to the Interval Mapping process, the result of which is the Biometric Hash vector, a k-dimensional vector of non-negative integer scalars, $b=(b_1, ..., b_k)$.

Note that due to the heterogeneous characteristics and physical capabilities of the digitizer tablets in the evaluation framework, not each of the currently 69 parameters shown in Table 6-1 can actually be taken into account for the hash value calculation in every case. If a feature is not available in this process (for example because the digitizer tablet is not capable to record the underlying physical trait, such as pen angle signals), the representative feature vector component in these cases will be set to the constant value of 0 for all samples.

6.2.3   Interval Matrix Algorithm

The Interval Matrix *IM*, being the helper data for mapping a set of statistical feature values into a stable Intra-Class value space adequate for key generation, is a matrix composed from two k-dimensional vectors:

$\Delta I=(\Delta I_1, ..., \Delta I_k)$, denoting the **Interval Length Vector** and
$\Omega=(\Omega_1, ..., \Omega_k)$, denoting the **Interval Offset Vector**.

The **Interval Matrix** *IM* is then defined as $IM=(\Delta I, \Omega)$, consequently, *IM* is of dimension of $k \times 2$.

The interval length and offset values are determined separately for each user during from the sampled signals during an enrollment process (see Section 2.4.1). We describe our algorithm for the *IM* determination in functional notation, using the following designators:

- let **ES** be the set of signals sampled during *e* **writing processes** of an enrollment of a subject, $ES=\{es_1, \ldots, es_e\}$ and let $\{n^{(1)}, \ldots, n^{(e)}\}$ **be the set of *e* statistical feature vectors derived from *ES***, each of which having a dimensionality of *k* (the process of extraction of reference features is drafted in Figure 6-4),
- let **MIN** be the **function** taking a set of *k*-dimensional vectors as arguments and returning a *k*-dimensional vector representing the **minimum for each component index** over the argument,
- let **MAX** be the **function** taking a set of *k*-dimensional vectors as arguments and returning a *k*-dimensional vector representing the **maximum for each component index** over the argument,
- let $I_{InitLow}$, $I_{InitHigh}$, I_{Low}, I_{High}, ΔI_{Init} be helper data as *k*-dimensional vectors for intermediate results of the algorithm,
- let *tv* be the *k*-dimensional Tolerance Vector: $tv=(tv_1, \ldots, tv_k)$,
- let *tf* be the scalar Tolerance Factor for a global factorization of each of the *tv* components, i.e. a global stretching or shortening factor for the mapping intervals,
- let **MOD** be the **component-wise modulo operation between two *k*-dimensional vector operands**, i.e. it yields one *k*-dimensional vector consisting of components obtained by the scalar modulo operation between each of vector components left and right of the operator *MOD*. Given this notation, the **IM generation algorithm** is defined as follows:

$$IM = (\Delta I, \Omega) \tag{6-3}$$

where *ΔI* defined as:

$$\Delta I = \begin{pmatrix} \Delta I_1 \\ \ldots \\ \Delta I_k \end{pmatrix} = I_{High} - I_{Low} = \begin{pmatrix} I_{High,1} \\ \ldots \\ I_{High,k} \end{pmatrix} - \begin{pmatrix} I_{Low,1} \\ \ldots \\ I_{Low,k} \end{pmatrix} \tag{6-4}$$

and I_{High}, I_{Low} are given as:

$$I_{High} = \begin{pmatrix} \lceil I_{InitHigh,1} + tv_1 * \Delta I_{Init,1} * tf \rceil \\ ... \\ \lceil I_{InitHigh,k} + tv_k * \Delta I_{Init,k} * tf \rceil \end{pmatrix} \tag{6-5}$$

$$I_{Low} = \begin{pmatrix} \lfloor I_{InitLow,1} - tv_1 * \Delta I_{Init,1} * tf \rfloor \; if \; (\lfloor I_{InitLow,1} - tv_1 * \Delta I_{Init,1} * tf \rfloor) > 0, 0 \; otherwise \\ ... \\ \lfloor I_{InitLow,k} - tv_k * \Delta I_{Init,k} * tf \rfloor \; if \; (\lfloor I_{InitLow,k} - tv_k * \Delta I_{Init,k} * tf \rfloor) > 0, 0 \; otherwise \end{pmatrix} \tag{6-6}$$

$$I_{InitHigh} = MAX(ES)$$
$$I_{InitLow} = MIN(ES) \tag{6-7}$$
$$\Delta I_{Init} = I_{InitHigh} - I_{InitLow}$$

and finally Ω is defined as:

$$\Omega = I_{Low} \; MOD \; \Delta I \tag{6-8}$$

The parameter specific Tolerance Vector *tv* is introduced to compensate the Intra-Class variability of each feature parameter and the additional Tolerance Factor *tf* allows for a linear factorization of the tolerance vector components with a global impact. A discussion on the overall impact of this parameter is given in the following Section 6.2.4 and methods how to estimate adequate parameterization values will follow within the evaluation discussion later in this chapter in Section 6.4. Note that **all vectors in our algorithm except *tv* are of non-negative integer type.** As *tv* represents a non-negative factorization vector, composed of real value type, we perform a rounding to the next higher and next lower integer value for the determination of the Interval border vectors I_{High} and I_{Low} respectively.

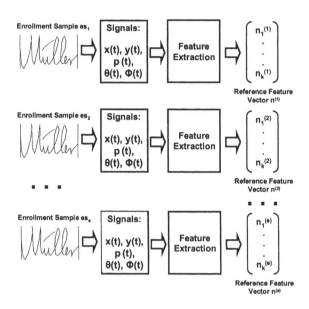

Figure 6-4. Schematic calculation of the set of reference feature vectors $\{n^{(1)}, ..., n^{(e)}\}$

6.2.4   Parameterization of the System: Tolerance Vector

As introduced earlier, for each of the $i \in \{1, ..., k\}$ Biometric Hash vector components the Tolerance Vector tv provides a value component tv_i, which is introduced in order to compensate the Intra-Class variability separately for each of the individual features. The entire Tolerance values are collected in the Tolerance Vector $tv=(tv_1, ..., tv_k)$. This compensation takes care of the observation, that each of the features which are represented by the Biometric Hash vector components $(b_1, ... , b_k)$ may possess a different degree of Intra-Class variability. The compensation does so be extending the interval length of each of the values in feature vector $n=(n_1, ... ,n_k)$, which are mapped onto identical hash vector component values by the mapping function described in the following Section 6.2.5. Figure 6-5 a), b) and c) illustrate the impact of the Tolerance Value for one exemplary component n_i from feature vector n.

For the exemplary feature value n_i, the initial determination of $I_{InitLow,i}$ and $I_{InitHigh,i}$ and the resulting initial Interval Length $\Delta I_{Init,i}$ are shown in the first diagram Figure 6-5 a). Suppose we have observed a minimum value of $I_{InitLow,i} = 58$ and a maximum value of $I_{InitHigh,i} = 74$ for feature n_i in our set of enrollment samples, *ES*, we thus get an initial interval length of $\Delta I_{Init,i} = 16$.

The resulting mapping intervals for $tv_i=0$, thus $\Delta I_i=\Delta I_{Init,i}$, $I_{Low,i}=I_{InitLow,i}$, $I_{High,i}=I_{InitHigh,i}$ (no Tolerance Value compensation), are shown in Figure 6-5 b), along with the result value of the Biometric Hash function in the ordinate. The horizontal dotted lines denote each of the mapping intervals of length $\Delta I_i=16$ and the Interval Offset yields $\Omega_i = I_{Low,i}\ MOD\ \Delta I_i=10$.

The effects of a different Tolerance Vector value of $tv_i=0.3$ are shown in Figure 6-5 c). With $I_{Low,i}=53$ and $I_{High,i}=79$, we observe an interval length of $\Delta I_i=26$ with an Interval Offset of $\Omega_i=1$.

The basic concept of the Biometric Hash algorithm is an interval mapping, which is formally described in the following Section 6.2.4. Graphically, in Figure 6-5 b) and c) this mapping can be explained as follows: the value scale for feature vector component n_i on the abscissa is partitioned in intervals of length ΔI_i with an Interval Offset of Ω_i, starting from 0. Each value of n_i within these intervals (denoted as horizontal, dotted lines) is mapped by a Biometric Hash Function $m(n_i, \Delta I_i, \Omega_i)$, to a unique value assigned to b_i of the Biometric Hash vector b. For the sake of completeness and in anticipation of the formal description of the interval mapping method in the following Section 6.2.5, we have included the function results for $m(n_i, \Delta I_i, \Omega_i)$ in the ordinate axis of Figure 6-5 b) and c).

Obviously, the effects of the increasing Tolerance value tv_i to the Biometric Hash function can be summarized as follows:

- with an **increasing Tolerance Vector** value tv_i, the **scale of feature values** n_i mapped to identical Biometric Hash values $m(n_i, \Delta I_i, \Omega_i)$ **increases linearly**,
- with an **increasing Tolerance Vector** value tv_i, the size of the **achievable value space** for the resulting Biometric Hash component b_i **decreases linearly**.

Consequently, the parameterization of the Tolerance Vector components of tv in the Biometric Hash function can be expected to expose a similar trade-off characteristics as other threshold-based biometric authentication systems, as discussed in Chapter 2, Section 2.4. With an increasing Tolerance value we expect that the ratio of wrongly non-identical hash values for authentic users decreases at the cost of an increasing false match of a non-authentic subject and vice versa. In order to validate this hypothesis, results of comprehensive evaluations are presented in the coming Sections 6.3 to 6.6. For these tests, three reference parameterizations for the Tolerance values will be suggested and the response characteristics of the Biometric Hash function described in this section are analyzed in various test scenarios, as presented in the following section.

a) IM Determination

b) Mapping Intervals for tv$_i$=0

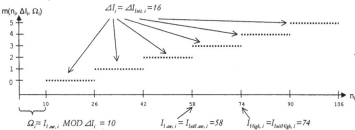

c) Mapping Intervals for tv$_i$=0.3

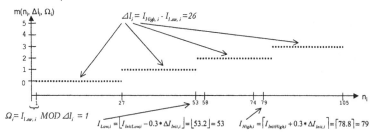

Figure 6-5. Impact of a Tolerance Vector compensation of tv_i=0.0 in graph b) and tv_i=0.3 in graph c) to mapping intervals

6.2.5 Biometric Hash Determination by Interval Mapping

The hash value computation is based on a mapping of each of the feature parameters of a test sample to an integer value scale. Due to the nature of the determination of the interval matrix, all possible feature values for two variables $n_i^{(1)}$ and $n_i^{(2)}$ within the interval $[I_{Low,i}, I_{High,i}]$ for each of the $i \in \{1, ..., k\}$ fulfill the following condition:

$$\left\lfloor \frac{(n_i^{(1)} - \Omega_i)}{\Delta I_i} \right\rfloor == \left\lfloor \frac{(n_i^{(2)} - \Omega_i)}{\Delta I_i} \right\rfloor \forall n_i^{(1)}, n_i^{(2)} \in \left[I_{Low,i}, I_{High,i} \right]: \qquad (6\text{-}9)$$

and

$$\left\lfloor \frac{(n_i^{(1)} - \Omega_i)}{\Delta I_i} \right\rfloor \neq \left\lfloor \frac{(n_i^{(2)} - \Omega_i)}{\Delta I_i} \right\rfloor \forall n_i^{(1)} \in \left[I_{Low,i}, I_{High,i} \right], n_i^{(2)} \notin \left[I_{Low,i}, I_{High,i} \right] \qquad (6\text{-}10)$$

That is, any given values of $n_i^{(1)}$ and $n_i^{(2)}$ within the interval $[I_{Low,i}, I_{High,i}]$ lead to identical integer quotients, whereas values below or above the interval border lead to different integer values. Thus, we define the scalar Biometric Hash function m_{Scalar} for each feature parameter n_i of a feature vector to:

$$m_{Scalar}(n_i, \Delta I_i, \Omega_i) = \left\lfloor \left| \frac{(n_i - \Omega_i)}{\Delta I_i} \right| \right\rfloor \tag{6-11}$$

Consequently, as the algorithm is applied to each of the $i \in \{1, \dots, k\}$ feature vector components n_i, the resulting Biometric Hash vector b consists of k components of non-negative integer values: $b = (b_1, \dots, b_k)$ and the resulting Biometric Hash function m, yielding the k-dimensional result vector b and taking an actual feature vector n and an Interval Matrix IM as arguments, can be written to:

$$m(n, IM) = m(n, \Delta I, \Omega) = \begin{pmatrix} m_{Scalar}(n_1, \Delta I_1, \Omega_1) \\ \dots \\ m_{Scalar}(n_k, \Delta I_k, \Omega_k) \end{pmatrix} = \begin{pmatrix} \left\lfloor \left| \frac{(n_1 - \Omega_1)}{\Delta I_1} \right| \right\rfloor \\ \dots \\ \left\lfloor \left| \frac{(n_k - \Omega_k)}{\Delta I_k} \right| \right\rfloor \end{pmatrix} \tag{6-12}$$

This functional definition of **$m(n,IM)$ implements the formal requirement of a biometric hash function, $m \in M, m : A \times C \to B$**, as postulated in the beginning of this chapter, with n representing an implementation of authentication information A and IM representing C.

6.3   Evaluation Methodology

With respect to the experimental setup and test scenarios, we apply the same methodology as defined in Chapter 5, Section 5.6, replacing the MQED algorithm by the introduced Biometric Hash function. However, in contrast to the typical evaluation strategy for biometric verification systems, where the classification accuracy is determined in terms of error rates, which are typically charted as False-Match/ False-Non-Match rates as function of a decision threshold T (see Chapter 2, Section 2.4.4), evaluation of the Biometric Hash generation requires a different metric. Here, no decision threshold parameter exists at the time of authentication attempt. Rather than that, as can be seen from Figure 6-3, the only parameter at the time of hash generation is the interval matrix *IM*, which needs to be determined in a-priori manner, as described earlier in this section. We have shown in the previous section that for the determination of this *IM*, three quantities are required: the scatter vectors of feature values during enrollment (derived by a Minumum/Maximum strategy from the set of Enrollment Samples, *ES*), the Tolerance Vector (*tv*) parameter for interval extension and a Tolerance Factor *tf* for global weighting.

In regards to the system parameterization by interval matrices, there exist two general scenarios, which can be observed. Firstly, a **global parameterization** at system level causes the Biometric Hash algorithm to use the same system settings for all users, whereas the second option of individualized parameters considers a local parameterization for each of the users. This second option is denoted as **local parameterization**. Both scenarios are relevant from an application point of view, as the first option allows the design of a biometric system with fixed internal parameters, where no user-specific information or parameterization is required. The second option is interesting for usage in scenarios, where the hash generation is based on the corequisite of possession of the user-specific Interval Matrix and the ability to generate appropriate biometric signals. In practical applications, this combination of possession and biometrics can be achieved, for example, by storage of the *IM* on a device, which remains in possession of the user (e.g. smart card). In this case, during the verification process, the user grants read-access to the authentication system to retrieve the *IM* template (representing the complementary information *C*) and also provides a sample of handwriting as authentication information *A*.

For a feasible test setting for this high dimensional parameter problem, we use our test database as a significant evaluation set to analyze one representative configuration of each of the scenarios in this section and compare the empirical results to the case of a zero-Tolerance Vector, representing the case of no Intra-Class variability compensation at all. The proceeding to find adequate *tv* values for the cases of global and local parameterization will be shown in the forthcoming subsection.

The **evaluation methodology of the Biometric Hash for key generation is identical to the methodology introduced in Chapter 5, Section 5.6 with respect to the experimental setup and the test scenarios.** For the later, **we extent the test scenarios** consisting of five semantic classes and five tablet categories (see Chapter 5, Section 5.6.3, Table 5-3) **by three different scenarios** for the Tolerance Vector parameterization: **Zero-Tolerance Vector, Individual *tv* Parameterization and Global *tv* Parameterization.** Consequently, our evaluation of the Biometric Hash for key generation consists of a total of 75 test runs.

The main evaluation goal in this examination is to evaluate, to which degree the Biometric Hash algorithm allows the generation of stable hash values for individual users and to which degree the system produces colliding results for the set of different users. As the result of a Biometric Hash function is quite different from a binary result of Authentication functions L, we require a different metric for our experiments, which is based on the analysis of Hamming Distances[9] (*HD*) distributions of Intra- and Inter-Class and forgery tests, which we describe in the following Section 6.3.1. Section 6.3.2 will then introduce a graphical representation scheme for our experimental results, the Hamming-Distance histogram.

6.3.1   Evaluation Metric: Hamming Distance

As introduced in Chapter 5, Section 5.6.1, the experimental setup includes three categories of tests: Intra-Class, Inter-Class and Forgery tests. We have shown, that within one experiment, also denoted as test environment, one Intra-Class test, one Inter-Class test (also denoted as Random-Forgery tests) and up to three forgery tests of different attack strengths (*Blind, Low-Force, Brute-Force*) are conducted. In this section, we present how evaluation metrics for the Biometric Hash algorithm are derived from these cases.

Intra-Class Stability Tests
In this mode, Biometric Hash values are calculated for each individual user with a given test scenario consisting of enrollment samples *ES* and verification samples *VS*. Each of the enrollment samples from an set $ES=\{es_1, ..., es_e\}$ in this case is used to generate one instance of the Interval Matrix *IM*, which is then used for the calculation of a Biometric Hash value from each of the verification samples of the same person from the given test set *VS*. All Biometric Hash values generated in this way are collected to a set $B_{Intra\text{-}Class}$ and are logged to the test protocol. From this set, the measure for Intra-Class stability of Biometric Hash vectors is determined for each of the enrollments and each of the users H as follows:

---

[9] In this context, we use an extended definition of the Hamming Distance adopted from [ANT2000]: *"The number of digit positions in which the corresponding digits of two binary words of the same length are different. Note 1: The Hamming distance between 1011101 and 1001001 is two. Note 2: The concept can be extended to other notation systems. For example, the Hamming distance between 2143896 and 2233796 is three, and between "toned" and "roses" it is also three."*. Within the scope of this book, the Hamming Distance refers to the number of non-equal vector components of two vectors of equal dimensionality at corresponding index positions.

- The first Biometric Hash vector in $B_{Intra\text{-}Class}$ with the highest number of occurrences will be denoted as the **reference Biometric Hash vector, $b_{Reference}$**.
- **Each** occurrence of Biometric Hash vectors b in $B_{Intra\text{-}Class}$ having a Hamming Distance to $b_{Reference}$ greater than 0 (i.e. $HD(b,b_{Reference})>0$) is **registered as mismatch**.
- The average **Hamming Distance distribution quantifies the degree of mismatch** is tabulated over the entire test set for this Intra-Class evaluation (see Section 6.3.2).

<u>**Inter-Class and Forgery Discriminatory Power Tests**</u>

This part of the evaluation considers scenarios where the algorithm is exposed to non-authentic writing samples. As introduced in Chapter 5, different types of non-authentic samples and also defined levels of attack strength are considered (*Random, Blind, Low-Force* and *Brute-Force Forgeries*). Separately for these classes of attacks, the reference Biometric Hash vector $b_{Reference}$ is determined in exactly the same way as described for the Intra-Class Stability tests. Then, for all forgeries registered in the selected attack strength, the Biometric Hash vector resulting from forgeries (including *Random* forgeries representing Inter-Class tests) is determined using the reference *IM*. Among the set of generated forgery hashes, all vectors having a **Hamming distance equal to 0** to the reference vector are considered as **false-matches** and the degree of similarity will be again be charted in a distribution diagram.

The test methodology can be summarized by the following algorithmic description:

- For each given test environment $te \in TE$
  - For each individual subject H in te
    - For each set of **enrollment samples** $es \in ES$ of person H
      - Determine **Interval Matrix IM** of H from es and Tolerance Vector tv by applying the Interval Matrix Algorithm described in Section 6.2.3
      - Determine the **set of all authentic Biometric Hash vector** instances $B_{Authentic}$ for each of the Verification Samples $vs \in VS$ belonging to H by applying the Interval Mapping function defined in Section 6.2.5
      - Set the **Reference Biometric Hash $b_{Reference}$** to the value of the vector of maximum number of occurrences in $B_{Authentic}$.

- **Protocol** the Hamming Distance distribution of all Biometric Hash vectors in $B_{Authentic}$ with respect to $b_{Reference}$ to the **Intra-Class distribution log**
- **For each of the given forgery classes** *{Random, Blind, Low-Force, Brute-Force}* within test environment *te:*
  - Determine the set of all **forgery Biometric Hash vector** instances $b_{Forgery} \in B_{Forgery}$ for each of the forgery samples attacking subject H
  - Protocol the hamming distance distribution of $B_{Forgery}$ with respect to $b_{Reference}$ to the **Inter-Class distribution log** for each forgery class

The results of this process are the following five different distribution logs:

1. **Intra-Class distribution** of authentic Biometric Hash vectors,
2. **Inter-Class distribution** between Biometric Hashes generated by different users (**Random Forgery Distribution**),
3. **Inter-Class distribution** of Biometric Hashes generated from **Blind Forgeries**,
4. **Inter-Class distribution** of Biometric Hashes generated from **Low-Force Forgeries**,
5. **Inter-Class distribution** of Biometric Hashes generated from **Brute-Force Forgeries**.

6.3.2   Experimental Results: Hamming Distance Histogram

For the evaluation of the results of our experiments, we introduce a histogram view. From an exemplary histogram, as shown the following Figure 6-6, it can be seen that the occurrence probability is plotted as function of the Hamming Distance separately for each distribution type and for each test.

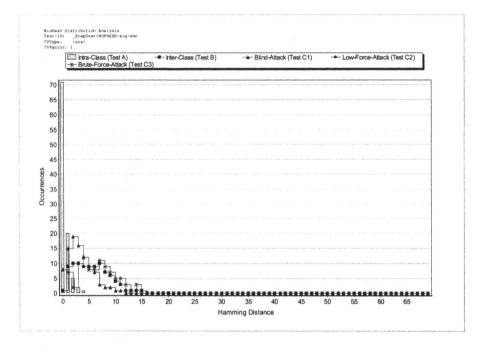

Figure 6-6. Histogram example of Hamming Distance distributions, semantic class *Signature*

The diagram in Figure 6-6 can be interpreted as follows: the degree of **Intra-Class stability** in this test scenario is represented by the percentage of occurrences of Biometric Hash vectors having a **Hamming Distance equal to zero to the reference vectors** $b_{Reference}$, which is indicated by the leftmost bar for the Intra-Class distribution (**solid gray bar at abscissa value 0**). In this example, stable Biometric Hash vectors were observed in approximately 71% of all cases, whereas in approximately 29% of cases (cumulated values of gray bars at abscissa values one to four), the test vectors show a deviation in at least one, but no more than four vector components between the generated Biometric Hashes and $b_{Reference}$.

For the evaluation of the **Inter-Class discriminatory power**, the main indicator is the relative occurrence probability of the corresponding graph at a Hamming Distance of zero. In other words, the percentage of cases in which handwriting within the same test environment produced by other subjects than the authentic ones, but with no forgery intention, were able to produce identical Biometric Hashes. This measure can also be seen as a collision probability of the algorithm in the parameterization of the test environment. Accumulations of non-zero occurrence probability at higher Hamming Distances indicate an increasing robustness of the discriminatory power, whereas a grouping in lower ranges indicates higher fragility. From the example given above, it can be observed that in approximately one percent of cases, collisions of Biometric Hashes occurred (see graph *Inter-Class*, denoted by square symbol, ■) and with respect to robustness it can be estimated, that parameterization of the algorithm in this test scenario towards higher Intra-Class stability will definitely result in a lower discriminatory power.

The interpretation of the **forgery distributions** is performed in analogy to the Inter-Class discriminatory power analysis, where the evaluation aspects are robustness of the algorithm with respect to intended forgeries. For the test example shown in Figure 6-6, it can be seen that up to a Hamming Distance of 4, *Blind Forgeries* (graph *Blind-Attack*, denoted by triangle symbols, ▲) showed a higher success rate than *Brute-Force Attacks* (graph *Brute-Force-Attack*, asterisk-pointed, *). At the practically significant operating point at a Hamming Distance of zero, in approximately 1% of cases *Brute-Force Forgeries* could successfully generate the authentic Biometric Hashes, whereas *Blind Forgeries* were successful in 8% of cases. Note in the exemplary test set, no *Low-Force Forgeries* were produced, thus the graph symbolized by diamonds (♦) is nonexistent.

Apparently the goal of our evaluation is to show the effect of the parameterization of the algorithm in different scenarios, which are composed by the test environments defined in Chapter 5, Section 5.6.3 under different settings of the Tolerance Vector *tv*. In order to do so, we consider three different parameter setting scenarios (two global and one user-specific setting) for *tv*, which are described in the following subsection.

6.4 Tolerance Vector Parameter Estimation

We have shown earlier, that the Tolerance Vector *tv* represents a significant parameter of the Biometric Hash function, which influences the characteristics of the interval matrix *IM* and thus the response characteristics of the algorithm. In the previous subsection, we have motivated the two general approaches of global and local parameterization and we now present the method of determining these parameters, which have been used within our evaluation task.

The approach, which we have taken, is based on the concept of three different parameterizations:

- **Zero-Tolerance Vector**: introduces no a-priori knowledge.
- **Individual Parameterization:** estimates *tv* individually for each user.
- **Global Parameterization:** estimates *tv* globally for all users of the authentication system.

In order to estimate the later two parameterizations, the evaluation scenarios described in the evaluation methodology in Chapter 5, Section 5.6.3 have been utilized.

The estimation of Tolerance vectors can either be done based on **pessimistic or optimistic assumptions** regarding the underlying empirical data. In the **pessimistic scenario**, we want to exclude correlation effects between the training set for parameter estimation and the actual evaluation data sets. Therefore, these sets are divided into **two disjoint subsets of equal size**. These subsets are denoted as $ES_{Estimation}$ and $ES_{Evaluation}$ **for the resulting Enrollment Samples** and $VS_{Estimation}$ and $VS_{Evaluation}$ **in case of Verification Samples**. This splitting is performed separately for each subject H, for each semantic class and each tablet category to ensure a balance in set sizes. As a result of this, we are using two disjoint subsets for each of the test environments: one for estimation of the tv parameterization and the other for the experimental evaluation of this setting.

In the **optimistic scenario**, we assume no correlation between training sets for parameter estimation and evaluation and consequently, we utilize all the entire empirical information without splitting into two disjoint sets.

In our presentation of test results in Section 6.6, we will clarify, that both estimation scenarios have a practical relevance. In this section we explain our algorithms for obtaining these Tolerance Vectors in the following three subchapters. Note that the algorithms are identical for pessimistic and optimistic scenarios and for the sake of clarity we will use the terms ES and VS synonymously for both set categories.

6.4.1   Zero-Tolerance Vector

In the first case, no a-priori knowledge about the intra-personal distribution of the feature values as assumed. Thus no reasonable selection for the Tolerance Vector tv can be made, and the Tolerance values are set to $tv_i=0$ for each of the $i \in \{1, ..., k\}$ Tolerance Vector components ($tv=(0,...,0)$). This category of Tolerance values will be denoted as zero-Tolerance Vector and represents a complete disregard of the parameterization of the system by Tolerance Vectors.

6.4.2   Individual Tolerance Vector

The second consideration, the individualized Tolerance Vectors, **considers a-priori knowledge about the intra-personal variability of each of the features n_i within the known dataset**. To find estimates for such an individual parameterization, a-priori evaluation of the statistical properties has to be performed separately for each of the subjects *H* using stored information of an authentication system.

In order to find sets of Tolerance values for this category, we have intuitively chosen a heuristic approach, which measures the statistical variability, based on the deviation of features originating from the Verification Samples *VS* (see Chapter 2, Section 2.4.1), compared to the corresponding Enrollment Samples *ES* individually for each of the users. In case of the third category of Tolerance Vectors (globally estimated), the approach leads to a single Tolerance Vector for a selection of tablets and semantic class, whereas in case of individual Tolerance value determination, **each of the users of the authentication system is assigned an individual** *tv* for a specific hardware and semantic context.

Our heuristic algorithm for determination of the individualized tolerances can be described as follows:

- **For each of digitizer tablet categories** {*Tablet-A, Tablet-B, MIDRES-PQ, HIRES-PQ-Angle, All*}
  - **For each of the semantic classes** {Signature, "8710", Passphrase, "Sauerstoffgefäß", Symbol}
    - **For each user *H*** having biometric data registered with the evaluation system in this tablet / semantic class category
      - **For each** of the $i \in \{1, ..., k\}$ **feature components in** *n*:
        - **For each** of the $es \in ES$ **Enrollment Samples and each of the** $vs \in VS$ **Verification Samples** of *H*, calculate the feature deviation as follows:
          - Determine **minimum and maximum enrollment feature values** $n_{ES,i,Min}$ **and** $n_{ES,i,Max}$ above all *ES* Enrollment Samples
          - Determine center of **average enrollment feature value[10]**:
            $$n_{ES,i,Average} = n_{ES,i,Min} + (n_{ES,i,Max} - n_{ES,i,Min})/2$$
          - Determine **minimum and maximum verification feature values** $n_{VS,i,Min}$ **and** $n_{VS,i,Max}$ above all *VS* Verification Samples
          - Calculate **maximum relative deviation** d_i of the verification feature values $n_{VS,i,Min}$ **and** $n_{VS,i,Max}$ from the average enrollment feature value $n_{ES,i,Average}$:

---

[10] Note that the term average enrollment feature value denotes a helper variable in our algorithm, with no intention to justify the mathematical definition of an average function. In fact, from a mathematical point of view, it should be considered as the center or middle of the feature value interval $[n_{ES,i,Min}, n_{ES,i,Max}]$.

- The **average of all** d_i for each user H **yields the individual tolerance vector component** tv_i
- **Collect feature deviations** for each user H **into individualized Tolerance Vector** $tv_H = (tv_1, ..., tv_k)$

In other words, each of the components of the Tolerance Vector tv_H obtained in this way is a scalar parameter denoting the degree of scatter between average feature values observed during enrollments and extreme feature values observed during verification processes of individual users.

Consequently, in this scenario, an individual parameter vector tv_H is assigned to each of the users of a biometric authentication system for a given environment. This individual parameterization aims to a local compensation of the Intra-Class variability of each user under specific ancillary conditions, which are subject to the natural variability of handwriting-based features and can thus be estimated statistically.

For the analysis of the impact of individualized tv_H, we have chosen to apply separate parameters depending on the two-dimensional classification of the evaluation database with respect to semantic classes and digitizer devices. Thus tv_H have been determined for each user, each semantic class and different sets of digitizer tablets and these configurations, representing well-defined subsets of the test database, have been used in the verification tests which are described later in this section.

Table 6-2 presents an example for such an individual parameterization, the estimated tv_H for one single user (*person index 164*) for tablet category *Tablet-A* and semantic class *Signature*. As typical characteristics, it is noticeable that the variability differs widely between the different parameters, in this case from 0% (for features n_7, n_9, n_{19}-n_{22} and n_{24}) to a maximum scatter of 8217% for n_{32}!

Table 6-2. Individualized *tv* estimation example for user *164*, *Tablet-A* category and semantic class *Signature*

Feature	Name	tv^*	Feature	Name	tv^*	Feature	Name	tv^*
n_1	TTotal	166	n_{24}	Average Azimuth	0	n_{47}	AreaX2	154
n_2	SampleCount	319	n_{25}	AverageAltitude	100	n_{48}	AreaX3	138
n_3	AspectRatio	651	n_{26}	Vx_TN	293	n_{49}	AreaX4	136
n_4	VxAbsolute	237	n_{27}	Vy_TN	500	n_{50}	AreaX5	103
n_5	VyAbsolute	343	n_{28}	TPenUp	132	n_{51}	AreaY1	302
n_6	SegmentCount	100	n_{29}	RatioTPenUp PenDown	137	n_{52}	AreaY2	200
n_7	VxMin	0	n_{30}	NoSamples	319	n_{53}	AreaY3	93

* all *tv* values presented in percent [%]

Table 6-2 (cont.)

Feature	Name	tv^*	Feature	Name	tv^*	Feature	Name	tv^*
n_8	VxMax	137	n_{31}	PathLength	271	n_{54}	AreaY4	190
n_9	VyMin	0	n_{32}	PixelCountR1C1	8217	n_{55}	AreaY5	96
n_{10}	VyMax	209	n_{33}	PixelCountR1C2	101	n_{56}	PenDPress	268
n_{11}	CentroidX	184	n_{34}	PixelCountR1C3	245	n_{57}	PenUPress	487
n_{12}	CentroidY	227	n_{35}	PixelCountR1C4	100	n_{58}	BaselineAngle	140
n_{13}	CentroidDist	202	n_{36}	PixelCountR2C1	3172	n_{59}	HistYZone1	162
n_{14}	MaxPressure	1580	n_{37}	PixelCountR2C2	108	n_{60}	HistYZone2	256
n_{15}	CentroidX_SN	157	n_{38}	PixelCountR2C3	133	n_{61}	HistYZone3	144
n_{16}	CentroidY_SN	177	n_{39}	PixelCountR2C4	285	n_{62}	AreaRatio1	212
n_{17}	Centroid Dist_SN	160	n_{40}	PixelCountR3C1	512	n_{63}	AreaRatio2	169
n_{18}	Centroid Azimuth_SN	286	n_{41}	PixelCountR3C2	188	n_{64}	AreaRatio3	274
n_{19}	MaxAltitude	0	n_{42}	PixelCountR3C3	122	n_{65}	PathRatio1	490
n_{20}	MinAltitude	0	n_{43}	PixelCountR3C4	102	n_{66}	PathRatio2	192
n_{21}	MaxAzimuth	0	n_{44}	IntegralX	164	n_{67}	PathRatio3	198
n_{22}	MinAzimuth	0	n_{45}	IntegralY	145	n_{68}	HistXLeft	125
n_{23}	AvgPressure	823	n_{46}	AreaX1	205	n_{69}	HistXRight	125

* all tv values presented in percent [%]

Due to the large number of different individual tv_H, which have been used throughout our tests, we refrain from including an exhaustive enumeration of all Tolerance Values. In the practice of our evaluation system, these values are determined dynamically from a subset of the test environment, which is disjoint to the data used for the evaluation itself. As this dynamic generation is reproducible, persistent storage of these parameters is not a requirement.

6.4.3 Global Tolerance Vector

The third consideration presumes that some global a-priori knowledge exists about the variability of each of the features n_i , but no localized knowledge about the intra-personal variability. Here, the Tolerance Vector components are estimated by a global analysis of biometric data collected from the users of the biometric authentication system. In the further considerations, we will refer to this category of tv as **Global Tolerance Vectors**.

The strategy chosen for estimating the Global Tolerance Vectors is based on the results of the estimation of individualized Tolerance Vectors (see previous Section 6.4.2) by averaging over all subjects. Consequently, this approach leads to one single Tolerance Vector per semantic class and digitizer tablet category.

Chapter 6

Examples for Tolerance values determined for the semantic class *Signature* for *Tablet-A* digitizer tablet category are given in the following table. Again, we refrain from enumerating all resulting 25 Global Tolerance Vectors, as the result directly from the individual *tv*, introduced in the previous subsection.

Comparing the two different Tolerance Vector examples, it can be seen that the characteristics of a globally estimated parameterization can be quite different from an individual, user-specific setting. For the examples presented in the previous two Tables 6-2 and 6-3, it can be observed that the maximum variation for the individual configuration was 8217% for feature n_{32} (pixel count in first row, first column), whereas the maximum in the global estimation for the same semantic class and digitizer tablet is observed for the same feature, but the value yields to a significantly lower value of 2997.

Table 6-3. Global Tolerance Vector estimation for Tablet-A tablet category and semantic class Signature

Feature	Name	tv_i^*	Feature	Name	tv_i^*	Feature	Name	tv_i^*
n_1	TTotal	729	n_{24}	AverageAzimuth	0	n_{47}	AreaX2	358
n_2	SampleCount	723	n_{25}	AverageAltitude	297	n_{48}	AreaX3	408
n_3	AspectRatio	653	n_{26}	Vx_TN	465	n_{49}	AreaX4	471
n_4	VxAbsolute	926	n_{27}	Vy_TN	534	n_{50}	AreaX5	374
n_5	VyAbsolute	970	n_{28}	TPenUp	523	n_{51}	AreaY1	507
n_6	SegmentCount	77	n_{29}	RatioTPenUpPenDown	393	n_{52}	AreaY2	434
n_7	VxMin	403	n_{30}	NoSamples	723	n_{53}	AreaY3	508
n_8	VxMax	1042	n_{31}	PathLength	628	n_{54}	AreaY4	510
n_9	VyMin	666	n_{32}	PixelCountR1C1	2997	n_{55}	AreaY5	541
n_{10}	VyMax	1118	n_{33}	PixelCountR1C2	332	n_{56}	PenDPress	457
n_{11}	CentroidX	889	n_{34}	PixelCountR1C3	2558	n_{57}	PenUPress	590
n_{12}	CentroidY	710	n_{35}	PixelCountR1C4	205	n_{58}	BaselineAngle	374
n_{13}	CentroidDist	890	n_{36}	PixelCountR2C1	2704	n_{59}	HistYZone1	908
n_{14}	MaxPressure	1552	n_{37}	PixelCountR2C2	2731	n_{60}	HistYZone2	409
n_{15}	CentroidX_SN	383	n_{38}	PixelCountR2C3	2862	n_{61}	HistYZone3	451
n_{16}	CentroidY_SN	582	n_{39}	PixelCountR2C4	857	n_{62}	AreaRatio1	422
n_{17}	CentroidDist_SN	371	n_{40}	PixelCountR3C1	1778	n_{63}	AreaRatio2	360
n_{18}	CentroidAzimuth_SN	488	n_{41}	PixelCountR3C2	1309	n_{64}	AreaRatio3	478
n_{19}	MaxAltitude	0	n_{42}	PixelCountR3C3	947	n_{65}	PathRatio1	535

* all *tv* values presented in percent [%]

Table 6-3 (cont.)

Feature	Name	tv_i^*	Feature	Name	tv_i^*	Feature	Name	tv_i^*
n_{20}	MinAltitude	0	n_{43}	PixelCountR3C4	1917	n_{66}	PathRatio2	358
n_{21}	MaxAzimuth	0	n_{44}	IntegralX	417	n_{67}	PathRatio3	375
n_{22}	MinAzimuth	0	n_{45}	IntegralY	534	n_{68}	HistXLeft	511
n_{23}	AvgPressure	1516	n_{46}	AreaX1	321	n_{69}	HistXRight	511

* all *tv* values presented in percent [%]

6.5 Statistical Outlier Compensation

The concept of the Biometric Hash is based on statistical features of the handwriting and the set of features which is used for the current implementation of the function has been presented in the previous Section 6.2.1. This set of statistical variables has been chosen entirely intuitively, without application of a-priori selection criteria with respect to their suitability. A significant domain in the scientific area of pattern recognition addresses problems of feature evaluation and selection and great number of publications can be found on this subject. The predominant goal of these disciplines is to determine these subsets of features within a given set, that optimize the discriminatory power and Intra-Class variability trade-off for a given classification problem. Based on empirical knowledge about the behavior of a specific system, the feature selection results typically represent parameters estimated on a-priori information, for optimization of classification results.

In the scope of this book, we have refrained from taking this a-priori approach. Rather than that, we assume that for an experimental proof of concept, a basic a-posteriori adjustment of the feature set is adequate to show the principal characteristics and suitability of the Biometric Hash function. System optimization is not a designated goal of this book. However, the potential for future work can be seen and therefore, the following section gives a brief overview on selected related work in the area. In differentiation to existing work, the subsequent Section 6.52 describes our approach, which is based on an elementary analysis of the Intra-Class distribution and masking of features showing statistical outlier characteristics.

6.5.1 Related Work: Feature Selection

Feature evaluation or selection, describing the process of identifying the most relevant features for a classification task, is a research area of broad application. Today, we find a great spectrum of activities and publications in this area. From this variety we have selected those approaches, that appear to show the most relevant basics and are most closely related to our work.

In an early work on feature evaluation techniques, Kittler has discussed methods of feature selection in two categories, measurement and transformed space [Kitt1975]. He has shown that methods of the second category are computationally simple, while theoretically measurement-based approaches lead to superior selection results. However, at the time of his publication, these methods were computationally too complex to be practically applied to real-world classification problems. In more recent work, the hypothesis that feature selection for supervised classification tasks can be accomplished on the basis of Correlation-based Filter Selection (CFS) has been explored by Hall [Hall1999]. Evaluation on twelve natural and six artificial database domains have shown that this selection method increases the classification accuracy of a reduced feature set in many cases and outperforms comparative feature selection algorithms. However, none of the domains in this test set is based on biometric measures related to natural handwriting data. Principal Component Analysis (PCA) is one of the common approaches for the selection of features, but it has been observed, that, for example, data sets having identical variances in each direction, are not well represented [FoPo2003]. Chi and Yan presented an evaluation approach based on an adopted entropy feature measure, which has been applied to a large set of handwritten images of numerals [ChYa1995]. This work has shown good results in detection of relevant features compared to other selection methods. With respect to the feature analysis for the Bio-Hash algorithm, it is required to analyze the trade-off between intra-personal variability of feature measures and the value space, which can be achieved by the resulting hash vectors over a large set of persons.

An exhaustive discussion of the enormous number of approaches that has been published on the subject is beyond the scope of this work. Thus, the work referenced at this point reflects a very limited number of activities, which appear to be of particular relevance in comparison to our approach, which will be presented in the following section.

6.5.2   Compensation by Feature Component Masking

Rather than in related work of feature selection, we take an a-posteriori approach, by defining a new masking procedure to compensate statistical outlier effects by component masking. We describe our new method in this section and develop a masking configuration, which will be used for our further experiments.

During initial tests, which have been conducted for test environments based on samples collected on those digitizer tablets, which provide quantized pressure signals, we have observed that the Hamming Distance distribution of all observed Intra-Class tests shows a distinct peak at a HD value of two. Figure 6-7 illustrates this phenomenon for the test environment defined for the semantic class *Signature* and recorded from the tablet category *HIRES-PQ-Angle*, see Chapter 5, Section 5.6.3.

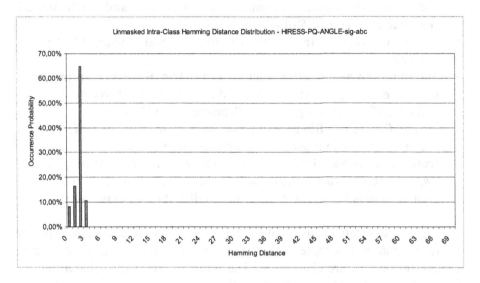

Figure 6-7. Example for an unmasked Hamming Distance distribution

In this case, a well-defined peak may be observed at the specific Hamming Distance of two, having an occurrence probability of approximately 0.65. As these characteristics has been observed for all test sets, including quantized pressure signals (see experimental setup, Chapter 5, Section 5.6.1) and independently of the parameterization of the Tolerance Vector, our explanation hypothesis for this effect are statistical outliers due to systematic noise in some of the feature variables.

In order to verify this hypothesis, a mismatch distribution for each single component of the Biometric Hash is determined according to the following algorithm:

- **For each of digitizer tablet categories** {*Tablet-A*, *Tablet-B*, *MIDRES-PQ*, *HIRES-PQ-Angle*, *All*}
- **For each of the semantic classes** {Signature, "8710", Passphrase, "Sauerstoffgefäß", Symbol}
- **For each user** *H* having biometric data registered with the evaluation system in this tablet / semantic class category **and each set of enrollment samples** *ES* of this user
- Determine **Interval Matrix** *IM* of *H* from *ES* and individual Tolerance Vector tv_H
- Determine the **set of all authentic Biometric Hash vector** instances $b_{Authentic} \in B_{Authentic}$ by calculation of the Biometric Hash vectors for each of the Verification Samples $vs \in VS$ belonging to *H* and *IM*
- Set the **Reference Biometric Hash** $b_{Reference}$ to the value of the first vector of maximum number of occurrences in $B_{Authentic}$.
- **Protocol the Intra-Class deviation occurrences** of each of the $i \in \{1, \ldots, k\}$ **Biometric Hash vector components** b_i of each of the Biometric Hash instances $b_{Authentic} \in B_{Authentic}$ **into a distribution diagram**

That is, we statistically analyze the probability of deviation between reference and test sample, separately for each Biometric Hash vector component on an Intra-class focus. The result of our analysis based on the four test environments for semantic class *Signature* and tablet categories *MIDRES-PQ*, *Tablet-B*, *Tablet-A* and *HIRES-PQ* are presented as a distribution diagram in Figure 6-8.

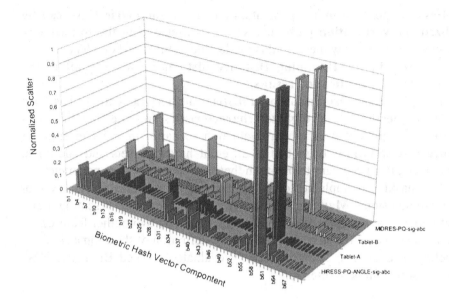

Figure 6-8. Deviation distribution by component for four different test sets, semantic class
Signature

The diagram visualizes the per-component scatter for each of the $i \in \{1,$ ..., $k\}$ hash vector components b_i (on the abscissa in Figure 6-8), observed during Intra-Class tests based on the four different test environments. Occurrence probabilities are normalized to the maximum value of all occurrences for each test separately and are plotted on the ordinate axis. Among the four distributions one common pattern becomes visually obvious: features n_{56} (*PenDPress, average pen-down pressure*) and n_{57} (*PenUPress, average pen-up pressure*) significantly account for the maximum scatter in all four test cases.

As this effect has been observed for all other semantic classes as well as for all tablet categories and furthermore, no other features show a similar degree of correlation between the test sets, we classify these two features as **systematic statistical outliers**. From these observations it can be concluded that the two outlier features are responsible for the peak shift illustrated in Figure 6-7 and thus they should be excluded from our feature set relevant for the Biometric Hash generation. For the implementation of this exclusion, rather than a reduction of the feature parameter set from the initial set presented in Table 6-1, we have chosen to mask out these components for all further evaluations of the key generation mode in this chapter. Masking is required mainly due to two reasons:

Besides operation in key generation mode, the **Biometric Hash can be utilized for verification** purposes, which is discussed in the forthcoming Chapter 7. As we show there, in this mode, due to the threshold dependency, **peak offsets in the Hamming Distance distribution do not affect the accuracy of the verification results.**

This particular **observation of statistical outliers in features** has been made for **specific sets of digitizer characteristics and the specific set of feature parameters** used in our evaluation scenario. In order to **support future re-evaluations** on potential different hardware sets and additional parameters, it is necessary to maintain these features as system parameters.

The masking is implemented by multiplying each Biometric Hash vector by a k-dimensional **Masking Vector** $mv=(mv_1, \ ... \ ,mv_k)$, representing a unit vector except at the component indices related to the two outlier features, n_{56} and n_{57}. Consequently, in supplement to the definition of the Biometric Hash function in Section 6.2, the effectively evaluated masked Biometric Hash vector b_{Masked} can be written to:

$$b_{Masked} = b * mv, \hspace{4cm} (6\text{-}13)$$

with $mv_i=1$ for all $i \in \{1, \ ..., \ 55, \ 58, \ ..., \ k\}$, $mv_i=0$ for all $i \in \{56, 57\}$

Note that the test results presented in this chapter are entirely based on the masked Biometric Hash, whereas the discussions on the verification mode in the following chapter will refer to the unmasked values.

In order to conclude the effects of our compensation by feature masking, we have repeated the tests introduced in the beginning of this section with masked versions of the Biometric Hash. The following Figure 6-9 illustrates the effects of the statistical outlier compensation for the same test set as shown in Figure 6-7.

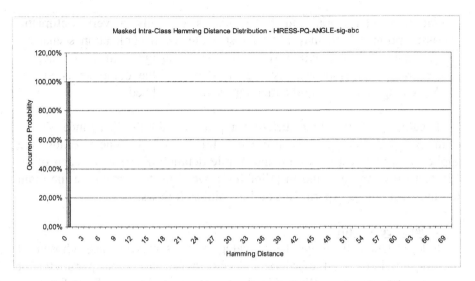

Figure 6-9. Masked Hamming Distance (HD) distribution, all Intra-Class hashes having
HD=0

6.6   Test Results

Basis of the Biometric Hash evaluation in key generation mode have
been tests performed using the test methodology described in Chapter 5,
Section 5.6, the Hamming-Distance metrics, as defined in Section 6.3.1 of
this chapter and the evaluation data sets described in Section 5.5.5 of
Chapter 5. As stated in Section 6.4, two approaches can be taken with
respect to the information source for the estimation of Tolerance Vector
parameters:

- In the **pessimistic estimation** approach, Tolerance Vectors are estimated
  on entirely disjoint data. For this purpose, enrollment and verification
  data of each of the 25 test environments have been split into two
  respective subsets of equal size, $ES_{Estimation}$, $ES_{Evaluation}$, $VS_{Estimation}$ and
  $VS_{Evaluation}$ in such way, that uniform distributions of the number of
  enrollment and verification samples are preserved for each subject in the
  dataset. This estimation approach ensures that no correlation between
  the parameterization and the test data exists; they are statistically
  independent.
- In the **optimistic estimation**, we assume that entire system information
  can be applied for the Tolerance Vector estimation, thus the same
  enrollment and verification data sets from the test environments are used

for parameterization and test. This is certainly a very optimistic assumption, which may not be justifiable in all application scenarios. However, this evaluation shall give some insights, to which degree accuracy may improved by the algorithm, if the complete empirical knowledge within an authentication system is utilized.

Together with the three different approaches for the Tolerance Vector estimation as discussed in Section 6.4, a total of five parameterizations are applied to all 25 test environments. While detailed diagrams of each of all 125 test runs can be found in [Viel2004], we want to summarize the main findings from these experiments at this point as follows:

Tolerance Vector
Independently from the tablet category or semantic class chosen, it becomes obvious, that the Tolerance Vector *tv* is a mandatory parameter for the generation of robust Biometric Hashes of authentic users. Even for those tests, that have been conducted on tablet categories of unique physical characteristics (*Tablet-A*, *Tablet-B*), authentic users were able to reproduce their Biometric Hash reference values in only 5-10% (False-Generation-Rate of 90-95%) of cases, if the Tolerance Vector was set to zero. With the inclusion of Tolerance values, independent of the estimation scope of these, a significant decrease in the False-Generation rates can be observed.

The two Figures 6-10 and 6-11 exemplify the effect of decrease in False-Generation rates by presenting the experimental results of the Biometric Hash distribution for the tablet category *HIRES-PQ-ANGLE*, semantic class *Symbol*. Based on identical test sets, Figure 6-10 shows the Hamming Distance distribution for the zero-Tolerance Vector configuration, whereas the distribution for individualized *tv* in an optimistic scenario is presented in Figure 6-11.

For simplification, in both charts only the Intra-class Hamming Distance (solid gray bar), together with the Random Forgery distance distribution (black square symbols "■") are plotted. In the first graph shown in Figure 6-10, the solid gray bar at a Hamming Distance equal to zero in the first diagram shows, a correct generation of stable Biometric Hash vectors by authentic users was achieved in only 6% of cases, thus a False-Generation rate of 94% was observed for authentic persons. By applying individually determined Tolerance Vectors, the correct hash generation rate of authentic users could be improved drastically. Figure 6-11 illustrates the effect for this particular example. With a factorization of *1.0*, the algorithm yields a False-Generation rate of 13% at a point, where no hash collisions have been observed. Note that the Inter-Class distribution (denoted in this figure by the graph marked by square symbols) indicates that the Inter-Class discriminatory power in this example leaves the potential for a parameterization towards even higher accuracy, as the closest hash values of any two different writers still expose Hamming Distances of 6. However exploitation of this optimization potential shall not be part of our analysis in this book.

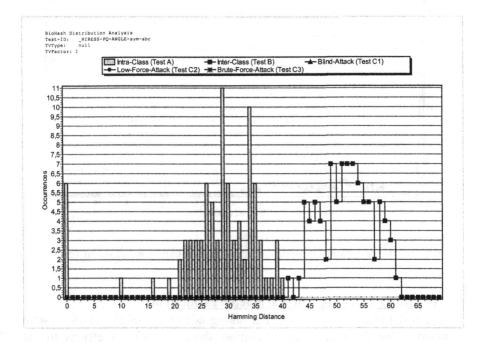

Figure 6-10. Correct Biometric Hash generations, non-parameterized

In both parameterizations we observe an outstanding discriminatory power, allowing to completely separating the two classes of authentic samples (*Intra-Class* graph, gray bar) from Random Forgeries (*Inter-Class* graph marked by squares).

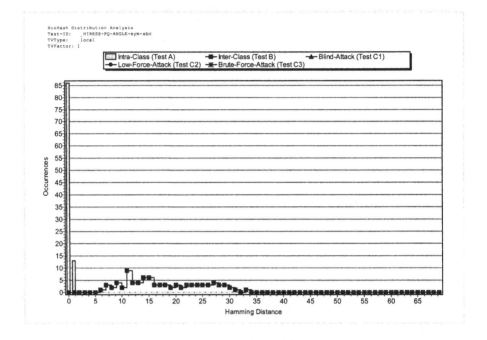

Figure 6-11. Correct Biometric Hash generations, parameterized by individual Tolerance Vector

Pessimistic vs. Optimistic Parameter Estimation

The test results have shown that taking advantage of the entire system knowledge for the parameter estimation shows significant effects to the accuracy of hash value generation. If confined at similar levels of accuracy in generating authentic Biometric Hash values, parameterizations based on estimations of the entire population possess a higher capability to discriminate forgeries from authentic writing samples. This effect is illustrated in the following two figures (Figures 6-12 and 6-13) for experimental scenario of tablet category *Table-A*, semantic class *"8710"*:

The two different distribution diagrams in Figures 6-12 and 6-13 show a significant decrease in the success probability of forgeries. Especially for the Low-Force forgery class (see *Low-Force Attack* graph marked by the dot symbols "●" in both diagrams), the success rate for generating the Biometric Hash values of authentic users was reduced by half from 15% (in Figure 6-12) to approximately 7% (in Figure 6-13). This tendency was observed throughout for the great majority of test results.

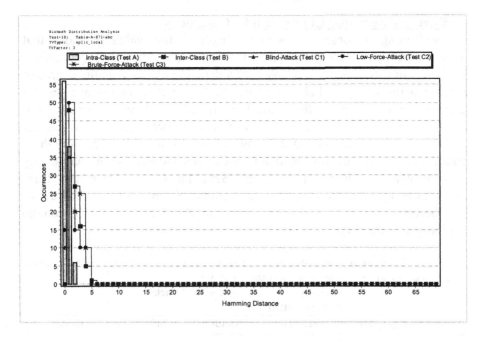

Figure 6-12. Pessimistic Tolerance Vector configuration results

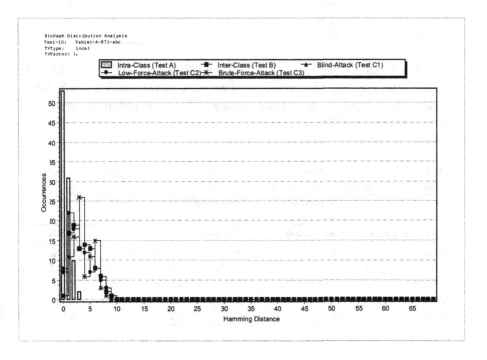

Figure 6-13. Optimistic Tolerance Vector configuration results

Effects of Semantic Classes, Tablet Categories
Confirming our observations from Chapter 5, the evaluation shows that
all semantic classes are potentially suitable for Biometric Hash generation.
However, like in Chapter 5, we observe a dependency between the degree of
heterogeneity of physical characteristics in the tablet set and error rates at a
given operating point of the algorithm. In Table 6-4, we summarize our
results for all five tablet categories. In terms of correct generation rate for
authentic users and forgery success rates of attacks, it can be seen from these
figures, that results in successful authentications and successful attacks vary
significantly, e.g. between 22% and 82% for correct Biometric Hash
generations by authentic subjects (see column "Correct BH" in Table 6-4)
and between 0% and 35.5% for successful Blind Forgeries (see column
"Blind" in Table 6-4).

Table 6-4. Summary of successful authentications vs. attacks, semantic class *Signature*,
pessimistic individual *tv* estimation, factorization *tf=3.0*

| Tablet Category ID | Successful Authentications | Successful Attacks | | | |
	Correct BH	Random	Blind	Low	Brute
All	41 %	1 %	7.5 %	16 %	14 %
Tablet-A	51.5 %	5.5 %	0 %	0 %	18 %
HIRES-PQ-Angle	60 %	0 %	n/a	n/a	0 %
MIDRES-PQ	22 %	1 %	0 %	n/a	3 %
Tablet-B	82 %	7 %	35.5 %	n/a	19 %

With respect to the sensitivity of the Biometric Hash algorithm to
semantic classes, we observe a smaller dependency within each tablet
category. For example, the tablet category *Tablet-B* produces generation
results as shown in Table 6-5.

Table 6-5. Successful authentications vs. attacks, each semantic class, pessimistic individual
tv estimation, factorization *tf=3.0*, tablet category *Tablet-B*

| Semantic Class | Successful Authentications | Successful Attacks | | | |
	Correct BH	Random	Blind	Low	Brute
Signature	82 %	7 %	35.5 %	n/a	19 %
"Sauerstoffgefäß"	66,5 %	5.5 %	n/a	10.5 %	11.5 %
"8710"	57 %	5 %	n/a	34 %	31.5 %
Passphrase	48 %	1 %	11 %	40 %	13 %
Symbol	55 %	0 %	n/a	n/a	n/a

Here, we observe the tendency, that the absolute operating point varies between correct generation rates of 55% and 82% (see column "Correct BH" in Table 6-5), at forgery success rates, for example, of Random forgery attacks, between 0% and 7% (see column "Random" in Table 6-5). Furthermore, we find the two ratio categories in transitive order; we thus assume that the dependency between semantic classes and accuracy of Biometric Hash generation is much less distinctive than the tablet category dependency.

There are two main conclusions of this analysis with respect to tablet categories and semantic classes. Firstly, to find a reasonable operating point for the Biometric Hash generation, the estimation of Tolerance Vector settings must be considered under the constraints of tablet category and semantic class. The additional Tolerance Vector factorization by the term *tf* allows for tuning at a specific accuracy either with respect to correctly generated authentic hash values or with respect to successful attacks.

The second conclusion, which we derive from the impact of different settings in the global *tf* parameter, is a tendency of super proportional increase of attack success rates. This particularly appears to happen, if the Tolerance Factor *tf* is configured such way, that it allows improvements in correct Biometric Hash generation probabilities in the area of 40% or higher. Thus for applications requiring low key collision probabilities, additional provisions have to be made, in order to limit the error probability.

Tolerance Vector Factorization

We have shown that the introduction of a Tolerance Vector *tv* is a suitable means to adjust the operating point of the Biometric Hash algorithm. In analogy to the threshold configuration in biometric verification systems, this term allows tuning of the False-Generation vs. False-Non-Generation error characteristics. As shown in the analysis of tablet category and semantic class dependency, the Tolerance Vector is a mandatory parameter for the Biometric Hash generation, which has to be determined with respect to these categories and configured in the system in an a-priori manner.

In conclusion, the test results are encouraging and show that the Biometric Hash algorithm is suitable for key generation applications. Although with the effects of the system parameterization to the False-Generation Rates we observe a trade-off problem similar to the compromise between False-Non-Matches and False-Matches known from biometric user verifications systems, we are able to configure the system in such way that reasonable accuracy can be achieved.

6.7   Summary

The Biometric Hash function introduced in this chapter is conceptually based on two main process steps: firstly, a **set** of predefined **statistical features** is extracted from the various sampled signal representations of the biometric authentication information into a feature vector *n*. Secondly, from the feature vector, the Biometric Hash vector is determined by an **interval mapping function**, parameterized by the parameters, Interval Matrix *IM,* a global tolerance factor *tf* and a vector of statistical features extracted from an actual handwriting verification sample, *vs.* We have suggested a substantial set of 69 statistical features (see Table 6-1), based on which we have discussed approaches of how to obtain settings for the Interval Matrix parameter by **a-priori analysis** of empirical data. Furthermore, we have revealed **statistical outlier effects** in some of the features and described a pragmatic approach to compensation of these effects. Evaluation results have been presented based on extensive tests by applying the methodology described in the previous chapter.

In view of our design objectives we can summarize the following observations. Due to the statistical nature of the Biometric Hash and the types of features chosen, the temporal and structural information of the sequences of the handwriting process is heavily suppressed. Thus, from the data representation of a Biometric Hash, a **reproduction** of the original handwriting signals is **infeasible** and a scanning approach by **systematic generation** of all possible originals requires computational efforts which grow exponentially with the dimensionality of the Biometric Hash vector and thus can be assumed as **computationally hard**. Consequently, we conclude that the visual appearance of original writing traces cannot be reverse engineered from the Biometric Hash, thus the proposed method can ensure **anonymity** for the user.

One of the most important motivations for our work on the Biometric Hash was the goal to find a method to derive **cryptographic keys** from the biometric authentication signals. The test results have shown, that this can be achieved with error likelihoods, which are correlated to the two factors of **tablet category** and **semantic class**. From our test results, we conclude that the **highest stability** in generation of correct hash values can be achieved, if **only digitizer tablets of one specific type** are utilized, whereas a cross-tablet generation leads to a higher degree of false generations. While in our evaluation scenario, we observe the highest accuracy for the semantics of *Signature*, both test results of this and the previous chapter indicate that other semantic classes are suitable as well, but may require a different parameterization during the Interval Matrix determination.

By definition of the number and types of the statistical features to be utilized for the Biometric Hash generation, the **dimensionality** of the hash vector can be scaled and adjusted to potential **capacity constraints**. In our evaluation scenario, with a dimensionality of $k=69$ for the Biometric Hash, we can achieve a maximum reference data size of 552 Bytes, if the components of the Interval Matrix (IM) are coded as 4 Byte Integer variables. In [Conc2002], we were able to prototypically show that this Biometric Hash enables storage on Smartcard devices. We are confident, that feature set dimensionality can be further reduced for these application scenarios requiring small reference sizes, by optimization of the coding of the Interval Matrix variables. Thus reference storage on future technology for mass markets, e.g. devices like low-cost RFID tags, appears to be viable.

Consequently, the result of the Biometric Hash algorithm yields **very compact data**, a vector of fixed dimensionality and non-negative Integer values. It therefore can be represented by an array of integer values. For further computational processing in authentication systems, this allows for very **efficient mathematical methods**. For example, to derive a cryptographic key of a size other than the dimensionality of the vector, either simple mathematical hash functions can be applied or the target key size can be achieved by padding. The positive impact of this low computational complexity leaves potential for an additional design goal besides key generation. This aspect will be discussed in detail in the following Chapter 7.

6.8 Notations and Abbreviations

The following Table 6-6 summarizes all notations and abbreviations introduced in this Chapter 6 in alphabetical order.

Table 6-6. Summary of notations and abbreviations introduced in Chapter 6

Designator	Name	Description	Introduced in
b	Biometric Hash Vector	Biometric Hash Vector from a set of $b \in B$, where each b is a vector of dimensionality k: $b=(b_1, \ldots ,b_k)$	Chapter 6
$CountMax(a(t))$	Sample Count Function	Determines the number of local maxima in a sampled signal representation given as argument	Section 6.2.1
$CryptoHash$	Cryptographic Hash Function	Cryptographic Hash Function, which takes a message of arbitrary size as argument and returns a cryptographic hash (or digest) value of pre-defined output size. Example Algorithms: MD2, MD4, MD5, SHA	Chapter 6

Table 6-6 (cont.)

Designator	Name	Description	Introduced in
CryptoSign	Cryptographic Signature Function	Cryptographic Signature Function, which takes two arguments: a *Hash* or digest of the Message *Msg* to be signed and the private key of an user *H*, $PrivateKey_H$. Returns the cryptographic signature *Sig*.	Chapter 6
CryptoVerify	Cryptographic Verification Function	Cryptographic Verification Function, which takes two arguments: a digital signature *Sig* and the public key of an user *H*, $PublicKey_H$. Retrieves *Hash* value from *Sig*	Chapter 6
ΔI	Interval Length Vector	k-dimensional Vector holding Interval Lengths as part of *IM*: $\Delta I=(\Delta I_1, \dots , \Delta I_k)$, $IM=(\Delta I, \Omega)$	Section 6.2.3
d_i	Maximum Relative Feature Component Deviation	Helper variable for the Tolerance Value estimation algorithm for storing the maximum relative deviation d_i of the verification feature values $n_{VS,i,Min}$ and $n_{VS,i,Max}$ from the average enrollment feature value $n_{ES,i,Average}$: $$d_i = MAX\left(\left\| \frac{n_{ES,i,Average} - n_{VS,i,Min}}{n_{ES,i,Average} - n_{ES,i,Min}} \right\|, \left\| \frac{n_{ES,i,Average} - n_{VS,i,Max}}{n_{ES,i,Average} - n_{ES,i,Max}} \right\| \right)$$	Section 6.4.2
Hash	Cryptographic Hash Value	Cryptographic Hash Value of an original message	Chapter 6
$Hash^*$	Cryptographic Hash Value	Cryptographic Hash Value retrieved from a cryptographic signature	Chapter 6
IM	Interval Matrix	The Interval Matrix *IM* is a helper function for the interval mapping performed by the Biometric Hash function. It is defined as $IM=(\Delta I, \Omega)$, consequently, *IM* is of dimension of $k \times 2$.	Section 6.2.3
m	Biometric Hash Function	Function from the set of Biometric Hash functions $m \in M$, which maps two arguments from the set of authentication information *A* and complementary information *C* to the set of Biometric Hash vectors $b \in B$, as per the following equation: $m \in M, m: A \times C \to B$	Chapter 6

Table 6-6 (cont.)

Designator	Name	Description	Introduced in
m_{Scalar}	Scalar Biometric Hash Function	Scalar Biometric Hash function m_{Scalar}, for mapping of each of the components n_i of a feature vector n to the corresponding component of a Biometric Hash vector, b_i : $$m_{Scalar}(n_i, \Delta I_i, \Omega_i) = \left\lfloor \frac{(n_i - \Omega_i)}{\Delta I_i} \right\rfloor$$	Section 6.2.5
MAC	Message Authentication Code	Key-dependent cryptographic hash function	Chapter 6
MAX	Component-wise Maximum Vector Function	Function MAX takes a set of k-dimensional vectors as argument and returns a k-dimensional vector representing the maximum for each component index over the argument	Section 6.2.3
$MaxVal(a(t))$	Maximum Sample Value Function	Determines the absolute maximum sample value from the discrete sampling points of a sampled signal representation given as argument	Section 6.2.1
MIN	Component-wise Minimum Vector Function	Function MIN takes a set of k-dimensional vectors as argument and returns a k-dimensional vector representing the minimum for each component index over the argument	Section 6.2.3
$MinVal(a(t))$	Minimum Sample Value Function	Determines the absolute minimum sample value from the discrete sampling points of a sampled signal representation given as argument	Section 6.2.1
MOD	Component-wise Vector Modulo Operation	MOD denotes the component-wise modulo operation between two k-dimensional vector operands, i.e. it yields one k-dimensional vector consisting of components obtained by the scalar modulo operation between each of vector components left and right of the operator MOD	Section 6.2.3
Msg	Message	A message or data to be cryptographically signed	Chapter 6
Msg_{Signed}	Signed Message	The signed Message, i.e. the digital signature concatenated to the original message or data	Chapter 6

Table 6-6 (cont.)

Designator	Name	Description	Introduced in
mv	Masking Vector	Masking Vector $mv=(mv_1, \ldots ,mv_k)$, for determination of a masked Biometric Hash vector b_{Masked} by suppressing at specific component indices: $b_{Masked} = b * mv$, with $mv_i \in \{0,1\}$, $i \in \{1, \ldots ,k\}$	Section 6.5.2
n	Statistical Feature Vector	Describes a k-dimensional vector of values retrieved by statistical analysis of biometric signals: $n=(n_1, \ldots ,n_k)$	Section 6.2.1
$\{n^{(1)}, \ldots, n^{(e)}\}$	Set of Statistical Feature Vectors	Describes a *set of e statistical feature vectors of type n.* Components of each of the vectors are denoted by lower indices, i.e.: $$\{n^{(1)}, ..., n^{(e)}\} = \left\{ \begin{pmatrix} n_1^{(1)} \\ ... \\ n_k^{(1)} \end{pmatrix}, ..., \begin{pmatrix} n_1^{(e)} \\ ... \\ n_k^{(e)} \end{pmatrix} \right\}$$	Section 6.2.3
Ω	Interval Length Vector	k-dimensional Vector holding Interval Offsets as part of *IM*: $\Omega=(\Omega_1, \ldots , \Omega_k)$, $IM=(\Delta I, \Omega)$	Section 6
$PrivateKey_H$	Private Key for Digital Signature	Private key of a key pair for digital signatures based on asymmetric cryptographic (RSA encryption)	Chapter 6
$PublicKey_H$	Public Key for Digital Signature	Public key of a key pair for digital signatures based on asymmetric cryptographic (RSA encryption)	Chapter 6
tf	Tolerance Factor	Tolerance Factor tf represents a scalar term for global weighting of the tolerance intervals of all features	Section 6.2.3
$T_{Total}(a(t))$	Total Writing Time Function	Function T_{Total} determines the total duration of a handwriting process from a sampled signal representation given as argument	Section 6.2.1
tv	Tolerance Vector	Tolerance Vector tv is a vector of dimensionality k with tv_i, $i \in \{1, \ldots, k\}$ and denotes the degree of scatter which is tolerated for each components of a statistical feature vector $n=(n_1, \ldots , n_k)$ to map to one unique component value by a Biometric Hash function, m	Section 6.2.3

Chapter 7

USER VERIFICATION
Biometric Hash: From Key Generation to User Verification

7.   USER VERIFICATION

In the previous chapter, the Biometric Hash function has been introduced as a method to generate individual hash values based on biometric handwriting signals of subjects. It has been shown that the concept is appropriate to generate stable intra-personal values with an inter-personal discriminatory power of a specific steadiness, which is mainly dependent on the system parameterization and the hardware classes for the digitizer tablets. Due to the stability of the generated hash values, this approach is relevant to a number of applications, as it allows the usage of cryptographic methods by providing means for key generation. Furthermore, it has been shown that the suggested approach introduces solutions for further open problems in biometric user authentication. It overcomes security concerns for storage of complementary information for the users, due to the high computational complexity for reconstruction of the original biometric signals from the biometric references represented by Interval Matrices. Also, the concept of Biometric Hash allows efficient calculation of the feature values due to their statistical nature and the low dimensionality leads to effectively small capacity requirements for the stored references.

In view of the challenges in handwriting-based user authentication highlighted in Chapter 4, the Biometric Hash, as presented in Chapter 6, thus first addresses the requirement for a direct key generation from the biometric modality and secondly provides techniques to overcome problems of reference storage. In this chapter, our intention is to inherit these positive properties of the Biometric Hash algorithm in view of the problem of reference storage, for applications requiring biometric user verification rather than the generation of cryptographic keys. Our goal is to find a biometric authentication approach based on threshold-based **handwriting verification**, utilizing **compact reference information** of low complexity, thus allowing for deposition on **low capacity storage devices** and execution of the **comparison algorithms on small computer devices** such as handhelds or smart cards. Furthermore, we want to adopt a data representation of the complementary information C of the reference template from the Biometric Hash algorithm for key generation from Chapter 6, which makes it **computationally hard to estimate the original handwriting signals from the reference data**. The authentication algorithm is **evaluated under different operational conditions** with respect to **tablet categories** and **semantic classes**, as introduced in Chapter 5, with the goal of a conclusion, to which degree accuracy of the approach depends on these environments.

Our aim is to present and evaluate an authentication scheme, which operates in **verification mode**. The output result of this verification mode is quite different from the key generation, with a Boolean result parameterized by a **threshold value T rather than a Biometric Hash vector b** of dimensionality k in the key generation mode. Therefore, a definition of this additional verification mode of the Biometric Hash function will be given in this section, which bases on the basic key generation approach presented in the previous chapter. Furthermore, a specific test metric for this operation mode is given and test results are determined by re-applying our experimental setup and the scenarios from Chapter 5, Section 5.6. These test results are discussed based on common evaluation result representations for biometric authentication systems: threshold-based error rate diagrams, as already used in the discussion of our experimental results in Chapter 5.

Analysis of threshold-based verification test results is a well-established method to examine the accuracy of biometric systems in general, as it allows empirical conclusions about the system's accuracy (see Section 2.4 of Chapter 2). However, it does not allow conclusions about the complexity for potential attackers having access to components of the authentication system. In Chapter 4, Section 4.3, we have shown, that among others, the possibility of **scanning, i.e. systematically testing a value range for the authentication information**, is one possible method, which can utilized to attempt malicious verification. In cases where an attacker has access to the information channel between a subject H and an authentication system U, he or she may take the same approach in case of biometric user verification. **Similarly to dictionary-based password attacks** to knowledge-based authentication systems, the complexity of such attacks decreases significantly with the knowledge of the key space distribution. In order to have an **estimator for the complexity of such an attack** to the Biometric Hash for user verification, we expand our discussions on an **entropy estimation approach**, present selected examples of this entropy evaluation and finally derive conclusions with respect to the scanning complexity.

This chapter is organized as follows: in the following Section 7.1 we describe the principle of how to use the Biometric Hash function for a verification problem, by introducing a distance measure and a threshold-based decision component. Closely relating to the previous chapter, we then describe the evaluation metric chosen for the Biometric Hash in verification mode in Section 7.2, followed by remarks on the system parameterization in Section 7.3. Section 7.4 contains a comprehensive discussion of the test results in selected configurations of tablet categories and semantic classes. An estimation technique for the effective key space of Biometric Hashes is introduced in Section 7.5, along with an exemplary calculation from our database to assess the theoretical efforts of a scanning attack. Finally, in the Section 7.6, we summarize the insights of this chapter, followed by a last section, providing a summary of notations and abbreviations introduced in this chapter in Section 7.7

7.1   From Key Generation to User Authentication

Besides the direct generation of keys from biometrics, for use, for example, by cryptographic applications as shown in the previous chapter, user authentication by using a distance measure can be a desirable goal. In this category, biometric user verification is the most common method, describing the automated, threshold-based approval or disapproval of a subject's declared identity as the authentication process, see Section 2.4.2 of Chapter 2.

In the previous chapter, we have presented a detailed discussion on the Biometric Hash designed for generation of keys, which may be applied for cryptographic solutions. Thus the design goal in Chapter 6 is the direct generation of keys from handwriting-based biometric signals. Formally and in view of our general model for authentication systems from Chapter 4, this operation mode can be described as:

Direct generation of a k-dimensional Biometric Hash vector $b=(b_1, ..., b_k) \in B$ from the authentication information input A and the complementary information C by a set of Biometric Hash functions $m \in M$. The resulting Biometric Hash vector aims to represent a collision free mapping of biometric measures of different users and thus is qualified for individual key generation. As defined in Chapter 6, the Biometric Hash function can be formalized as $m \in M, m: A \times C \rightarrow B$ and in Section 6.2.5, we have introduced an implementation of such functions in the specific characteristics *m(n,IM)*, where *n* instantiates Authentication Information *A* in form of a statistical feature vector and *IM* instantiates *C* in form of an Interval Matrix.

Given this method for direct key generation, we define an additional and complementary authentication operation mode for the Biometric Hash, which can be seen as an extension to the key generation process. The concept for this adaptation is based on the consideration to determine a **reference value for the Biometric Hash value** b_{Ref} of each subject at the time of enrollment. At time of authentication, an actually calculated Biometric Hash value is then compared against the stored reference value and only if a certain similarity between reference and actual vector is achieved, the user gets authenticated. Formally, we describe this verification operation mode for the Biometric Hash as follows:

Authentication by some **verification** function $l \in L$, $l:A \times C^{*} \rightarrow \{true,$ *false}*, as shown in Chapter 4: in this mode, the **each instance of the full reference information** $c^{*} \in C^{*}$ is a collection **composed** of the **implementation of** complementary information $c \in C$ **by an Interval Matrix** *IM*, as defined in Chapter 6, Section 6.2.3, **supplemented by a reference Biometric Hash value** b_{Ref} , which has been obtained at time of enrollment: $c^{*} = \{IM, b_{Ref}\}$. An authentication process *l* can then be modeled as Biometric Hash calculation followed by a verification function, see the following formalization:

$$Let\ a\ be\ represented\ by\ n$$

$$Let\ c\ be\ represented\ by\ IM$$

$$Let\ c^{*}be\ represented\ by\ \{IM, b_{Ref}\}\ , thus\ C \subseteq C^{*} \qquad (7\text{-}1)$$

$$Let\ b\ be\ implemented\ by\ the\ Biometric\ Hash\ function\ m(n,IM)$$

$$l \in L, l:A \times C^{*} \rightarrow \begin{cases} true, if\ m(n,IM)\ is\ similar\ to\ b_{Ref} \\ false\ otherwise \end{cases}$$

Apparently, the authentication function *l* can be modeled by two subsequent processes, instantiating a hash generation function *m* and a similarity decision. In this case, the final result of *l* is determined by a comparison function, which estimates if two instances of a Biometric Hash *m(n,IM)* (resulting from the actual authentication information *A*) and b_{Ref} (as part of the complementary information C^{*}) are similar enough to be considered of the same origin, thus yielding to a positive authentication or not. As pointed out in the definition of another experimental metric in Chapter 5, Section 5.6.2, the similarity between two terms can be determined by a general distance function δ and a threshold-based decision criterion, in comparison to some upper bound T. In our particular algorithm, the threshold value of T is a global system parameter and with the definition of a vector distance function δ_{Vector}, which yields a scalar distance value between two vectors of identical dimensionality, we can write l to:

$$l(A, C^*) = \begin{cases} true, if\ \delta_{Vector}(m(n, IM), b_{Ref}) \leq T \\ false, otherwise \end{cases} \tag{7-2}$$

The authentication function l in our system layout is a function of three values: the result of a Biometric Hash function m, b_{Ref} and a global decision threshold T. For the selection of the distance measure function δ_{Vector}, a wide spectrum of mathematical functions exists. Written in our notation for a distance measure between two k-dimensional Biometric Hash vectors b and b_{Ref}, we can limit to the most commonly used for biometric verification:

- **p-Minkowski Metrics** (special cases are *City-Block Distance* for p=1 and *Euclidean Distance* for p=2), see for example [Tous2004]:

$$\delta_{p-Minkowski}(b, b_{Ref}) = \left(\sum_{i=1}^{k} |b_i - b_{Ref,i}|^p \right)^{\frac{1}{p}}, \tag{7-3}$$

thus for $p=1$ the **City-Block** (or Manhattan-Taxi) **Distance**:

$$\delta_{1-Minkowski}(b, b_{Ref}) = \sum_{i=1}^{k} |b_i - b_{Ref,i}| \tag{7-4}$$

and for $p=2$ the **Euclidean Distance**:

$$\delta_{2-Minkowski}(b, b_{Ref}) = \sqrt{\sum_{i=1}^{k} |b_i - b_{Ref,i}|^2} \tag{7-5}$$

- **Mahalanobis Distance** (see e.g. [WiSV2003]):

$$\delta_{Mahalanobis}(b, b_{Ref}) = \sqrt{(b - b_{Ref})V^{-1}(b - b_{Ref})'} \tag{7-6}$$

with V^{-1} being the sample covariance matrix of all authentic Biometric Hash values.

- **Hamming Distance (HD)** (e.g. [Daug1993])

$$\delta_{Hamming}(b, b_{Ref}) = HD(b, b_{Ref}) = \frac{\#(b_i \neq b_{Ref,i})}{k}, \qquad (7\text{-}7)$$

where $\#(b_i \neq b_{Ref,i})$ denotes the count function of non-identical value for each of the $i \in \{1, ..., k\}$ vector components.

- **Levensthein Distance** has been adapted from an original string comparison function [Leve1966] to a distance measure between biometric features in. The basic idea behind the Levensthein Distance is to transform one sequence of code words from to another under the constraint of cost minimization of the three modification operations insert, delete and replace. Details of the adapted algorithm can be found in [ScVD2004].

- ...

Due to the initial goal of the Biometric Hash approach, the robust and collision-free mapping of statistical features into a vector space, we expect rather high stability for each of the vector components in this scenario. At the same time, in the verification scenario, the Biometric Hash vector can be considered as a feature vector of higher dimensionality and for similar problems, the Hamming Distance function has already been applied successfully [Daug1993]. Therefore and also due to its computational low complexity, we apply the Hamming Distance function in our verification scenario as well. This decision can be justified, because at this point we do not consider optimization of the concept, but want to prove the general feasibility of the approach.

A block diagram differentiating the two operation modes for authentication based on Biometric Hashes is presented in Figure 7-1.

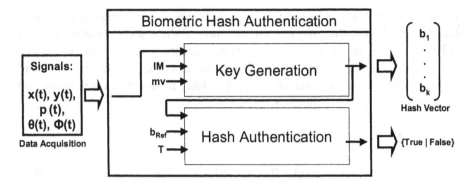

Figure 7-1. Block diagram of the key generation versus verification mode

For operation in key generation mode, the two parameters Interval Matrix (*IM*) and Masking Vector (*mv*) are required in addition to the biometric signals. The result of this operation is the *k*-dimensional Biometric Hash vector, as introduced in Chapter 6. In order to utilize the authentication functionality, the actual Biometric Hash vector, being the result of the key generation process, is fed into the secondary optional process of hash authentication. This process requires two additional parameters: the reference Biometric Hash vector b_{Ref} and the decision threshold T. The system output will be a binary value denoting if the claimed identity of the subject is confirmed or not.

Apparently, the concept of a Biometric Hash is suitable in theory to serve in both modes. However, there is a significant difference with respect to the demands of the expected output results of the two configurations. In authentication mode, the introduction of a threshold value T allows for the adjustment of the operating point of the authentication system at time of verification. Depending on the application requirements, the system may be configured towards higher security with respect to false acceptances, taking into account higher false-rejections or vice versa, as discussed in Chapter 2, Section 2.4.4 in the context of general aspects of biometric authentication systems. Independently of the enrollment process, the operating point may be chosen arbitrarily at time of verification.

In key generation mode, the main demand to a Biometric Hash is the Intra-Class stability and Inter-Class dissimilarity. The optimum operating point in this mode is a configuration, in which every user of the biometric system can generate exactly one unique Biometric-Hash vector at any time from one particular semantic, while no other subject is able to reproduce the same value using the same system. In practice such optimal configuration is hard to achieve and thus, occurrences of non-identical hash values for authentic users with a specific probability and collisions of hash values between different users have to be expected. Here, as no thresholding-based decision is taken at the time of hash generation, the system parameters need to be estimated and configured a-priori and accuracy of the chosen settings can only be evaluated a-posteriori. Due to these aspects of the two different operation modes, the evaluation presented later in this section is discussed separately for the two different scenarios.

7.2   Evaluation Metric

In the authentication mode, Biometric Hash values are used as immediate feature representations. Reference values are determined in form of Biometric Hashes of enrollment samples and are compared to Biometric Hashes derived from actual handwriting signals at time of verification using a distance measure and a decision threshold. During the enrollment phase, for each reference sample set of each user in the test set, a number of interval matrices together with an associated reference Biometric Hash vector are computed. During the verification test, for each of the test samples of authentic users, Biometric Hash values are computed for each of the enrollment *IM* and Hamming Distances to each of the determined reference Biometric Hashes are computed. For the classification, the distance measure of minimum value is chosen, thus implementing a Nearest-Neighbor Classifier [Zhan2000]. This minimum distance is then compared to a threshold value for the authentication decision, which implements the smallest event unit being recorded during the test, also called primitive verification experiment. For visualization of the test results, the observed ratio of False-Non-Match occurrences is plotted in a FNMR graph as function of varying thresholds. False-Match Rates (FMR) are determined in an analog manner, comparing forgeries of subjects other than the authentic ones to the enrollment data.

Compared to the key generation mode analysis, this evaluation consists of additional processing steps for the computation of reference data at time of test execution. To illustrate this proceeding in a compact way, the **procedure of our verification experiments** can be described by the following algorithm:

- for each **given test environment** *te* $\in TE$
  - for each individual subject *H* in *te*
    - **for each** set *es* $\in ES$ of the **enrollment samples** of person *H*
      - **Initialize** $IM_{Ref}=\{\}$, $B_{Ref}=\{\}$
      - **for each of the** $i \in \{1, ..., e\}$ **sampled signals** in $es=\{es_1, ..., es_e\}$
        - **generate** *IM* from es_j, $j \in \{1, ..., e\}$, $j \neq i$, append *IM* to IM_{Ref}
        - **generate** *b* from *IM* and es_i , append *b* to B_{Ref}

- **for each** of the **verification samples** $vs \in VS$ belonging to H in test environment *te*:
  - **Initialize** $B_{Test}=\{\}$
  - **for each of the Interval Matrix set members** $IM_{Ref,i} \in IM_{Ref}$, $i \in \{1, ..., e\}$
    - **calculate test Bio Hash vector** b_{Test} by determining n from vs and using Biometric Hash function $m(n, IM_{Ref,i})$. Append resulting hash vector b_{Test} to B_{Test}
  - calculate **minimum Hamming Distance between any** $b_{Test} \in B_{Test}$ **and** $b_{Ref} \in B_{Ref}$: $Min(HD(B_{Test}, B_{Ref}))$
  - **authentication_result** $l=TRUE$, if $Min(HD(B_{Test}, B_{Ref})) \leq T$, *FALSE* otherwise
  - if $l==FALSE$, **then protocol one case of False-Non Match** to the log file, otherwise protocol one case of correct verification

Here, $IM_{Ref} = \{IM_{Ref,1}, ..., IM_{Ref,e}\}$ denotes a set of e reference Interval Matrices and B_{Ref} the set of corresponding authentic Biometric Hash references. *ES* identifies the set of enrollment data of a particular authentic user, consisting of e writing samples. B_{Test}, being a helper variable for the set of Biometric Hash values for the nearest neighbor test, is determined from an actual verification sample vs and each Interval Matrix in IM_{Ref}. The minimum Hamming Distance HD between any of the test vectors in B_{Test} and any of the reference vectors in B_{Ref} is determined by the minimum function *Min* and is then compared to a given decision threshold T for the authentication result.

In analogy to the algorithmic description of the *Verification Tests* above, we perform forgery tests by replacing the authentic verification samples $vs \in VS$ by forgery sample sets of the respective attack category (*Random, Blind, Brute-Force, Low-Force*), see description of the experimental setup in Chapter 5, Section 5.6.1. In this case, False-positive authentications are logged to the respective False-Match category FMR_{Random}, FMR_{Blind}, $FMR_{Low-Force}$ and $FMR_{Brute-Force}$.

For the sake of consistency to other experimental evaluations in the context of this book, test series are again performed in accordance to the methodology and using the experimental scenarios, as defined in Chapter 5, Section 5.6.3, using the metric described above.

7.3 Parameterization of the System

As explained in Section 6.4 of Chapter 6, the introduction of Tolerance Vectors (*tv*) addresses the compensation of Intra-Class variability of individual features and for the problem of estimating reasonable values for this parameter has been discussed thoroughly. We have suggested three principles to obtain the Tolerance Vector (*tv*) parameter, two of which are based on statistical evaluation of a-priori knowledge:

- **Zero-Tolerance Vector**: introduces no a-priori knowledge and suppresses this parameter entirely,
- **Individual Parameterization:** estimates *tv* individually for each user,
- **Global Parameterization:** estimates *tv* globally for all users of the authentication system.

Further, we have introduced a Tolerance Factor *tf* for the later two categories, which increases globally the system accuracy in generating authentic hash values at the cost of increase of attack success likelihoods. It has been shown in the previous chapter that these parameters can be estimated in an optimistic or an pessimistic manner, depending on the aspect if the evaluation sets chosen for the estimation are disjoint or not.

In this part of the book, we correspond to this parameterization approach by evaluating again these three different principles with respect to the Tolerance Vector (*tv*) configuration, depending on the degree of presumed a-priori knowledge. For the local feature weighting by *tv*, we apply the **same settings** determined **in the *tv* estimation as discussed in Chapter 6, Section 6.4** of the previous chapter. However, since we focus on a threshold-based verification mode, one previously existing goal of the system parameterization can be withdrawn: the intention to achieve stable Biometric Hashes for authentic users becomes obsolete in this scenario. Here, the actual operating point of the verification process can be configured at time of verification by analysis of the system at different threshold setting. Thus, we have decided **not to apply any a-priori parameterization** by the Tolerance Factor, effectively setting *tf=1.0*.

Further, in the previous chapter we have shown that two approaches for the parameter estimation exist: firstly, these can be estimated in a pessimistic manner by dividing the test data in two disjoint subsets and secondly, in the optimistic approach, they can be determined on the entire system information available at time of authentication. The test results have shown that both approaches are qualified for the Biometric Hash technique, where the optimistic estimation approach possesses the potential of higher accuracy with observed improvements in the range of 10 percent. Due to the fact that this aspect of the Biometric Hash has already been discussed in a very comprehensive manner, we limit our evaluation in this part to the optimistic scenario concluding by analogy, that pessimistic parameter estimation will lead a similar degradation of system accuracy of approximately 10 percent.

7.4 Test Results

To evaluate the accuracy of the Biometric Hash in verification mode, we test the system at different threshold levels and determine the error characteristics for authentic writing samples and forgeries of different qualities, by analyzing the error rate diagrams of False-Matches and False-Non-Matches (see also Chapter 2, Section 2.4.4). We evaluate these experimental results in form of error rate diagrams in three aspects: the general characteristics observed the impact of different parameterizations and effects of using different semantic classes and tablet categories in the system. In this section, we summarize the relevant conclusions from our experiments.

General Evaluation

We observe a typical characteristic of a threshold-based biometric system throughout the tests. The property of monotonic increase of false acceptances with increasing threshold together with a monotonic decrease of false rejections underlines the discriminatory capability. Furthermore, we are able to determine the Equal-Error Rate (EER) parameter in all cases. Figure 7-2 illustrates the test results for semantic class *Signature*, tablet category *Tablet-A* and an optimistic *tv* parameterization. In the diagram, error rates for authentic *Verification* attempts are given by the graph marked with squares, denoted by FNMR, whereas success rates of *Random Forgeries* are given by the *FMR-Random* graph, labeled by circles "●". *Blind, Low-Force* and *Brute-Force Forgeries* graphs are labeled by the triangle "▲", cross "+" and rhombus "◆"graphs respectively and denoted as *FMR-Blind, FMR-LowForce* and *FMR-BruteForce* in Figure 7-2.

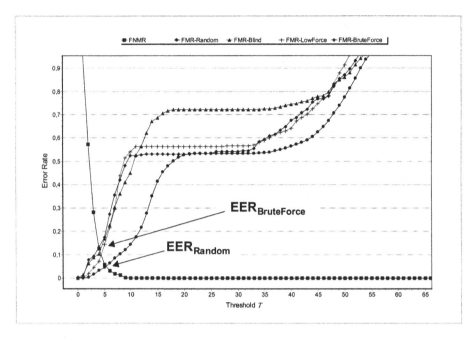

Figure 7-2. Biometric Hash verification errors for semantic class *Signature* and tablet category *Tablet-A*

In confirming to the trend observed in Chapter 5, the False-Match error rates strongly depend on the attack strength applied to the system. In all cases, the error rates generated by random forgeries (Inter-Class tests) are noticeably lower than those produced by intended forgeries (see graph Random-Forgeries, circle labels in Figure 7-2). Within the class of intentional counterfeits, *Blind Forgeries* (graph *FMR-Blind*) are typically less successful than *Low-* or *Brute-Force* attacks (graphs *FMR-LowForce* and *FMR-BruteForce*). However, we observe that in a number of cases, the gradients of success rate functions of *Blind* attacks are very close to those of *Low-* and *Brute-Force* error curves and in some cases, *Blind Forgeries* are even more often successful than other forgeries. Figure 7-2 is an adequate example for this characteristic, where we observe an EER, i.e. the error rate value on the ordinate at intersections of FMR and FNMR curves, of approximately 5% for *Random Forgeries* (for example, see EER_{Random} in diagram). For the other attack strength categories, error rates of 10% for *Low-Force*, 11% for *Blind* and 12% and *Brute-Force* attacks are observed (see intersections of graphs *FMR-LowForce*, *FMR-Blind* and *FMR-BruteForce* with FNMR curve in Figure 7-2). We ascribe this observation to different skills and motivations of forgers in the experiments.

System Parameterization

The experimental results confirm that the parameterization of the Biometric Hash by the Tolerance Vector (*tv*) has a remarkable impact on the verification accuracy. To discuss this observation, we refer to error characteristics diagram determined for the example of tablet category *Tablet-A*, semantic class *Passphrase*, as shown in Figure 7-3. The graphs represent the error characteristics for parameterizations zero (upper left graph), global estimation (upper right) and local individual estimation (lower graph). Particularly EER_{Random}, being the intersection between FNMR curve and the FMR graph for Random Forgeries, reduces significantly from left to right. Also, we observe in this scenario that the $EER_{LowForce}$ can be reduced by more than 50 percent from the unparameterized settings to local parameter estimation.

The summary of the experimental results shown in Figure 7-3 are presented in form of equal error rates (EER) in the following Table 7-1. As can be seen, with an individual parameterization, the system accuracy can be significantly improved, in this case from 6% down to 0% in the case of *Random Forgeries* and from 38 % to 25 % for *Brute-Force* attacks.

Table 7-1. Equal Error Rates for three different parameterizations

	Equal Error Rate (EER)			
tv Parameterization	**Random**	**Blind**	**Low-Force**	**Brute-Force**
Zero	6 %	15 %	48 %	38 %
Global Estimation	4 %	15 %	55 %	40 %
Individual Estimation	0 %	4 %	22 %	25 %

Observations from our further experimental results based on other subsets of the test database have confirmed this conclusion.

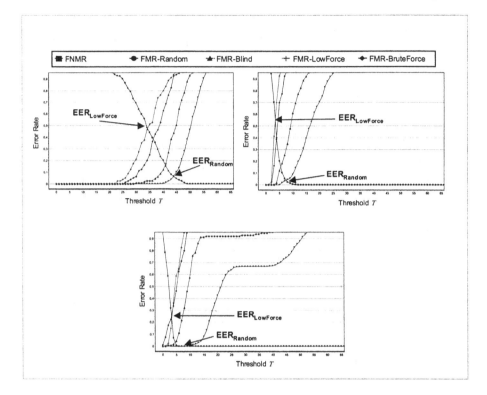

Figure 7-3. Error rate example for *Zero-tv* (upper left), *global tv* estimation (upper right), *local tv* estimation (lower)

Effects of Tablet Categories

Again, we observe a dependency of the Biometric Hash algorithm on the tablet category. The trend of increasing accuracy with a higher spatial resolution, which has been observed already in Chapter 5, has been confirmed in this test. For example, the error rate characteristics of the semantic class *Signature* are shown in Figure 7-4 for the three different tablet categories: *Tablet-B* and *Tablet-A* having a medium spatial resolution according to the classification given in Chapter 5, Section 5.5.3 plus *Hires-PQ-Angle* with a high spatial resolution. We observe EER_{Random} in the range of 5% for the first two categories, having almost identical digitizer resolutions, whereas this term becomes zero in the third experiment.

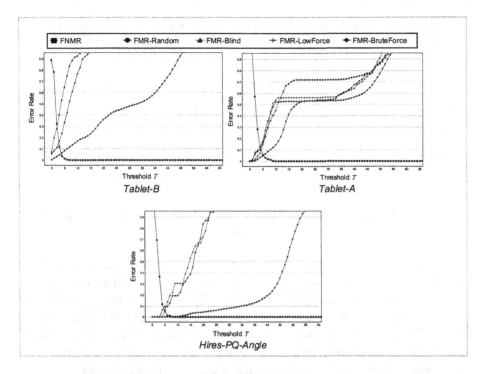

Figure 7-4. Error rates for semantic Signature, tablet categories *Tablet-B* (upper left), *Tablet-A* (upper right) and *Hires-PQ-Angle* (lower)

Also, the EER for the class of intended forgeries are significantly lower for the category of higher resolution tablets, in average the False-Match Rates reduce to about half of those observed for lower resolutions.

Looking at the test result diagrams for the merged sets *All* and *Midres-PQ* for semantic class *Signature* as shown in Figure 7-5, it can be seen that the highest error rates are observed for the category of medium resolution tablets, with an EER_{Random} of more than 20 % and False-Match Rates for intended forgeries of more than 30%.

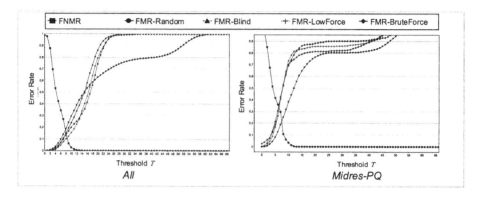

Figure 7-5. Error rates for semantic Signature, tablet categories *All* (left) and *Midres-PQ* (right)

As summarized in Table 7-2, the test environment *All*, comprising tablets of all categories, shows an accuracy characteristic, which exhibits an interesting property: among the different attack levels, EER_{Random} yields the highest value, 18%, whereas the lowest errors occurred in the case of *Low-Force Forgeries*. Consequently, in this heterogeneous scenario in view of the tablet characteristics, randomly chosen writing samples are more likely to be accepted by the algorithm than intended and skilled forgeries.

Table 7-2. Equal Error Rates for three different tablet categories, semantic *Signature*

| | **Equal Error Rate (EER)** | | | |
Tablet Category	**Random**	**Blind**	**Low-Force**	**Brute-Force**
All	15 %	14 %	11 %	18 %
Tablet-A	5 %	12 %	10 %	13%
Hires PQ-Angle	0 %	n/a*	5 %	8 %
Midres PQ	22 %	34 %	33 %	33 %
Tablet-B	5 %	29 %	n/a*	16 %

* n/a test data not available

Effects of Semantic Classes

The general observation is that the alternative semantic classes, which have been tested in the system besides the *Signature*, are adequate for user authentication by the Biometric Hash in verification mode. Especially those semantic classes including individual knowledge (*Passphrase* and *Symbol*) result in rather accurate authentication results. An example of this observation is given in Figure 7-6, showing the error rate diagrams for the same tablet category, *All*, and the four semantic classes complementary to *Signature*. The two semantic classes *"8710"* and *"Sauerstoffgefäß"*, based on fixed textual content, lead to EER between 20 % (diagram

"Sauerstoffgefäß", EER_Random , i.e. intersection of graphs *FMR-Random* and FNMR) and 55% (diagram *"8710", EER_Blind* , i.e. intersection of graphs *FMR-Blind* and FNMR). Compared to these, the results for the other two semantic classes are obviously much more accurate, with a minimum EER of 0% (diagram *Passphrase, EER_Random*) and 35% (diagram *Symbol, EER_BruteForce* , i.e. intersection of graphs *FMR-BruteForce* and FNMR). In summary, the evaluation of alternative semantic classes to be used as authentication information for the Biometric Hash verification approach confirms the results presented in Chapter 5, Section 5.7, that all semantic classes are adequate for authentication, and particularly the knowledge-based semantics may even improve the overall system accuracy.

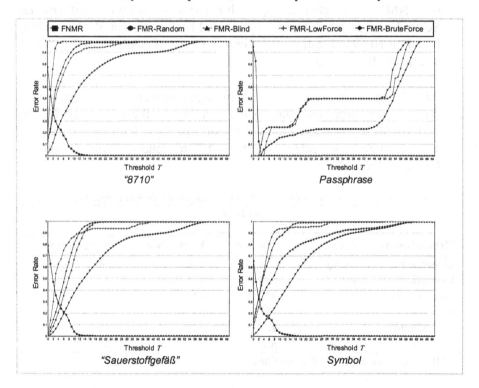

Figure 7-6. Error rate diagrams for different semantic classes, tablet category *All*

The main conclusions, which can be drawn from our accuracy evaluation of the Biometric Hash in verification mode, are:

* The overall **accuracy** of the Biometric Hash algorithm in verification mode is **increasing with a higher degree of spatial resolution and higher degree of homogeneity** of the physical characteristics of digitizer tablets. On the other side, with increasing heterogeneity of the

tablet characteristics in the authentication system, the **success chances of attackers generally increase**, but are influenced in such way, that the **relative gain in success rates by increased forgery efforts becomes smaller** with an increasing heterogeneity of the hardware devices.

- The **recognition results** can be **classified as rather good** in comparison to other published results based on global statistical features and the semantic class *Signature*. Schmidt [Schm1999] has published results of a statistical approach based on 13 features and reported a FNMR of 12.8% at a FMR of 13.7% with an estimated EER of 13.3%. These results were discussed in view of work of Lee et al. [LeBA1996], reporting an EER of 2,5% and an asymptotic performance of 7% FMR at 0% FNMR for a statistical approach based on 49 features. Furthermore, Schmidt compared to a system presented by Bromley et al. [Bro+1993] based on 10 global statistical features, where performances of 20% FMR at 3% FNMR were reported.

Table 7-3 gives an overview of our recognition results in comparison to the mentioned approaches. Due to the fact that in the referenced related work, tests were conducted only on one specific digitizer device, we compare to three tablet categories of great homogeneity (*Hires-PQ-Angle*, *Tablet-A* and *Tablet-B*).

Table 7-3. Error rates comparison for semantic class Signature (n/a = not available)

Method/Tablet Category	Error Rate		
	Best Case	Worst Case	No. Signatures
Biometric Hash –Hires-PQ-Angle	0 % (EER)	8 % (EER)	2258
Biometric Hash –Tablet-A	5 % (EER)	13 % (EER)	2318
Biometric Hash – Tablet-B	5 % (EER)	29 % (EER)	2318
[Schm1999]	13.3 %	n/a[11]	2383
[LeBA1996]	2.5 %	n/a[1]	> 10.000
[Bro+1993]	n/a[1]	20% / 3% [*]	956

* FMR / FNMR values, no EER determined

All test set sizes are in ranges that allow comparison of results and as can be seen from Table 7-3, we are able to determine an **operating point for the Biometric Hash verification** which outperforms other approaches in the

---

[11] From the test results presented in [Schm1999] and [LeBa1993], it has not been possible to differentiate into random and intended forgeries, as an explicit differentiation is not specified. Thus their results are presented in the column "Best Case". [Bro+1993] have exposed the system only to intended forgeries of different quality, thus we assign their results to the "Worst Case" column.

literature, if we limit the view to only one tablet category, *Hires-PQ-Angle*. Assuming a best case scenario[1] for tests of [Schm1999] and [LeBA1996], we conclude that all three categories of tablets show better rates in our scenario. In comparison to a test scenario where exclusively skilled forgeries have been considered, as described in [Bro+1993], we observe a similar accuracy level of our approach.

7.5   Entropy Analysis of Biometric Hashes

The accuracy of our user verification scheme based in Biometric Hashes has been empirically analyzed in the previous section. It has been shown that this approach is characterized by different error rate functions, depending on the digitizer category, semantic classes and forgery strength. However, we have not discussed yet the theoretical boundaries of the achievable key value space of Biometric Hashes. This discussion, however, is important mainly because of two reasons: **complexity estimations for scanning attacks** and **individuality of features** in view of their ability to **discriminate subjects**.

In this section, we focus our discussion on theoretical efforts for an attacker in a scenario, where he or she has access to components of an biometric authentication system and attempts to get knowledge about reference data, which is either encrypted individually for each user, using a key derived from the Biometric Hash, as described in the motivation for Chapter 6, or which may be represented by a reference Biometric Hash b_{Ref}, as introduced in Section 7.1. We start our analysis by firstly determining a theoretical upper boundary based on the size of storage variables for the integer vector components in Section 7.5.1, followed by a short reflection on the motivation to use entropy for individuality analysis of biometric features in Section 7.5.2. A summary of related approaches of entropy-based analysis of biometric systems for modalities other than handwriting is given in Section 7.5.3. In Section 7.5.4, we exemplify one application of entropy, entropy coding, of Biometric Hash values and motivate our approach of entropy analysis, which is presented in Section 7.5.5.

7.5.1   Scanning Attacks

Firstly, an attacker having logical access to system components of a biometric authentication system as shown in Section 4.3.1 can apply the method of key space scanning to attempt malicious authentication by the system. This proceeding, however, requires that he or she is aware of the dimensionality and the data typing of the authentication information A. If this knowledge is available to an attacker, an approach of systematic generation and testing of all possible values in the resulting value space could be taken. In the Biometric Hash scenario, the key is represented by a Biometric Hash vector $b=(b_1, ..., b_k)$ and assuming that each of the vector components b_i, $i \in \{1, ... ,k\}$ is coded by a r-bit, non-negative Integer value, the value range for each of these components is $0 \leq b_i < 2^k$. Further assuming that a key is generated by concatenation of each of the vector components (with $//$ denoting the concatenation operation): $b_1 // b_2 // ... // b_k$, then the number of bits assigned for such a key yields $k*r$ bits and the size, or **cardinality *CARD*, of the resulting key space results to *CARD(b)*=$2^{(k*r)}$**.

Obviously, from this theoretical boundary, the complexity for a potential attacker lies in the size of the key space. For example, the implementation of the Biometric Hash discussed in the context of this book, with a dimensionality of $k=69$ and a data typing by $r=64$ bit Integer values would lead to a maximum number of different key values to be scanned equal to 2 $^{(4416)} \approx 2.2 * 10^{(1329)}$, a number which is certainly too high to expect a successful scanning in reasonable time. However, this boundary practically is far too optimistic, because of:

- **Sparse Population:** we expect that by far not all possible values in the key space actually occur in application,
- **Distribution Inhomogeneity**: specific key values might show a higher occurrence than others.

If an attacker knows about the empirical distribution of key values in a real-world application, these two characteristics are helpful for an attacker in the scanning attempt. He or she can limit the scan region by excluding key values, which are unlikely to occur or by prioritizing those values having higher occurrence probabilities. This knowledge is the basic idea behind so-called dictionary attacks, whereby the computational effort of scanning can be reduced drastically [BiKl1995].

7.5.2   Individuality of Features

Although the size of the test database used in our evaluations in context of this book can be considered as rather large compared to other databases for handwriting authentication found in the literature, it still is limited with respect to the number of test subjects. We have already presented operating figures of collisions probabilities in terms of accidental matches between Biometric Hashes generated from two different authentic persons, by discussing the Inter-Class *Random-Forgery* success rates. However, conclusions from these False-Match rates from the population size in our tests to larger populations can only be drawn, if we have some knowledge about the practically achievable value space of the Biometric Hashes which can be attained. From the publications considered for the research presented in this book, such systematic analyses beyond statistical tests have not been performed yet for the biometric modality of handwriting. Thus we have chosen to perform such analysis by applying the method of entropy evaluation, which has already been applied successfully for other feature selection problems [ChYa1995].

7.5.3 Entropy Analysis for Non-Handwriting Modalities

A well-established method for evaluation information content of digital systems known from coding theory is the information entropy analysis, which had been introduced by Claude E. Shannon more than half a century ago [Shan1948]. It is a measure for the information density within a set of values with known occurrence probabilities. Knowledge of the information entropy, describing a term of the effective amount of information contained in a finite set, is the basis for design of several efficient data coding and compression techniques. Among the wide range of entropy-based applications the most commonly known method is the Huffman code [NeGa1995] (see example in the following Section 7.5.4) and in the domain of multimedia technology, a wide spectrum of applications based on entropy exist, e.g. for image compression [TuTr2002], speech recognition [Jeli1998] and many others.

In biometric authentication research, information entropy analysis has been applied mainly for iris recognition technology (see Chapter 3, Section 3.3.2). Daugman has performed an initial estimation on the uniqueness of IrisCodes based on statistical decision theory in [Daug1992], where he assumes that each of the 2048 binary feature vector components of the IrisCode are statistically independent. With a second assumption of a binomial distribution of Inter-Class Hamming Distances and based on a test database of 2064 pair wise comparisons of unrelated IrisCodes, Daugman estimates an equivalent of 173 independent binary degrees of freedom in the 2048-bit IrisCode. Consequently the theoretical average False-Match probability can be determined to 10^{-52}. In subsequent work [Daug2003], it has been shown that by optimizing the feature extraction of the IrisCode, increased entropy of 249 bit was observed in a test including approximately 9.1 million comparisons of different IrisCodes. Although these figures clearly unveil the degree of redundancy, Davida et al. have rated these entropy estimates as large and emphasize the benefit of reducing vector dimensionality [DaFM1998].

7.5.4   Entropy Coding Example: Huffman Code

One of the most relevant applications based on entropy analysis is entropy coding techniques for data compression. The goal of these techniques is to reduce the number of bits required to represent some information (e.g. a string), composed of a sequence of states (or symbols such as characters), by finding an optimized code under consideration of the occurrence probabilities of each of the states.

The basic idea behind entropy coding is to assign short codes to those states having a high occurrence probability and long codes to those having a lower probability. A boundary for such coding is the system entropy as defined by Shannon [Shan1948], denoting a lower boundary for the number of bits needed for the represented symbols. One of the most commonly applied entropy coding techniques today is the Huffman code, introduced in [Huff1952]. In order to exemplify the Huffman code applied for the coding of one component of a Biometric Hash vector component b_i, we rewrite the original definition of entropy from [Shan1948] as follows:

- let $N_{States}(b_i)$ be the total number of different states (values) observed for variable b_i
- let p_j **be the occurrence probability** of the j-th state of b_i , $j \in \{1, ..., N_{States}(b_i)\}$
- we define the **Entropy of b_i**, *Entropy(b_i)* as follows:

$$Entropy(b_i) = - \sum_{j=1}^{N_{States}(b_i)} p_j \bullet \log_2 p_j \qquad (7\text{-}8)$$

For an hypothetical example, where we observe $N_{States}(b_i)$=5 different symbols for b_i : $b_i \in \{1,2,3,4,5\}$ with occurrence probabilities of p_1=0.4, p_2=0.2, p_3=0.1, p_4=0.2 and p_5=0.1 respectively, we yield:

Entropy(b_i)= - 0.4 log$_2$ 0.4 - 0.2 log$_2$ 0.2 - 0.1 log$_2$ 0.1 - 0.2 log$_2$ 0.2 - 0.1 log$_2$ 0.1 = 2.122

This means, that the **lower boundary of the bit size for representing** this system for b_i is equal to 2.122 bit. Practically, to find a Huffman coding for our system, we can utilize a binary tree as shown in Figure 7.7. The tree is developed from those states having the lowest occurrence probabilities in the deepest leaves via the nodes denoting the combined probabilities towards the root of the tree. The Huffman code for each of the symbols can be found by traversing the tree from root to the leaf denoted with the required symbol and concatenating the edge designators.

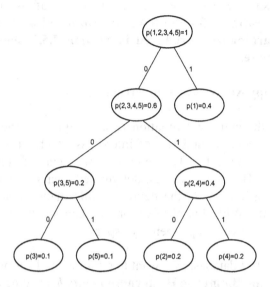

Figure 7-7. Huffman coding of our example, represented as a binary tree

For the example in Figure 7-7, we can find the binary coding (note that the assignment of 0/1 values of the complementary branches in the Huffman tree can be chosen arbitrarily, thus the same system may lead to different codes), as presented in Table 7-4:

Table 7-4. Huffman codes resulting from example in Figure 7-7

Symbol	p$_j$	Huffman Code	Symbol Size
1	0.4	1	1 bit
2	0.2	010	3 bit
4	0.2	011	3 bit
3	0.1	000	3 bit
5	0.1	001	3 bit

Consequently, from the point of view of storage capacity, when applying this code to our exemplary system, we can expect an average coding size in bits per Symbol of: $1*0.4 + 3*0.2 + 3*0.2 + 3*0.1 + 3*.01 = 2.2$ *bit*. This value is slightly above the theoretical lower boundary, given by our initial determination of: *Entropy(b$_j$)= 2.122*.

From the point of view of our scanning attacker scenario, we can conclude that an attacker will have to scan a range of $2.^{1.22} = 4.323$ different symbols in average for this single component, if the knowledge about the coding and the underlying statistical symbol distribution is available to him or her.

With this example, we motivate our approach of **using the entropy function as an estimate for the lower boundary of a scan value range, whereas the cardinality introduced in Section 7.5.1 denotes an upper boundary estimate.**

7.5.5   Entropy Analysis of Biometric Hashes

Apparently, the entropy estimation is an adequate method to determine some theoretical lower boundaries of Inter-Class distributions of Biometric Hash vector components. The entropy of each of the components $b=(b_1, ..., b_k)$, for Biometric Hashes, determined over sets of different users, represents a measurement of the degree of information content in each of these components. With this observation, we can structure the goal of our entropy analysis in two complementary aspects:

- based on our test database, we want to empirically determine the **entropy for each of the Biometric Hash components** b_i in some of our different test scenarios, as defined in Section 5.6.3. This allows conclusions, **to which degree the statistical features** n_i , being the basis for the calculation on b_i , **contribute information content** to the entire Biometric Hash vector b.
- From the individual entropy values of each of the Biometric Hash components b_i , we want to derive a **lower boundary estimate of the size of the key space** represented by the entire collection of Biometric Hashes b, which an **attacker would be required to scan**, if he or she is aware of the statistical distribution of the Hash values.

As such analysis has not been published for the modality of handwriting-based biometrics before, we decide to perform an entropy analysis of the Biometric Hash approach for selected data sets of our evaluation system. The goal is to systematically outline boundaries of the algorithms at specific operating points of the Biometric Hash by choosing distinct operational test sets performing the analysis and discussing the expected impact on large scale applications.

Initially, we have included the entropy analysis in the area of handwriting-based biometrics in the context of determination of adequate feature sub-sets for Biometric Hashes [ViSt2004]. In this section we extent this approach towards boundary estimation of key vectors of higher dimensionality. For this estimation, we base the entropy calculation in our rewritten definition of the component-wise entropy of a collection of

Biometric Hashes, *Entropy(b$_i$)^{12}*, from Section 7.5.4. Furthermore, in analogy to the considerations of Daugman [Daug2003], we are assuming a statistical independency of the vector components for the entropy analysis. This is a simplifying assumption, which we justify by the fact that our goal is to find a theoretical estimation for the boundaries. With this simplification, we have the freedom to analyze the entropy of each of the components of the Biometric Hash separately. In order to do so, we proceed separately for each test environment *te* according to the following algorithmic description:

- for each **given test environment** *te* $\in$ *TE*
  - for each **individual subject** *H* in *te*
    - **for each** set *es* $\in$ *ES* of the **enrollment samples** of person *H* in *te*
    - Determine **Interval Matrix** *IM* from *es*
    - **for each** of the **verification samples** *vs* $\in$ *VS* belonging to *H* in *te:*
      - Determine the Biometric Hash Vector *b* from *vs* and *IM*
      - **Protocol** the occurrence probability of each distinct value of each the *i* $\in$ *{1, ..., k}* vector components of *b=(b$_1$, ..., b$_k$)*

From the resulting evaluation protocol, we produce a statistics separately for each vector component *b$_i$* , tabulating the number of occurrences of each unique value observed, which are the symbols for the entropy determination.

The entropy analysis has been performed for two representative tablet categories (*All* and *MIDRES-PQ*) under two different parameterizations for and *tv* and *tf*. The following Figure 7-8 shows one example of the result of the entropy test by visualizing the entropy distribution of one specific test environment for the semantic class of *Signatures* and the tablet category *All*, separately for each of the Biometric Hash vector components (*b$_1$, ..., b$_k$*).

---

[12] We refrain from using the commonly accepted notation *H(X)* for the information entropy, as introduced by Shannon, in order to avoid confusion with designator *H*, introduced for denoting the human subject in the general model for an authentication system in Chapter 4.

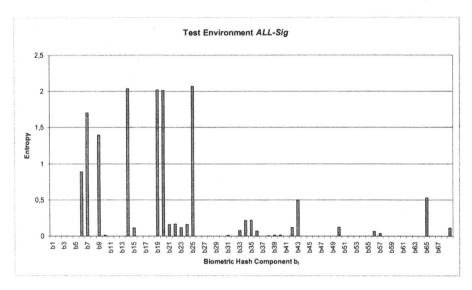

Figure 7-8. Feature entropy of test environment *All*, semantic class *Signature*, global *tv*,
tf=5.0

We evaluate the results of the entropy analysis with respect to the following three aspects:

- **Empirical key space estimation**: Taking into account the above observations with respect to redundancy and our assumption of statistical independence of the vector components b_i , we can safely assume that the overall system entropy is less or equal to the overall sum of entropy of all Biometric Hash components in each of the test environments. The resulting size of the key space of Biometric Hashes is less or equal to the space spanned by the orthogonal vectors. Thus, we can write the overall system entropy to:

$$Entropy(b) = \sum_{i=1}^{k} Entropy(b_i) \qquad (7\text{-}9)$$

For the example in Figure 7-8, we observe *Entropy(b)=14.99*, from which we deduct that for an optimum entropy coding, we require a coding by at least $\lceil 14.99 \rceil = 15$ *bit* and consequently, an attacker performing a scanning attack will have to scan at least $2^{15}=32,768$ different values to succeed.

- **Redundancy**: we define redundancy as the percentage of components having entropy of zero out of the total number k. We do so, because from the point of view of information theory, this means that this **fraction of the vector components of the Biometric Hash do not contribute to the information content** within the given system. For the coding efficiency of the Biometric Hash vector in different evaluation scenarios (i.e. tablet categories, semantic classes), this indicates the degree of redundancy. For the example in Figure 7-8, we observe that 33 out of 69 vector components result in entropy values equal to zero, thus we observe a redundancy degree of 47.8 %.

Table 7-5 summarizes our evaluation with respect to redundancy and key space estimates of the entropy analysis for the various test sets. Note that the values observed for Redundancy, as well as for Key Space Estimate, vary to a large extent, depending on tablet category as well as semantic classes. The lowest Redundancy was observed for tablet category *All*, semantic class *Symbol*, with a Estimate of 2^{23} different keys. On the other end of the scale, the smallest value was observed for the same tablet category and semantic class *Passphrase*, with an estimated Key Space of 2^{8} different values.

Table 7-5. Summary of entropy analysis results

Tablet Category	Semantic Class	Redundancy	Key Space Estimate
All	*Signature*	47.83 %	2^{15}
All	*"Sauerstoffgefäß"*	37.68 %	2^{22}
All	*"8710"*	71.01 %	2^{19}
All	*Passphrase*	85.51 %	2^{8}
All	*Symbol*	30.43 %	2^{23}
MIDRES-PQ	*Signature*	73.91 %	2^{12}
MIDRES-PQ	*"Sauerstoffgefäß"*	73.91%	2^{11}
MIDRES-PQ	*"8710"*	85.51 %	2^{12}
MIDRES-PQ	*Passphrase*	84.06 %	2^{13}
MIDRES-PQ	*Symbol*	79.71 %	2^{12}

In view of the two goals given at the beginning of this chapter, the analysis results of this example can be concluded as follows:

- the **effort for scanning the entire key space** can be reduced to the problem of trying out a minimum of 2^{8} to 2^{23} different hash values, if the attacker has knowledge about the value distribution. Therefore he or she would have to consider a minimum range of app. $2.5 \cdot 10^{2}$ to $8 \cdot 10^{6}$ different hash values and it can be expected that in average half of these will be necessary to achieve a malicious authentication. The scan range increases with greater heterogeneity of the tablet categories (highest key space estimate for Tablet category *All* is 2^{23}, for *MIDRES-PQ*, it is 2^{13}).

- The **Redundancy of Biometric Hashes is rather high**, but **depends significantly on the semantic class used and the tablet categories**. For semantic class *Signature*, for example, redundancies of 73.91 % were observed in the tablet category *MIDRES-PQ*. Consequently, only 18 out of the k=69 components of the Biometric Hash vectors actually have an entropy higher than zero, thus contribute to the discriminatory information in the system represented by this scenario. Apparently, the redundancy reduces with greater heterogeneity of tablet characteristics, as for the category All, only approximate half of the vector components possess an entropy of zero.

7.6   Summary

We have shown that the Biometric Hash function possesses qualities, which facilitate an **additional operating mode** to the original goal of key generation: user authentication by **handwriting verification**. In order to achieve this additional functionality, we have extended the authentication system based on Biometric Hash generation by three components:

- amendment of a Biometric Hash reference vector $b_{Reference}$ in Complementary Information $C^* = \{IM, b_{Ref}\}$,
- determination of a feature distance measure δ and inclusion of it in authentication functions L,
- authentication by a threshold T-based decision module.

From the wide range of possible feature distance measures, we have selected the **Hamming Distance**, which has been successfully applied to authentication problems of another biometric modality, iris recognition. This measure has significant advantages compared to other distance measures in terms of computational low complexity.

With the evaluation methodology presented in Chapter 5, we were able to demonstrate in general, that the system performs as expected by showing **typical error rate characteristics**. Furthermore, in analogy to test scenarios discussed earlier in this book in Chapter 5, Section 5.6.3, we have inspected the system behavior under different configurations with respect to tablet categories, semantic classes and forgery qualities. Again, we observe a **noticeable dependency on all three parameters, confirming earlier conclusions** from Chapter 5 and 6. We have observed that with the semantic class of *Signatures*, we are able to produce the best test results of EER between 0% for random, and 5% for *Brute-Force* skilled forgeries, using only tablets with a high spatial and pressure signal resolution. On the other side, we have observed that the application of different tablets of very heterogeneous physical characteristics in the test scenarios leads to a degradation of the system accuracy, represented by an EER in the range of 15% to 20%. However, even in this category of digitizer devices, we were able to produce EER as low as 0% (EER_{Random}) to 5% ($EER_{BruteForce}$) by applying *Passphrase* as an alternative semantic class.

Another **outstanding conclusion** of the error rate evaluation is that biometric user verification based on Biometric Hashes can achieve a degree of accuracy, which is **rather high in comparison to other recent approaches** based on statistical analysis found in the literature.

In order to get some **theoretical insights** in efforts for **one specific attack method** presented earlier, **scanning**, we have presented **entropy analysis** as a new technique for estimating the lower boundary of the size of the key space, which is effectively achieved by the Biometric Hash system. Although similar techniques have been applied and published for biometric modalities based on iris analysis, it is the first approach of utilizing such methods of the decision theory for the modality of handwriting, according to related work. The results of our pessimistic estimation based on entropy analysis indicate that the size of the **achievable key space varies widely depending on the semantic class** used. Our observations are scales in the range of 2^8 (semantic class *Passphrase*) to 2^{23} (semantic class *Symbol*). Also the **degree of redundancy varies depending on the semantic class**. While for the semantic class *Symbol*, only approximately one third of the features contribute to the discriminatory power, this is the case only for roughly half of the same features for semantic class *Signature*. This observation may have an impact on the design of future biometric authentication and verification systems, where a semantic-specific feature selection appears possible.

7.7 Notations and Abbreviations

Table 7-6 summarizes all notations and abbreviations introduced in this Chapter 7 in alphabetical order.

Table 7-6. Summary of notations and abbreviations introduced in Chapter 7

Designator	Name	Description	Introduced in
b_{Ref}	Reference Biometric Hash vector	Reference value for the Biometric Hash value $b_{Ref} \in B_{Ref}$ of each subject, determined at time of enrollment.	Section 7.1
B_{Ref}	Set of Biometric Hash Reference Vectors	B_{Ref} denotes the set of authentic Biometric Hash references corresponding to IM_{Ref}	Section 7.2

Table 7-6 (cont.)

Designator	Name	Description	Introduced in
B_{Test}	Set of Biometric Hash Test Vectors	B_{Test} denotes the temporary set of authentic or forged Biometric Hash vectors for verification tests	Section 7.2
C^*	Complementary Information	Complementary Information representation for user authentication by Biometric Hash verification: $c^* \in C^*$. It is a collection composed of the implementation of complementary information $c \in C$ by an Interval Matrix IM, supplemented by a reference Biometric Hash value b_{Ref}: $c^* = \{ IM, b_{Ref} \}$	Section 7.1
$\delta(b, b_{Ref})$	Vector Distance Function	General Vector Distance Function to determine distance between two Biometric Hash Vectors b and b_{Ref}: $\delta(b, b_{Ref})$	Section 7.1
$\delta_{Hamming}$	Hamming Distance Function	Hamming Vector Distance Function for Biometric Hash Vectors: $$\delta_{Hamming}(b, b_{Ref}) = HD(b, b_{Ref}) = \frac{\#(b_i \neq b_{Ref,i})}{k}$$ where $\#(b_i \neq b_{Ref,i})$ denotes the count function of non-identical value for each of the $i \in \{1, \ldots, k\}$ vector components	Section 7.1
$\delta_{Mahalanobis}$	Mahalanobis Distance Function	Mahalanobis Vector Distance Function for Biometric Hash Vectors: $$\delta_{Mahalanobis}(b, b_{Ref}) = \sqrt{(b - b_{Ref})V^{-1}(b - b_{Ref})'}$$ with V^{-1} denoting the sample covariance matrix of all authentic Biometric Hash values	Section 7.1
$\delta_{p\text{-}Minkowski}$	p-Minkowski Vector Distance Function	p-Minkowski Vector Distance Function for Biometric Hash Vectors: $$\delta_{p\text{-}Minkowski}(b, b_{Ref}) = \left(\sum_{i=1}^{k} |b_i - b_{Ref,i}|^p \right)^{\frac{1}{p}}$$	Section 7.1
δ_{Vector}	Vector Distance Function	δ_{Vector} yields a scalar distance value between two vectors of identical dimensionality	Section 7.1

Table 7-6 (cont.)

Designator	Name	Description	Introduced in
$Entropy(b_i)$	Biometric Hash Entropy	Entropy of Biometric Hash vector component b_i in a given system of Biometric Hashes: $$Entropy(b_i) = -\sum_{j=1}^{N_{States}(b_i)} p_j \bullet \log_2 p_j$$	Section 7.5.4
IM_{Ref}	Set of Reference Interval Matrices	Set of e reference Interval Matrices: $IM_{Ref} = \{IM_{Ref,1}, \dots, IM_{Ref,e}\}$	Section 7.2
N_{States}	Number of States	$N_{States}(b_i)$ denotes the total number of different states (symbols) observed for variable b_i	Section 7.5.4
r	Integer Variable Size	Integer Variable Size in bit	Section 7.5.1

Appendix

APPENDIX A: TECHNICAL DETAILS OF DIGITIZER TABLETS

The following Table A-1 summarizes the technical specifications of all digitizer tablets, which have been used for the collection of our test database. Note n/a describes features not available for a specific device, whereas specifications, which have not been provided by manufacturers and were experimentally determined, are denoted with an asterisk symbol (*).

Table A-1. Technical specifications of the digitizer tablets in our test set, n/a=not available, *=experimentally determined

Tablet-IDs	Active physical Size (width x height) [mm]	Interface	Sampling Rate [Hz]	Position x(t)/y(t) [lpi]	Pressure p(t) [levels]	Altitude φ(t) [°]	Azimuth φ(t) [°]	Remark
1,21	127 x 106	Serial	<= 200	2540	1024	0.1°	0.1°	
2	160x160	Craddle, USB	45*	160x160	2	n/a	n/a	Built-in digitizer display
4, 22, 23, 29	127 x 106	USB	<= 200	2540	1024	0.1°	0.1°	
5, 28	302 x 226	USB	90*	1016	256	n/a	n/a	Digitizer display
6	359 x 287	USB	66 – 125	72,47 horizontal, 90,62 vertical	2	n/a	n/a	Touch-screen technology

Table A-1 (cont.)

Tablet-IDs	Active physical Size (width x height) [mm]	Interface	Sam-pling Rate [Hz]	Position x(t)/y(t) [lpi]	Pressure p(t) [levels]	Altitud e φ(t) [°]	Azimut h φ(t) [°]	Remark
7	302 x 226	USB	<= 205	508	512	n/a	n/a	Digitizer display
8, 24, 25	127 x 106	USB	<= 200	2540	1024	0.1°	0.1°	
9, 26	127,6 x 92,8	USB	80 *	1000	512	n/a	n/a	
11	203mm x 152mm	USB	150 *	<= 3048	512	n/a	n/a	
12	127 x 106	USB	<= 200	2540	1024	0.1°	0.1°	Inking pen
16, 17, 27	88 x 51	USB, serial	400	1092	127	n/a	n/a	Pressure-sensitive panel
19	88 x 51	USB, serial	400	546	127	n/a	n/a	Pressure-sensitive panel
16	127,6 x 92,8	USB	80 *	1000	512	n/a	n/a	Inking pen

APPENDIX B: THE PLATASIGN EVALUATION SYSTEM

In this appendix, we provide a technical description of the PlataSign evaluation system. The entire system is programmed using Borland Delphi™ Software Developments Kit (SDK), MtxVec™ numerical library and mysql.pas database interface API© by Matthias Fichtner.

The software system consists of three main modules, Evaluator, Database and Recorder (see Figure 5-7 in Chapter 5), which are interfaced by a TCP/IP network and can be utilized in a distributed manner in a given network infrastructure. At this point, an overview of the main functions of the two other modules, Recorder and Evaluator will be given.

PlataSign Recorder

The main purpose of this component is to record the sampling of input signals from digitizer tablets, for the visualization of the writing process as well as reproduction of writing processes previously stored. During the sampling process, information is stored dynamically and from the application menu of the user interface, sets of sampled handwriting sequences can be persistently stored to and loaded from the database. The PlataSign recorder at the current state supports three API for digitizer tablets: Mouse emulation, Wintab™ interfaces and one proprietary interface for StepOver™ digitizer tablets. The following screenshot shows the main writing canvas as the spacious white area, covering most of the screen, with a configuration dialog on top, allowing to configure the tablet driver, among other parameter.

Figure B-1 shows a screenshot of the recorder application. The footer area of the PlataSign Recorder module displays statistical information about the actual writing sample (lower left area) such as number of sampling points ("*Points*"), overall duration of the writing sample ("*Sampleduration*") and the dimensions of the bounding box of the writing sample in pixels

("*Bounding Box*"). Further, it provides some animation controls for the generation of forgeries (e.g. "*TimeLine*"-control for replay of writing process on the lower right area).

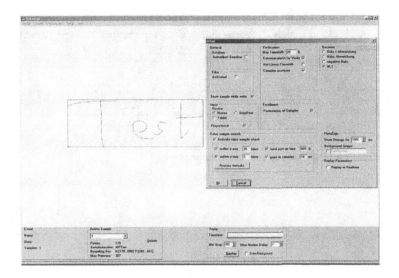

Figure B-1. Screenshot of the PlataSign recorder module

While the recording of handwriting samples is the most relevant task of this module, it contains additional functions for visualization of handwriting signals, as shown for example in the following Figure B-2. We refrain from an enumeration of each of the additional program functions of PlataSign recorder, as they possess limited relevance in the context of the evaluation work.

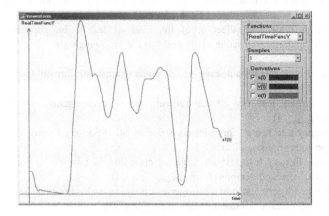

Figure B-2. Visualization example for vertical position signal in PlataSign recorder module

An exemplary screenshot of PlataSign Evaluator, the other main module of the PlataSign System, is provided in the following Figure B-3.

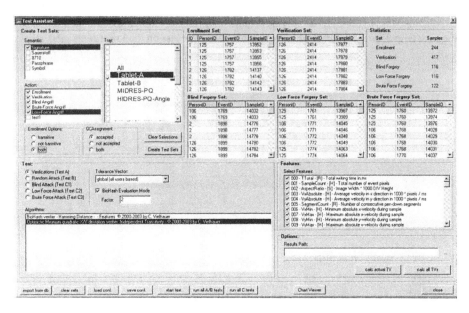

Figure B-3. Test profile setup screen in PlataSign Evaluator

This module is in charge of the automated execution of the tests, based on predefined and persistently stored test environments. The window title in our example displays the ID of the actually loaded test environment, in this case for tablet category *All* and semantic class *Signature*. The five list boxes in the upper right area represent groups of user IDs, events and samples for each of the action categories *Enrollment, Verification, Blind-, Low-Force-* and *Brute-Force* forgeries within this test environment. The list box in the lower left area serves for the selection of one of the algorithms available in the system environment (as dynamic library DLL-Plug-In). While the remaining controls are mainly to support the filtering of data and definition of appropriate test sets, the basic test process is initiated simply by selection of one of the algorithms and selection of the kind of test to be performed. The most comprehensive batch run will sequentially perform the following tests:

- *Verification* test: test all authentic verifications against enrollments from corresponding users (*FNMR*, Test A).
- *Random* forgery test: test all non-authentic verifications against enrollments of other users ($\rightarrow$ *FMR_{Random}*, Test B).
- *Blind* forgery test: test all forgeries classified as Blind Forgery against all enrollments of all attacked persons (*FMR_{Blind}*, Test C1).
- *Low-Force* forgery test: test all forgeries classified as Low-Force Forgery against all enrollments of all attacked persons (*FMR_{LowForce}*, Test C2)
- *Brute-Force* forgery test: test all forgeries classified as Brute-Force Forgery against all enrollments of all attacked persons (*FMR_{BruteForce}*, Test C3)

Threshold ranges and step widths are autonomously determined by the verification DLL and interrogated by the evaluator module at runtime. All test results are logged to text files for further reference and processing.

DLL-Plug-In Interface

A brief description of the DLL interface functions, which have to be served by any verification algorithm to be evaluated in the PlataSign system, is given in the following Table B-1.

Table B-1. Functional description of the plug-in-DLL verification algorithm interface

Function Name	Description
Load_Enrollment	Load and activate a set of handwriting samples provided as input parameter as Enrollments.
Load_TestSample	Load and activate one handwriting sample to be verified.
GetThresholdBoundaries	Identifies the minimum and maximum threshold values of the algorithm and suggests a step width.
Verify_To	Performs a verification of the actually loaded test sample (via **Load_TestSample**) in comparison the actually loaded enrollment (via **Load_Enrollment**).
IdentifyAlgorithm	Returns a short identification string of the verification algorithm (to be displayed in the PlataSign Evaluator selection box).
GetFullDescription	Returns a string with the full description of the algorithm.
Unload_Enrollment	De-activates the actual enrollment and releases memory for it.
Unload_TestSample	De-activates the actual test sample and releases memory for it.
Get_Distance	Returns the value of the distance measure distance between the actually loaded test sample (via **Load_TestSample**) and the actually loaded enrollment (via **Load_Enrollment**). Per definition this value lies within the boundaries provided by **GetThresholdBoundaries**.
GetLastErrorMessage	Returns a string containing the error message causing the last error exception.
Init	Initializes the verification algorithm, needs to be called once prior to any other function call.

Other brands and product names may be trademarks or registered trademarks of their respective owners.

References

[AbCD2002] C.B. Abdelkader, R. Cutler, L. Davis, Stride and Cadence as a Biometric in Automatic Person Identification and Verification, In: Proceedings of the 5th International Conference on Automatic Face and Gesture Recognition, Vol. 12, No. 9, pp. 1120 - 1131, ISSN: 1057-7149, 2002

[ANST2000] American National Standard for Telecommunications - Telecom Glossary 2000, http://www.atis.org/tg2k/t1g2k.html, requested January 2004

[BaNi2005] A.I. Bazin, M.S. Nixon, Gait Verification Using Probabilistic Methods, In: Proceedings of the 7th IEEE Workshop on Applications of Computer Vision, Breckenridge, CO, U.S.A., pp. 60 - 65, ISBN 0-7695-2271-8, 2005

[BaSE1997] M. Ballan, F.A. Sakarya, B.L. Evans, A Fingerprint Classification Technique Using Directional Images, In: Proceedings of the. IEEE Asilomar Conference on Signals, Systems and Computers, Vol. 1, pp. 101 - 104, Pacific Grove, CA USA, 1997

[BBBH2003] E. Bailly-Baillière, S. Bengio, F. Bimbot, M. Hamouz, J. Kittler, J. Mariéthoz, J. Matas, K. Messer, V. Popovici, F. Porée, B. Ruiz, and J.-P. Thiran, The BANCA database and evaluation protocol, In: Proceedings of the 4th International Conference on Audio- and Video-Based Biometric Person Authentication, AVBPA. Springer-Verlag, 2003

[BBEC+2004] A. Berezin, I. Berezin, S. ElKalfi, Y. Chouri, M. Chhiba, jKeyStroke - ein Software-Projekt im Rahmen der Lernveranstaltung "Datenschutz und Datensicherheit im digitalen Netz", http://wwwiti.cs.uni-magdeburg.de/biometricsGroup/jKeyStroke.pdf, 2004 (in German)

[BeRi1999] C. Becchetti, L.P.Ricotti, Speech recognition theory and C++ implementation, Wiley, Chichester NY, U.S.A., ISBN 0-471-97730-6, 1999

[Beut1994] A. Beutelspacher, Cryptology, The Mathematical Association of America, 1994

[BiKl1995] M. Bishop, D.V. Klein, Improving system security via proactive password checking, Computers & Security, Vol. 14, No. 3, pp. 233 - 249, 1995

[BioA2001] BioAPI consortium, BioAPI specification version 1.1, http://www.bioapi.org/BIOAPI1.1.pdf, March 2001, requested April 2004

[Bioi2004] Bioinformatics Organization Homepage, http://bioinformatics.org, requested 2004

[Bish2003] M. Bishop, Computer Security, Addison-Wesley, Boston, U.S.A, ISBN 0-201-44099-7, 2003

[BoJo2001] A.F. Bobick, A.Y. Johnson, Gait recognition using static activity-specific parameters, In: Proceedings of IEEE Computer Vision and Pattern Recognition Conference (CVPR 2001), Kauai, Hawaii, U.S.A., pp. 423 - 430, 2001

[Bro+1993] J. Bromley, I. Guyon, Y. LeCun, E. Säckinger, R. Shah, Signature Verification using a "Siamese" Time Delay Neural Network, In: J. D. Cowan, G. Tesauro, J. Alspector (Eds.), Advances in Neural Information Processing Systems 6 (7th NIPS Conference, Denver, Colorado, U.S.A., 1993), pp. 737 - 744, ISBN 1-55860-322-0, 1994

[BrRo1993] M. Brown, S. Rogers, User identification via keystroke characteristics of typed names using neural networks, In: International Journal of Man-Machine Studies 39, pp. 999 - 1014, 1993

[BrZu2003] A. Brömme, S. Al-Zubi, Multifactor Biometric Sketch Recognition, In: A. Brömme, C. Busch, BIOSIG 2003, Proceedings of the 1st Conference on Biometrics and Electronic Signatures of the GI Working Group BIOSIG, Darmstadt, Germany, ISBN 3-88579-360-1, 2003

[BuBu1999] M. Burge, W. Burger, Ear biometrics, In: A. Jain, R. Bolle, S. Pankanti (Eds.), Biometrics Personal Identification in Networked Society, Kluwer Academic Publishers, pp. 273-286, 1999

[BuGM1993] D. Bullock, S. Grossberg, C. Mannes, A neural network model for cursive script production, In: Biological Cybernetics 70, Springer, Berlin, pp. 15 - 28, 1993

[Camp1997] J. Campbell, Speaker Recognition: A Tutorial, In: Proceedings of the IEEE, Vol. 85, No. 9, pp. 1437 - 1462, 1997

[CaRe1999] J.P. Campbell, D.A. Reynolds, Corpora for the Evaluation of Speaker Recognition Systems, In: Proceedings of the IEEE International Conference On Acoustics, Speech and Signal Processing (ICASSP), Vol. 2, pp. 829-832, 1999

[CBEF2001] The National Institute of Standards and Technology (NIST), Common Biometric Exchange File Format (CBEFF), http://www.itl.nist.gov/div895/isis/bc/cbeff/, January 2001, requested April 2004

[CEMM2000] R. Cappelli, A. Erol, D. Maio, D. Maltoni, Synthetic Fingerprint-image Generation, In: Proceedings of International Conference on Pattern Recognition (ICPR2000), Vol. 3, pp. 3475 - 3478, 2000

[CFVS2002] L. Croce Ferri, M. Frank, C. Vielhauer, R. Steinmetz, Biometric Authentication for ID Cards with Hologram Watermarks, In: Proceedings of SPIE - Security and Watermarking of Multimedia Contents, San Jose, CA, U.S.A., Vol. 4675, pp. 629 - 640, 2002

[ChDM2002] C. C. Chibelushi, F. Deravi, J.S.D. Mason, A review of speech-based bimodal recognition, In: IEEE Transactions on Multimedia, Vol. 4, No. 1, pp. 23 - 37, 2002

[ChYa1995] Z. Chi; H. Yan, Feature Evaluation and Selection based on an Entropy Measure with Data Clustering, Optical Engineering, Vol. 34, No. 12, pp. 3514 - 3519, 1995

[Citi2000] University of Michigan, Center for Information Technology Integration (citi), Sectok Library and Applications, http://www.citi.umich.edu/projects/smartcard/ sectok.html, requested April 2004

[ClKL2003] T.C. Clancy, N. Kiyavash, D. J. Lin, Secure Smartcard Based Fingerprint Authentication, In: Proceedings of the ACM Workshop on Biometrics Methods and Applications, Santa Barbara, CA, U.S.A., 2003

[CMSU2004] Central Missouri State University, Criminal Justice Department, Criminal Justice, http://www.cmsu.edu/cj/index.html, requested April 2004

[Cohe2003] C. Cohen, The Gesture Recognition Home Page, 2003, http://www.cybernet.com/~ccohen/, requested March 2004

[Conc2002] L.-P. Conçalves, Konzeption und Evaluierung von biometrischen Hashverfahren für Smart Card, Master Thesis, Faculty for Electrical Engineering and Information Technology, Technical University Darmstadt, 2002 (in German)

[CrSm1995] J.M. Cross, C.L. Smith, Thermographic imaging of the subcutaneous vascular network of the back of the hand for biometric identification, In: Proceedings of the International Carnahan Conference on Security Technology, Sanderstead, UK, pp. 20 - 35, ISBN 0-7803-2627-X, 1995

[CYET2004] H.E. Cetingul, Y. Yemez, E. Erzin, A.M. Tekalp, Discriminative Lip-Motion Features For Biometric Speaker Identification, In: Proceedings of the IEEE International Conference on Image Processing (ICIP'04), pp. 2023 - 2026, Singapore, 2004

[DaFM1998] G. I. Davida, Y. Frankel, and B. J. Matt, On enabling secure applications through off-line biometric identification, In: Proceedings of the 1998 IEEE Symposium on Security and Privacy, pp. 148 - 157, May 1998

[Daug1992] J. Daugman, High confidence personal identification by rapid video analysis of iris texture, In: Proceedings of the 1992 IEEE International Carnahan Conference on Security Technology, pp. 1 - 11, 1992

[Daug1993] J. Daugman, High confidence visual recognition of persons by a test of statistical independence, IEEE Transactions on Pattern Analysis and Machine Intelligence, Vol. 15, No. 11, pp. 1148 - 1161, 1993

[Daug1994] J. Daugman, Biometric Personal Identification System Based on Iris Analysis, U.S. Patent No. 5,291,560 issued March 1, 1994

[Daug2003] J. Daugman, The importance of being random: Statistical principles of iris recognition, Pattern Recognition, Vol. 36, No. 2, pp. 279 - 291, 2003

[Daug2004] J. Daugman, How Iris Recognition Works, In: IEEE Transactions on Circuits and Systems for Video Technology, Vol. 14, No. 1, pp. 21 - 30, 2004

[DDN+1995] H. Dullink, B. van Daalen, J. Nijhuis, L. Spaanenburg, H. Zuidhof, Implementing a DSP Kernel for Online Dynamic Handwritten Signature Verification Using the TMS320 DSP Family, Texas Instruments technical paper, http://www.freeinfosociety.com/electronics/schematics/computer/dynamicsignaturerecognition.pdf, 1995, requested January 2004

[DhPe2000] R. Dhamija, A. Perrig, Déjà Vu: User Study Using Images for Authentication, In: Proceedings of the 9th USENIX Security Symposium, http://citeseer.ist.psu.edu/326534.html, 2000, requested April 2005

[DiPW1997] U. Dieckmann, P. Plankensteiner, T. Wagner, Sesam: A Biometric Person Identification System Using Sensor Fusion, In: Pattern Recognition Letters, Vol. 18, No. 9, pp. 827 - 833, 1997

[Eff2004] Electronic Frontier Foundation, Surveillance Monitor Web Site, http://www.eff.org/Privacy/Surveillance/surveillancemonitor.html, requested April 2004

[EGGS+2003] J. Eisenstein, S. Ghandeharizadeh, L. Golubchik, C. Shahabi, D. Yan, R. Zimmermann, Device Independence and Extensibility in Gesture Recognition, In: Proceedings of the Virtual Reality Conference (VR 2003), Los Angeles, CA, U.S.A., 2003

[EuCo2000] Official Journal of the European Communities, DIRECTIVE 1999/93/EC OF THE EUROPEAN PARLIAMENT AND OF THE COUNCIL of 13 December 1999 on a Community framework for electronic signatures, http://europa.eu.int/eur-lex/pri/en/oj/dat/2000/l_013/l_01320000119en00120020.pdf, 2000, requested April 2005

[FaLL2003] K.-C. Fan, C.-L. Lin, W.-L. Lee, Biometric Verification Using Thermal Images of Palm-dorsa Vein-patterns, In: Proceedings of the 16th IPPR Conference on Computer Vision, Graphics and Image Processing (CVGIP), pp. 188 - 195, Kinmen, R.O.C., 2003

[FoPo2003] D. A. Forsyth, J. Ponce, Computer Vision - A Modern Approach, Prentice Hall, New Jersey U.S.A., pp. 505 - 515, ISBN 0-13-085198-1, 2003

[FrDi2000] R. Frischholz, U. Dieckmann, BioID: A Multimodal Biometric Identification System, In: IEEE Computer, Vol. 33, No. 2, pp. 64 - 68, 2000

[FuGD2002] M. Fuentes, S. Garcia-Salicetti, B. Dorizzi, On-line Signature Verification: Fusion of a Hidden Markov Model and a Neural Network via a Support Vector Machine, In: Proceedings of the International Workshop on Frontiers of Handwriting Recognition, Niagara on the Lake, Canada, pp. 253 - 258, 2002

[Furu1994] S. Furui, An overview of speaker recognition technology, In: Proceedings of the ESCA Workshop on Automatic Speaker Recognition, Identification and Verification, pp. 1 - 9, 1994

[FVC2004] FVC2004: the Third International Fingerprint Verification Competition, http://bias.csr.unibo.it/fvc2004, 2004, requested April 2005

[Garf2001] S. Garfinkel, Database Nation - The Death of Privacy in the 21st Century, O'Reilly, Sebastopol, CA, U.S.A., ISBN 0-596-00105-3, 2001

[Garf2002] S. Garfinkel, Web Security, Privacy and Commerce, 2nd Edition, O'Reilly, Sebastopol, CA, USA., ISBN 0-596-00045-6, 2002

[GoMM1997] M. Golfarelli, D. Maio, D. Maltoni, On the Error-Reject Trade-Off in Biometric Verification Systems, In: IEEE Transactions on PAMI, Vol. 19, No. 7, pp. 786 - 796, 1997

[GoMP2000] S. Gong, S. J McKenna, A. Psarrou, Dynamic Vision: From Images to Face Recognition, , Imperial College Press and World Scientific Publishing, London, UK, 2000

[GoTh1965] J.J. van der Gon, J.P. Thuring, The guiding of human writing movements, In: Kybernetik 2, pp. 145 - 148, 1965

[GuCa1997] J. Gupta, A. McCabe, A Review of Dynamic Handwritten Signature Verification, Technical report at James Cook University, Australia, 1997

[Hall1999] M.A. Hall, Correlation-based Feature Selection for Machine Learning, Ph.D. Thesis at the University of Waikato, New Zealand, 1999

[HaYH2000] S. Hangai, S. Yamanaka, T. Hamamoto, On-Line Signature Verification based on Altitude and Direction of Pen Movement, In: Proceedings of the IEEE International Conference on Multimedia and Expo (ICME), Vol. 1, pp. 489 - 492, 2000

[HeFr2003] O. Henniger, K. Franke, Biometrische Benutzerauthentisierung auf Smartcards mittels handschriftlicher Unterschriften, In: R. Grimm, H. B. Keller, K. Rannenberg, INFORMATIK 2003 - Mit Sicherheit Informatik, Schwerpunkt "Sicherheit - Schutz und Zuverlässigkeit", pp. 351 - 362, ISBN 3-88579-330-X, 2003 (in German)

[HeFr2004] O. Henniger, K. Franke, Biometric User Authentication on Smart Cards by Means of Handwritten Signatures. In: Biometric Authentication, First International Conference, ICBA 2004, Hong Kong, China, Proceedings. Lecture Notes in Computer Science Vol. 3072 Springer, pp. 547 - 554, 2004

[Hill1978] R.B. Hill, Apparatus and method for identifying individuals through their retinal vasculature patterns, US Patent No. 4109237, 1978

[Hill1999] R.B. Hill, Retina Identification, In: A.K. Jain et al. (Eds.), Biometrics: Personal Identification in Networked Society, Kluwer Academic Publishers, Boston, MA, U.S.A., 1999

[HKCF1992] T. Hastie, E. Kishon, M. Clark, J. Fan, A Model for Signature Verification, Technical report AT&T Bell Laboratories, 1992

[Holl1981] J.M. Hollerbach, An Oscillation Theory of Handwriting, In: Biological Cybernetics 39, pp. 139 - 156, 1981

[Howa1997] J.D. Howard, An Analysis Of Security Incidents On The Internet, Doctorial Thesis, Carnegie Mellon University, Pittsburgh, Pennsylvania, U.S.A., http://www.cert.org/research/JHThesis/Start.html, 1997, requested April 2005

[Huff1952] D.A. Huffman, A Method for the Construction of Minimum Redundancy Codes, In: Proceedings of IRE 40, pp. 1098 - 1101, 1952

[IBGr2005] International Biometric Group, Liveness Detection in Biometric Systems, http://www.biometricgroup.com/reports/public/reports/liveness.html, requested March 2005

[ICAO2004] Biometrics Deployment of Machine Readable Travel Documents – Technical Report, Version 2.0 Final, 2004

[IKHK+2001] S.-K. Im, Y.-W. Kim, S.-C. Han, S.-W. Kim, C.-H. Kang, An biometric identification system by extracting hand vein patterns. In: Journal of the Korean Physical Society, Vol. 38 No. 3: pp. 268 - 272, 2001

[Inte2004] Interpol Web Site - Forensic Fingerprint, http://www.interpol.int/Public/Forensic/fingerprints/default.asp, requested April 2005

[JaGC2002] A.K. Jain, Friederike D. Griess, S.D. Connell, On-line Signature Verification, Pattern Recognition, Vol. 35, No. 12, pp. 2963 - 2972, 2002

[JaRo2004] A.K. Jain, A. Ross, Multibiometric Systems, Communications of the ACM, Special Issue on Multimodal Interfaces , Vol. 47, No. 1, pp. 34 - 40, 2004

[Jeli1998] F. Jelinek, Statistical Methods for Speech Recognition (Language, Speech, and Communication), MIT Press, Cambridge, MA, U.S.A., ISBN 0-262-10066-5, 1998

[JoGu1990] R. Joyce, G. Gupta, Identity authorization based on keystroke latencies, In: Communications of the ACM, Vol. 33, No. 2., pp. 168 - 176, 1990

[KaHH2002] Y. Kato, T. Hamanoto, S. Hangai, A Proposal of Writer Verification of Hand Written Objects, In: Proceedings of the IEEE International Conference on Multimedia and Expo (ICME), Lausanne, Switzerland, August 2002, pp. 585 - 588, ISBN 0-7803-7305-7, 2002

[Kais2001] J. Kaiser, Vertrauensmerkmal Unterschrift - Gestaltungskriterien für sichere Signierwerkzeuge, In: Proceedings of GI Jahrestagung, pp. 500 - 504, 2001 (in German)

[KaSt2001] G. Kao, K. Stumph, Graphical Authentication System, HP Journada Projects at MONET, University of Illinois at Urbana-Champaign, http://cairo.cs.uiuc.edu/HPJournada/cs391-jornada_files/frame.htm, 2001, requested April 2005

[KHNT1997] R.S. Kashi, J. Hu, W.L. Nelson, W. Turin, On-line Handwritten Signature Verification using Hidden Markov Model Features, In: Proceedings of the 4th International Conference Document Analysis and Recognition (ICDAR), Ulm, Germany, Vol. 1, pp. 253 - 257, 1997

[KiPK1995] S.H. Kim, M.S. Park, J. Kim, Applying personalized weights to a feature set for on-line signature verification, Proceedings of the 3rd International Conference Document Analysis and Recognition (ICDAR), Montreal, Canada, Vol. 2, pp. 882 - 885, 1995

[Kitt1975] J. Kittler, Mathematical Methods of Feature Selection, Pattern Recognition, International Journal of Man-Machine Studies, pp. 609 - 637, 1975

[KWSJ2003] A. Kumar, D. C.M. Wong, H.C. Shen, A.K. Jain, Personal Verification Using Palmprint and Hand Geometry Biometric, In: Proceeding of 4th International Conference on Audio- and Video-Based Biometric Person Authentication (AVBPA), pp. 668 - 678, Guildford, UK, 2003

[LBR+2004] B. Ly-Van, R. Blouet, S. Renouard, S. Garcia-Salicetti, B. Dorizzi, G. Chollet, Signature with Text-Dependent and Text-Independent Speech for Robust Identity Verification. In: Proceedings, IEEE Workshop on Multimodal User Authentication, pp. 13 - 18, 2003

[LeBA1996] L.L. Lee, T. Berger, E. Aviczer , Reliable On-Line Human Signature Verification Systems, IEEE Transactions on Pattern Analysis and Machine Intelligence, Vol. 18, No. 6, pp. 643 - 647, ISSN 0162-8828, 1996

[LePl1994] F. Leclerc, R. Plamondon, Automatic Verifictaion and Writer Identification: The State of the Art 1989-1993, International Journal of Pattern Recognition and Artificial Intelligence, Vol. 8, pp. 643 - 660, 1994

[LeSP1996] C.-H. Lee, F.K. Soong, K.K. Paliwal (Eds.), Automatic Speech and Speaker Recognition - Advanced Topics, The Kluwer International Series in Engineering and Computer Science, Kluwer, New York, U.S.A. , Vol. 355, ISBN: 0-7923-9706-1, 1996

[Leve1966] V.I. Levenshtein, Binary codes capable of correcting deletions, insertions, and reversals, Soviet Physics, Vol. 10, pp. 707 - 710, 1966

[LuZW2003] G. Lu, D. Zhang, K. Wang: Palmprint recognition using eigenpalms features, In: Pattern Recognition Letters Vol. 24 No. 9-10, pp. 1463 - 1467, 2003

[LVBL+1993] M. Lades, J. C. Vorbrüggen, J. Buhmann, J. Lange, C. von der Malsburg, R. P. Würtz, W. Konen, Distortion Invariant Object Recognition in the Dynamic Link Architecture, In: IEEE Transactions on Computers, Vol. 42, pp. 300 - 311, 1993

[MaCl1996] R. Martens, L. Claesen, On-Line Signature Verification by Dynamic Time Warping, In: Proceedings of the 13th IEEE International Conference on Pattern Recognition (ICPR), Vienna, Austria, Vol. 1, pp. 38 - 42, ISBN 0-8186-7282-X, 1996

[MaCl1997] R. Martens, L. Claesen, Dynamic programming optimization for on-line signature verification, In: Proceedings of the 4th IEEE Int. Conf. On Document Analysis and Recognition, Ulm, Germany, Vol. 1, pp. 653 - 656, 1997

[MaHi2004] T. Matsumoto, M. Hirabayashi, Vulnerability analysis of iris recognition, In: Proceedings of SPIE - Optical Security and Counterfeit Deterrence Techniques V, Vol. 5310, 2004

[MaHS2004] T. Matsumoto, M. Hirabayashi, K. Sato: A Vulnerability Evaluation of Iris Matching (Part 3), In: Proceedings of the 2004 Symposium on Cryptography and Information Security (SCIS), Institute of Electronics, Information and Communication Engineers, pp. 701 - 706, 2004

[MaPr2002] A.F. Martin, M.A. Przybocki, NIST's Assessment of Text Independent Speaker Recognition Performance, In: The Advent of Biometrics on the Internet, A COST 275 Workshop in Rome, Italy, 2002

[MiSi2002] K.D. Mitnick, W. L. Simon, The Art of Deception: Controlling the Human Element of Security, Wiley, Hoboken, NJ, U.S.A, ISBN 0-471-23712-4, 2002

[MMCW+2004] D. Maio, D. Maltoni, R. Cappelli, J.L. Wayman, A.K. Jain, FVC2004: Third Fingerprint Verification Competition, In: Proceedings of the International Conference on Biometric Authentication (ICBA04), Hong Kong, pp. 1 - 7, July 2004

[MMJP2003] D. Maltoni, D. Maio, A.K. Jain, S. Prabhakar, Handbook of Fingerprint Recognition, Springer, New York, U.S.A., ISBN 0-387-95431-7, 2003

[MMYH2002] T. Matsumoto, H. Matsumoto, K. Yamada, S. Hoshino, Impact of Artificial 'Gummy' Fingers on Fingerprint Systems, In: Proceedings of SPIE - Optical Security and Counterfeit Deterrence Techniques IV, Vol. 4677, 2002

[MoRu2000] F. Monrose, A.D. Rubin, Keystroke Dynamics as a Biometric for Authentication. In: Future Generation Computing Systems (FGCS) Journal: Security on the Web (special issue), pp. 351 - 359, 2000

[MoRW2002] F. Monrose, M.K. Reiter, S. Wetzel. Password Hardening based on Keystroke Dynamics, In: International Journal on Information Security, Vol. 1, No. 2, pp. 69 - 83, Springer, 2002

[MoSV1999] B. Moreno, Á. Sánchez,, J.F. Vélez, On the Use of Outer Ear Images for Personal Identification, In: Security Applications. IEEE 33rd Annual International Carnahan Conference on Security Technology, pp. 469 - 476, 1999

[MRLW2001] F. Monrose, M.K. Reiter, Q. Li and S. Wetzel, Using voice to generate cryptographic keys, Proceedings of Odyssey 2001, In: Proceedings of the Speaker Verification Workshop, 2001

[MuPe1998] M.E. Munich and P. Perona, Camera-Based ID Verification by Signature Tracking, In: Proceedings of the 5th European Conference on Computer Vision EECV'98, Freiburg, Germany, pp. 782 - 796, 1998

[MySQ2005] www.mysql.com, requested April 2005

[Naik1990] J.M. Naik, Speaker Verification: A Tutorial, In: IEEE Communications Magazine, pp. 42 - 48, 1990

[NeGa1995] M. Nelson, J. Gailly, The Data Compression Book, M&T Books, New York, ISBN 1-55851-434-1, 1995

[NiAd1994] S.A. Niyogi, E.H. Adelson, Analyzing and Recognizing Walking Figures in XYT, In: Proceedings of the IEEE Conference on Vision and Pattern Recognition, pp. 469 - 474, 1994

[NiCa2004] M.S. Nixon,J.N. Carter, Advances in Automatic Gait Recognition. In: Proceedings of IEEE Face and Gesture Analysis, pp. 11 - 16, Seoul Korea, 2004

[Nich1999] R.K. Nichols, ICSA Guide to Cryptography, McGraw-Hill, pp. 650 - 675, ISBN 0-07-913759-8, 1999

[NIST2003] http://www.nist.gov/srd/biomet.htm, requested April 2005

[Nyqu1928] H. Nyquist, Certain topics in telegraph transmission theory, In: Transactions of AIEE, Vol. 47, pp. 617 - 644, 1928

[PaRR2004] N. Pavešic, S. Ribari, D. Ribari, Personal authentication using hand-geometry and palmprint features – the state of the art, In: C. Vielhauer, S. Lucey, J. Dittmann, T. Chen (Eds.): Proceedings of the 1st workshop "Biometrics: challenges arising from Theory to Practice (BCTP), Univ. Magdeburg, Magdeburg, Germany, ISBN 3-929757-3, 2004

[PGMB+2003] P. J. Phillips, P. Grother, R. J. Micheals, D. M. Blackburn, E. Tabassi, M. Bone, Face Recognition Vendor Test 2002: Overview and Summary, http://www.frvt.org/DLs/FRVT_2002_Overview_and_Summary.pdf, 2003, requested April 2005

[Phil2004] P. J. Phillips, Face Recognition Grand Challenge, Presentation at the Biometric Consortium Conference, Crystal City, Arlington, VA September 2004, http://www.frvt.org/FRGC/, requested April 2005

[PiTV2004] J. Picard, C. Vielhauer, N. Torwirth, Towards Fraud-Proof ID Documents using Multiple Data Hiding Technologies and Biometrics, to appear in: SPIE Proceedings - Electronic Imaging, Security and Watermarking of Multimedia Contents VI, SPIE and IS&T, Vol. 5306, pp. 416 - 427, ISBN 0-8194-5209-2, 2004

[PlLo1989] R. Plamandon, G. Lorette, Automatic Signature Verification and Writer Identification - the State of the Art, Pergamon Press plc., Pattern Recognition, 22, Vol. 2, pp. 107 - 131, 1989

[PlYB1992] R. Plamondon, P. Yergeau, J.J. Brault, A Multi-Level Signature Verification System, In: S. Impedovo, J.C. Simon (Eds.), From Pixels to Features III, Elsevier, New York, pp. 293 - 301, 1992

[PNGG+2003] G. Potamianos, C. Neti, G. Gravier, A. Garg, A.W. Senior, Recent Advances in the Automatic Recognition of Audio-Visual Speech, In Proceedings of the IEEE, Vol. 91, No. 9, 2003

[PrMa1998] M.A. Przybocki, A.F. Martin, NIST speaker recognition evaluations, In: Proceedings of the International Conference on Language Resources and Evaluation (LREC), Grenada, Spain, pp. 331 - 335, 1998

[RaBo2003] N. Ratha, R. Bolle (Eds.), Automatic Fingerprint Recognition Systems, Springer, Berlin, Germany, 2003

[RaEf2003] W. Rankl, W. Effing, Smart Card Handbook, 3rd Edition, John Wiley & Sons, ISBN 0-470-85668-8, 2003

[RaJu1993] L. Rabiner and B.-H. Juang, Fundamentals of Speech Recognition, Prentice Hall, ISBN: 0-130-15157-2, 1993

[Rama2002] F. Ramann, Entwicklung und Evaluierung eines adaptiven Wichtungsverfahrens zur Kombination von Online- und Offline-Merkmalen für die Benutzerverifikation für Handschrift, Master Thesis, HAS University of Applied Sciences, Department of Computer Science, Köthen, Germany, 2002 (in German)

[RaSc1978] L.R. Rabiner, R.W. Schafer, Digital Processing of Speech Signals, Prentice-Hall (Signal Processing Series, ISBN 0-132-13603-1), 1978

[ReCa1995] D. Reynolds, B. Carlson, Text-dependent speaker verification using decoupled and integrated speaker and speech recognizers, In: Proceedings of EUROSPEECH, Madrid, Spain, pp. 647 - 650, 1995

[Reyn2002] D.A. Reynolds, An Overview of Automatic Speaker Recognition Technology, In: Proceedings of the IEEE International Conference on Acoustics, Speech, and Signal Processing, pp. 4072 - 4075, 2002

[RiDr2003] J. Richiardi, A. Drygajlo, Gaussian mixture models for on-line signature verification, In: Proceedings of the ACM SIGMM Workshop on Biometrics methods and applications, Berkeley, USA, pp. 115 - 122, 2003

[RiSA1978] R.Rivest, A. Shamir, L. Adleman, A Method for Obtaining Digital Signatures and Public-Key Cryptosystems, Communications of the ACM, Vol. 2, pp. 120 - 126, 1978

[RoJa2004] A. Ross, A.K. Jain, Multimodal Biometrics: An Overview, In: Proceedings of the 12th European Signal Processing Conference (EUSIPCO), Vienna, Austria, pp. 1221 - 1224, 2004

[Rose2002] P. Rose, Forensic Speaker Identification, Taylor & Francis, ISBN 0-415-27182-7, 2002

[RoSt1997] A.R. Roddy, J.D. Stosz, Fingerprint Features - Statistical Analysis and System Performance Estimates, In: Proceedings of IEEE, Vol. 85, No. 9, pp. 1390 - 1421, 1997

[SaKo1982] Y. Sato, K. Kogure, Online Signature Verification Based on Shape, Motion, and Writing Pressure, In: Proceedings of the 6th International Conference on Pattern Recognition, pp. 823 - 826, 1982

[Sass2004] M.A. Sasse, Assessing the Biometrics Enterprise: the present situation and future challenges, In: Proceedings of the IEE Seminar on the Challenge of Biometrics, London, UK, ISBN 0-8634-1480-X, 2004

[ScGa1996] L.R.B. Schomaker, G. P. Van Galen, Computer Models of Handwriting, In: T. Dijkstra, K. de Smedt, Computational Psycholinguistics, Taylor & Francis, London, U. K., ISBN 0-7484-0465-1, 1996

[Schm1999] C. Schmidt, On-line Unterschriftenanalyse zur Benutzerverifikation, Shaker Verlag, Aachen, Germany, ISBN 3-8265-6607-6, 1999 (in German)

[Schn1996] B. Schneier, Applied Cryptography, Addison-Wesley, Boston, MA, U.S.A., ISBN 0-471-11709-9, 1996

[Schn1999] B. Schneier, Modeling Security Threats, In: Dr. Dobb's Journal, 1999, http://www.schneier.com/paper-attacktrees-ddj-ft.html, requested April 2005

[Scho1991] L.R.B. Schomaker, Simulation and Recognition of Handwriting Movements, Doctoral Dissertation (NICI TR-91-03), Nijmegen University, The Netherlands, 1991

[ScTT1989] L.R.B. Schomaker, A.J.W.M.Thomassen, H.-L. Teulings, A computational model of cursive handwriting, In: R.P. Lamondon, C.Y. Suen, M.L. Simner (Eds.), Computer Recognition and Human Production of Handwriting, Singapore: World Scientific, pp. 153 - 177, 1989

[ScVD2004] S. Schimke, C. Vielhauer and J. Dittmann, Using Adapted Levensthein Distance for Online Signature Verification, accepted for publication in: Proceedings of the IEEE International Conference on Pattern Recognition (ICPR), Cambridge, U.K., 2004

[ScVD2005] T. Scheidat, C. Vielhauer, J. Dittmann, Distance-Level Fusion Strategies for Online Signature Verification, To appear in: Proceedings of the IEEE International Conference on Multimedia & Expo, 2005

[SGNC2002] J.D. Shutler, M.G. Grant, M.S. Nixon, J.N. Carter, On a Large Sequence-based Human Gait Database, In: Proceedings of Recent Advances in Soft Computing, pp. 66 - 71, 2002

[Shan1948] C.E. Shannon, A mathematical theory of communication, Bell System Technical Journal, Vol. 27, pp. 379 - 423 and 623-656, 1948

[SiGa1996] S. Garfinkel, G. Spafford, Practical Unix & Internet Security, O'Reilly & Associates, pp. 247 - 250, ISBN 1-56592-148-8, 1996

[Simi2004] Similar Network of Excellence - The European taskforce creating human-machine interfaces, http://www.similar.cc/, requested April 2005

[SKVK2005] S. Schimke, S. Kiltz, C. Vielhauer, T. Kalker, Security Analysis for Biometric Data in ID Documents, In: SPIE Proceedings - Electronic Imaging, Security and Watermarking of Multimedia Contents VII, pp. 474 - 485, ISBN 0-8194-5654-3, 2005

[StCh1994] O. Stettiner, D. Chazan, A Statistical Parametric Model for Recognition and Synthesis of Handwriting, In: Proceedings of the 12th International. Conference on Pattern Recognition (ICPR), Vol. 2, pp. 34 - 38, 1994

[Sted1995] The American heritage Stedman's medical dictionary, Houghton Mifflin Company, Boston, MA, U.S.A., 1995

[StNa2004a] R. Steinmetz, K. Nahrstedt, Multimedia Applications, Springer Verlag, Berlin, Germany, ISBN 3-540-40849-5, 2004

[StNa2004b] R. Steinmetz, K. Nahrstedt, Multimedia Systems, Springer Verlag, Berlin, Germany, ISBN 3-540-40867-3, 2004

[Stru2001] B. Struif, Use of Biometrics for User Verification in Electronic Signature Smartcards, In: Smart Card Programming and Security - Proceedings of the International Conference on Research in Smart Cards (E-smart), Cannes, France, pp. 220 - 228, 2001

[SVC2004] First International Signature Verification Competition, to be held in conjunction of the first International Conference on Biometric Authentication (ICBA), Hong Kong, China, 2004, http://www.cs.ust.hk/svc2004/, requested April 2004

[Tann2001] A.S. Tanenbaum, Modern Operating Systems Second Edition, Prentice-Hall, Upper Saddle River, NJ, U.S.A., pp. 591 - 606, ISBN 0-13092-641-8, 2001

[TMTR2002] C. Tisse, L. Martini, L. Torres, M. Robert, Person identification technique using human iris recognition, In: Proceedings of 15th International Conference on Vision Interface, pp. 294 - 299, 2002

[Tous2004] G.T. Toussaint, Teaching course on Pattern Recognition academic year 2003-2004, McGill University, Montreal, Quebec, Canada, http://www-cgrl.cs.mcgill.ca/~godfried/teaching/pr-web.html, requested April 2005

[TüSc2003] U. Türk, F. Schiel, Speaker Verification Based on the German VeriDat Database, In: Proceedings of EUROSPEECH, Geneva, Switzerland, pp. 3025 - 3028, 2003

[TuPe1991] M. Turk, A. Pentland. Eigenfaces for Recognition. In: Journal of Cognitive Neuroscience, Vol. 3, No. 1. 71-86, 1991

[TuTr2002] C. Tu, T.D. Tran, Context-based entropy coding of block transform coefficients for image compression, IEEE Transactions on Image Processing, Vol. 11, pp. 1271 - 1283, ISSN 1057-7149, 2002

[UlRJ2004] U. Uludag, A. Ross, A.K. Jain, Biometric Template Selection and Update: A Case Study in Fingerprints, to appear in Pattern Recognition, 2004

[UPPJ2004] U. Uludag, S. Pankanti, S. Prabhakar, A.K. Jain, Biometric Cryptosystems: Issues and Challenges, In: D. Kundur, C.-Y. Lin, B. Macq, H. Yu (Eds.), Proceedings of the IEEE, Special Issue on Enabling Security Technology for Digital Rights Management, Vol. 92, No. 6, pp. 948 - 960, 2004

[VaGD2004] B. Ly Van, S. Garcia-Salicetti, B. Dorizzi, Fusion of HMM's Likelihood and Viterbi Path for On-line Signature Verification, Biometric Authentication Workshop (BioAW), Lecture Notes in Computer Science (LNCS) 3087, Prague, Czech Republic, pp. 318 - 331, 2004

[Vale2002] V. Valencia, Biometric Liveness Testing, In: J. D. Woodward, Jr., N. M. Orlans, P. T. Higgins (Eds.), Biometrics, Osborne McGraw Hill, New York, ISBN 0-072-22227-1, 2002

[Viel2000] C. Vielhauer, Handschriftliche Authentifikation für digitale Wasserzeichenverfahren, In: M. Schumacher, R. Steinmetz (Eds.), Sicherheit in Netzen und Medienströmen, Springer Verlag, pp. 134 - 148, ISBN 3-540-67926-X, 2000 (in German)

[Viel2004] C. Vielhauer, Handwriting Biometrics for User Authentication: Security Advances in Context of Digitizer Characteristics, Ph.D. Thesis, Faculty for Electrical Engineering and Information Technology, Technical University Darmstadt, 2004

[ViKa2004] C. Vielhauer, T. Kalker, Security for Biometric Data, In: Proceedings of SPIE - Security and Watermarking of Multimedia Contents, SPIE and IS&T, Vol. 5306, pp. 642 - 652, ISBN 0-8194-5209-2, 2004

[ViKD2002] C. Vielhauer, K. Keus, J. Dittmann, Trustworthy User Authentication - a Combination of Handwriting and Electronic Signatures, In: Proceedings of the Multimedia & Security Workshop at ACM Multimedia, Juan-les-Pins, France, ISBN 1-58113-639-0, 2002

[ViSM2002] C. Vielhauer, R. Steinmetz, A. Mayerhöfer, Biometric Hash based on Statistical Features of Online Signatures, In: Proceedings of the IEEE International Conference on Pattern Recognition (ICPR), Quebec City, Canada, Vol. 1, pp. 123 - 126, ISBN 0-7695-1696-3, 2002

[ViSS2004] C. Vielhauer, T. Scheidat, R. Steinmetz, Forensik und Biometrie zur Benutzererkennung, In: P. Horster (Ed.), D-A-CH Security 2004 - Bestandsaufnahme, Konzepte, Anwendungen, Perspektiven, pp. 192 - 205, ISBN 3-00-013137-X, 2004 (in German)

[ViSt2001] C. Vielhauer, R. Steinmetz, Sicherheitsaspekte biometrischer Verfahren: Klassifizierung von sicherheitsrelevanten Vorfällen und wesentlicher Größen zur Beurteilung der Funktionssicherheit, In: Tagungsband 7. Deutscher IT-Sicherheitskongress des BSI, SecuMedia Verlag, pp. 127 - 140, ISBN 3-922746-36-5, 2001 (in German)

[ViSt2003] C. Vielhauer, R. Steinmetz, Handschriftliche biometrische Signaturen, In: P. Horster (Ed.), D-A-CH Security, IT Security & IT Management, pp. 344 - 353, ISBN 3-00-010941-2, 2003 (in German)

[ViSt2004] C. Vielhauer, R. Steinmetz, Handwriting: Feature Correlation Analysis for Biometric Hashes, In: H. Bourlard, I. Pitas, K. Lam, Y. Wang (Eds.), EURASIP Journal on Applied Signal Processing, Special Issue on Biometric Signal Processing, pp. 542 - 558, Hindawi Publishing Corporation, Sylvania, OH, U.S.A., ISSN 1110-8657, 2004

[WaCr1953] Watson, James, and Francis Crick, "Molecular structure of nucleic acids (http://biocrs.biomed.brown.edu/Books/Chapters/Ch%208/DH-Paper.html), A structure for Deoxyribose Nucleic Acid". April 2, 1953. (paper on the structure of DNA)

[Waym1997] J.L. Wayman, Biometric Identifier Standards Research Final Report, College of Engineering, San Jose State University, 1997, http://www.aamva.org/Documents/ stdBiomStdResearch.pdf , requested April 2005

[Waym1999] J.L. Wayman, Technical Testing and Evaluation of Biometric Identification Devices, In A.K. Jain et al. (Eds.), Biometrics: Personal Identification in Networked Society, Kluwer Academic Publishers, Boston, MA, U.S.A., pp. 345 - 368, 1999

[Waym2000] J.L. Wayman (Ed.), National Biometric Test Center - Collected Works Version 1.3, http://www.ece.unh.edu/biometric/biomet/public_docs/nbtccw_TEST.pdf, 2000, requested April 2005

[WaZS2004] J. Wang, C. Zhang, H.-Y. Shum, Face Image Resolution versus Face Recognition Performance Based on Two Global Methods, In. Proceedings of the Asia Conference on Computer Vision (ACCV'2004), Jeju Island, Korea, 2004

[Wech2004] H. Wechsler, Biometrics and Forensics Lab, http://cs.gmu.edu/~wechsler /FORENSIC/, requested April 2005

[WePB+2002] H. Wechsler, P. J. Phillips, V. Bruce, et al. (Eds.), Face Recognition From Theory to Applications, Springer, Berlin, Germany, 2002

[Wien1949] N. Wiener, Cybernetics or control and communication in the animal and the machine, New York, Wiley, 1949

[Wild1997] R. P. Wildes. Iris Recognition: An Emerging Biometric Technology, In: Proceedings of the IEEE, Vol. 85, No. 9, pp. 1348 - 1363, 1997

[Wirt1995] B. Wirtz, Stroke-based Time Warping for Signature Verification, In: Proceedings of the 3rd International Conference on Document Analysis and Recognition (ICDAR), Montreal, Canada, Vol. 1, pp. 179 - 182, 1995

[WiSV2003] M. Wirotius, A. Seropian, N. Vincent, Writer Identification from Gray Level Distribution, In: Proceedings of the 7th IEEE International Conference on Document Analysis and Recognition (ICDAR), Edinburgh, Scotland, U.K., pp. 1168- 1172, ISBN 0-7695-1960-1, 2003

[WSKM1997] L. Wiskott, J.-M. Fellous, N. Krüger, C. von der Malsburg, Face Recognition by Elastic Bunch Graph Matching, In: Proceedings of the 7th International Conference on Computer Analysis of Images and Patterns (CAIP), Springer, Heidelberg, Germany, pp. 456 - 463, 1997

[WuJL1997] Q.-Z. Wu, I-C. Jou, S.-Y. Lee, On-Line Signature Verification Using LPC Cepstrum and Neural Networks, IEEE Transactions on Systems, Man, and Cybernetics-Part B: Cybernetics, Vol. 27, No. 1, pp. 148 - 153, 1997

[XiDa1995] X.-H. Xiao, R.-W. Dai, A hierarchical on-line Chinese signature verification system, In: Proceedings of the 3rd International Conference on Document Analysis and Recognition (ICDAR), Montreal, Canada, Vol. 1, pp. 202 - 205, 1995

[YaOk1977] M. Yasuhara, M. Oka, Signature Verification Experiment Based on Nonlinear Time Alignment: A Feasibility Study, IEEE Transactions on Systems, Man, and Cybernetics, pp. 212 - 216, 1977

[YCXG+2004] D. Y. Yeung, H. Chang, Y. Xiong, S. George, R. Kashi, T. Matsumoto, G. Rigoll, SVC2004: First International Signature Verification Competition, In: Proceedings of the International Conference on Biometric Authentication (ICBA), pp. 16 - 22, 2004

[ZCPR2003] W.-Y. Zhao, R. Chellappa, A. Rosenfeld, P.J. Jonathon Phillips, Face Recognition: A Literature Survey, ACM Computing Survey, Vol. 35, No 4, 399-458, 2003

[Zhan2000] D. Zhang, Automated Biometrics, Kluwer, ISBN 0-7923-7856-3, May 2000

[Zhan2004] D. Zhang, Palmprint Authentication, Kluwer Academic Publishers, USA, 2004

[Zott2003] F. Zotter, Emotional Speech, Technical Report, Technische Universität Graz, http://spsc.inw.tugraz.at/courses/asp/ ws03/talks/zotter_report.pdf , 2003 (requested April 2005)

[ZoVi2003] F. Zöbisch, C. Vielhauer, A Test Tool to support Brut-Force Online and Offline Signature Forgery Tests on Mobile Devices, In: Proceedings of the IEEE International Conference on Multimedia and Expo 2003 (ICME) , Baltimore, MD, U.S.A., Vol. 3, pp. 225 - 228, ISBN 0-7695-1062-0, 2003

Index